A Future for the Aged

THE HOGG FOUNDATION RESEARCH SERIES

Wayne H. Holtzman, Editor

Tornadoes over Texas by Harry Estill Moore

Electrical Stimulation of the Brain edited by Daniel E. Sheer

Inkblot Perception and Personality by Wayne H. Holtzman, Joseph S. Thorpe, Jon D. Swartz, and E. Wayne Herron

Changing Parental Attitudes through Group Discussion by Carl F. Hereford

Tomorrow's Parents by Bernice Milburn Moore and Wayne H. Holtzman

Across the Tracks by Arthur Rubel

A FUTURE for the AGED

Victoria Plaza and Its Residents

by Frances Merchant Carp

PUBLISHED FOR THE HOGG FOUNDATION FOR MENTAL HEALTH
BY THE UNIVERSITY OF TEXAS PRESS, AUSTIN & LONDON

THIS INVESTIGATION WAS SUPPORTED IN PART BY RESEARCH GRANTS FROM THE HOGG FOUNDATION FOR MENTAL HEALTH, THE UNIVERSITY OF TEXAS, AUSTIN, TEXAS

AND

IN PART BY A RESEARCH GRANT FROM THE SOCIAL SECURITY ADMINISTRATION, DEPARTMENT OF HEALTH, EDUCATION, AND WELFARE, WASHINGTON, D.C.

AND

IN PART BY TRINITY UNIVERSITY, SAN ANTONIO, TEXAS.

Library of Congress Catalog Card Number 66–16469

Printed by the University of Texas Printing Division, Austin
Bound by Universal Bookbindery, Inc., San Antonio

For PMM, WBM, and BNC

FOREWORD

Man has always had a special interest in old age, and the elderly have always had their lobbies, the Fifth Commandment being one of their earlier accomplishments. Somewhat later than that, but still in the pre-Christian era, Cicero stopped shouting at Catiline long enough to write *Concerning Old Age,* in which, while recognizing that "old age cannot be pleasant in extreme poverty," he vigorously defended its pleasures, one of the most honorable of which, he observed, is "to be consulted." Dr. Carp may have taken a hint from Cicero in her research for this work, since her methodology entailed much consulting with a group of elderly people.

Its timing, too, was felicitous. It began six months before the subjects moved into their new environment, and its cogent insights relating to "adjustability" are thus fortified by a knowledge which makes the impact of the changes in the lives of these people almost measurable.

While our wisdom may not yet match that of the ancients, we know a lot more about the elderly than they did. All that is needed to be persuaded of how *little* we know is to become involved in the kind of undertaking that resulted in Victoria Plaza. In the decade since that work was started research in this field has moved apace and its accomplishments have been tremendous.

Old age is a state toward which each of us, from birth, is moving willy-nilly. Not all achieve it, but the number of those who do is ever increasing and in fact, these days, "exploding." Well over 40 per cent of the 100,000 public-housing units authorized by the United States Congress in 1961 were allocated for occupancy by the elderly. This swell of activity has created a new profession, that of designing and managing housing for older people, and this profession, together with the older people themselves, will be the principal beneficiary of this study.

As Cicero saw, old age is not a happy state for those in need. Thanks to Victoria Plaza, the housing development, it has perhaps been somewhat happier for a few than it would otherwise have been; and thanks to *A Future for the Aged,* the study of Victoria Plaza, old age will be even happier for many others in the future.

MARIE C. MCGUIRE, *Commissioner*
Public Housing Administration
Washington, D.C.

ACKNOWLEDGMENTS

For simplicity this statement of appreciation follows the chronological sequence of major events in regard to research for this study. Recognition of individuals and institutions for their special assistance is expressed within this framework.

This procedure has the additional advantage of establishing priority. The calendar, not evaluation of importance, determined precedence of names. Unfortunately, this arrangement does no better than any other in guaranteeing inclusion of all who contributed. In addition to those mentioned here, some people are recognized in footnotes to titles of chapters which report their contributions. Though regrettable, it is also probable that some individuals deserving of mention have been omitted, simply because of the lapse of time and the variety of activities undertaken since that day, five years ago, when the concept of community action on behalf of older citizens in Bexar County was broadened to include the possibility of such research.

In October, 1956, the San Antonio Housing Authority had decided to build living quarters for aged people in Bexar County. Their plans included construction of a nine-story building with a community center on the ground floor and eight identical residential floors. Ground was broken in September, 1958.

Public housing, since its inception in 1937, has always provided older people with accommodations which were available and for which they could qualify. In San Antonio approximately six hundred low-income, elderly persons were living in public housing prior to erection of the new facility. However, Victoria Plaza was to be different in several ways. In the first place, it was planned to accommodate people within a limited age group. Second, it was the first high-rise public-housing building, and the tallest apartment house, in the area. Third, it embodied special features in design intended to make it more suitable for aged occupants.

Without a research capability of its own, the Housing Authority staff recognized the need for objective evaluation of their plan and in the fall of 1959 actively sought it. The novel, and even controversial, building had been under construction for a year, with all the problems attendant upon such a venture. Staff members had their hands full, not only with architects and engineers and plumbers and painters, but also with applicants for apartments in the new building, while at the same time they were trying to carry out their normal obligations to other public-housing units. Interpretation to the community, as the building became increasingly visible, also drained time and energy. Tribute surely must be paid to these people who not only accepted the additional imposition of a research effort, but campaigned for it. Though Housing Authority staff members were not involved in data collection or analysis, research preparations and procedures cost them many an hour and many a headache.

In preparation for the new facility the Community Welfare Council played a cooperative role with the Housing Authority, giving particular assistance in the development of plans for inclusion of a community center, open to all elder citizens, and in the mobilization of local organizations and institutions to provide services and benefits through it. The Council also perceived the possibility of advancing knowledge through research, and joined with the Housing Authority to invite the opinion of the Hogg Foundation for Mental Health.

The Foundation's administrators, immediately recognizing the value of this research opportunity, in late October of 1959 called to meet with members of their staff (Dr. Robert L. Sutherland, director; Dr. Wayne H. Holtzman, associate director; and Dr. Bernice M. Moore), representatives of the local organizations involved (Marie McGuire, director, San Antonio Housing Authority[1]; Olin LeBaron, executive director, Community Welfare Council), consultants (Dr. Robert Peck and Dr. Ivan Belknap, University of Texas; Dr. William Hales, NIMH, Fern M. Colborn, National Committee on the Aging, Dallas; Ollie A. Randall, National Council on Aging, New York; Ruther Shurter, USPHS, Dallas), and members of the local community who might be interested (Sister M. Frances Jerome, C.D.P., and C. J. Collins, The Worden School of Social Work, Our Lady of the Lake College; Dr. Abraham Carp, Air Force Personnel Research Laboratory; and Dr. Frances M. Carp, Trinity University).

As the result of a series of discussions and conferences, two recommendations were made. The first was immediate collection of initial demographic and personality descriptions of applicants to provide background data for any studies which might be made subsequently with this group of people. The second suggestion was that local machinery be set up to handle applications for such research projects.

Regarding preliminary information on applicants, pressure of time was intense, since Victoria Plaza was nearing completion. Assessment of the impact of housing change was an obvious research possibility; improved selection was another. As a base for these and other studies, information about applicants prior to the opening of the Plaza must be obtained.

For this preliminary study the Hogg Foundation for Mental Health made a grant of money to be administered through the Community Welfare Council, and a local research committee was set up, consisting of

[1] Now commissioner of the Public Housing Administration, Washington, D.C.

Sister Frances Jerome, professor of sociology, The Worden School of Social Work, Our Lady of the Lake College; Dr. Abraham Carp, technical director, United States Air Force Personnel Research Laboratory; and Dr. Frances M. Carp, chairman, Psychology Department, Trinity University.

Unfortunately, Sister Frances Jerome was unable to continue participation in the project, because of unexpected responsibilities at the Worden School and later receipt of a research grant which took her to Louisiana. She was most helpful in the planning stages of the study of applicants, and the contributions of her viewpoint, fine background, and delightful self were much missed. Other commitments made it necessary for Dr. Abraham Carp also to withdraw from active participation. He has continued to be an "unofficial" consultant beyond compare throughout all of the studies reported here.

Only months after completion of background data collection in the summer of 1960, the Hogg Foundation reproduced and distributed a working paper which summarized much of the information obtained from applicants (Carp and Carp, 1961). This preliminary description of the people was made available to anyone interested in planning his own study with them.

A second recommendation of the conference group was specification of procedures for processing proposals for studies, at any time in the future, requiring data collection on this group of older people. It was agreed that, if residents of Victoria Plaza were to be involved, application must be made to Victoria Plaza's Committee of Management, a standing committee of the Community Welfare Council. This group was to be advised regarding research merit by a subcommittee of local professional people in sociology, social work, and psychology.

In addition to the aim of endorsing only worthwhile research, attention was given to the timing and coordination of projects. Regarding research proposals, the Committee's primary consideration was the well-being of people who lived in the new building. It sought to protect their rights as home-renters and to avoid perception of them as laboratory inmates.

In early 1960 the proposal for the studies reported here was submitted to the Committee of Management and to the Hogg Foundation. The necessary data collection was approved by the Committee, and the Foundation provided financial support by means of a grant administered through Trinity University. Collection of data on the development of interpersonal relationships among Victoria Plaza residents was begun three months after the first people moved in. Data to provide assessment of the impact of housing change and to check predictions of adjustment in Victoria Plaza were collected nine months to a year later.

Opportunity for the data collection was dependent upon a cooperative effort involving nonresearch people variously situated in the community.

Here, in addition to Mr. LeBaron and Mrs. McGuire, special mention must be made of Marilynn Wacker[2] and Marjorie White of the Housing Authority office and Dorothy O'Neill[3] of the Community Welfare Council staff, whose assistance was unflagging and good-natured, even when the research effort added to their already overwhelming work loads.

Fundamentally, of course, credit for these studies must go to the people who served as subjects. They gave generously of their time and attention, for no personal gain, but to assist in the accumulation of information about people in their age group which might benefit others in the future.

The low refusal rate and the fullness of response from participants attest to the technical skills and personal qualities of the two women who collected most of the information, Effie May Sanders and Eleanor Russell. Their natural, warm interest in people was irresistible in establishing and maintaining rapport. Endless patience and much skill were required to lead subjects through consideration of the material needed without alienating them. To facilitate data collection these two women furnished transportation for shopping, fed puppies by bottle, trapped escaped parakeets, and unplugged drains. They became well known and liked among the people interviewed. The data reflect their effectiveness.

The same two women prepared the material for machine processing, no small task in view of the open-ended nature of the interview questions and the fact that responses were recorded as fully as possible. Response categories were determined only after all had been interviewed so that respondents would not be limited or directed. Individual answers to each item were then coded in IBM card format, following the system of categorization which had emerged from the data themselves.

Many others were involved in machine data processing. Dr. Wayne Holtzman, associate director of the Hogg Foundation for Mental Health, supervised punching the 1960 data into IBM cards and chi-square computation of overall initial sex differences and differences between subjects who subsequently became residents of Victoria Plaza and those who did not. Lola Netter, research assistant at Trinity University, had the thankless job of computing by hand the additional tests necessary to clarify interpretation of these overall differences.

Dr. Paul Kelley, of the Testing and Counselling Center, The University of Texas, supervised card punching of 1961 data and the compilation of frequency distributions of some variables.

In planning the assessment of residence effect, Dr. Robert Bottenberg and Dr. Raymond Christal, both of the Air Force Personnel Research Laboratory, were statistical consultants. Continuous variable data were processed in two phases. Dr. Earl Jennings, The University of Texas,

[2] Now assistant executive director, San Antonio Housing Authority.

[3] Now executive director, Senior Community Services, Inc., San Antonio.

supervised machine work on the first phase, using a program originally written by Dr. Joe Ward, Jr., of the Air Force Personnel Laboratory, which Dr. Jennings modified. The second phase of continuous variable processing and the chi-square treatment of dichotomous variables were programmed and run by Peter Kolmus, at St. Mary's University, San Antonio.

Regression analyses for prediction of adjustment in the Plaza were performed at The University of Texas during a 1964 summer workshop sponsored by The National Science Foundation. Statistical clerks were Nancy Shubat and Walter Costello.

Complete identification with the project and total effort on it characterized all participants. One, however, must have special mention. Effie May Sanders, employed as an interviewer, remained with the project to its conclusion, adapting herself to its changing requirements. No task was too small or too great for her, from routine filing to operating a computer. Throughout, she showed exceptional human-relations skill with subjects and coworkers. From beginning to end her effort was tireless, devoted, and effective.

A Social Security grant and Trinity University's cooperation provided a year's leave of absence and the assistance of a typist for report writing. This facilitation of reporting was especially valuable, since much money and effort are being spent, across the country, in attempts to deal with the special problems of older people, and the results of relevant studies should be made available, as quickly as possible, to those charged with decision making.

Typists at various times were Theodora Troyanos, Laural Winston, Beverly Fortune, and Jo Anne Lemasters. Mrs. Lemasters prepared the final manuscript.

Richard Carp made preliminary drawings of the figures in Chapter 7 and provided moral support and a sense of humor during such stresses as computer breakdowns and loss of half the manuscript in the move to a new office.

Vaughn M. Bryant, Jr., brought intelligence and skill to the task of preparing final copy for the figures.

Several people gave of their time, special backgrounds, and professional skill, to read the manuscript. Their favorable comments were energizing, their negative opinions both chastening and clarifying. Among the people who made this salutatory contribution were Dr. Abraham Carp, Bert W. Carp, Dr. Wilma Donahue, Dr. Wayne H. Holtzman, Olin LeBaron, Dr. Marjorie Fiske Lowenthal, Marie McGuire, Dr. Bernice M. Moore, Dorothy O'Neill, Dr. Robert Peck, Marilynn Wacker, and Marjorie White.

FRANCES MERCHANT CARP

CONTENTS

ILLUSTRATIONS

Following Page 126

(Photographs are by the staff photographer of the San Antonio Housing Authority and R. J. Leydon and Associates.)

FIGURES

TABLES

A Future for the Aged

CHAPTER 1

Why the Studies Were Made

A LITTLE OLD LADY in a faded, misshapen bathrobe opened the door to her expected visitor. Apathetically she turned back into the room, allowing the caller to follow her. Shuffling in her dilapidated, run-over carpet slippers, she slowly made her way to the unmade bed and slumped down on its edge. The guest had to clear a chair of odd pieces of old clothing and torn magazines. During most of the time they talked, tears ran unheeded down the old woman's cheeks. Occasionally she would brush a hand across her face, or run it through her uncombed gray hair. The air was stale and musty, dirty dishes were carelessly stacked in a corner, and the woman herself probably had not bathed or washed for several days.

She was worried about poor health and described her many ailments, including at least five heart attacks. For many weeks she had not been out of her home, and no one had been to see her except her son. The only good thing in her life was this son, who stopped to see her each morning on the way to work and every evening on the way home to his family. In addition, he paid for her phone and called her half a dozen times each day. Except for him, she had no reason to go on living, and his wife begrudged his attention.

Fourteen months later, this woman greeted the same visitor with a bright smile and warm handclasp. She attentively seated her visitor at a small table, set with a spotless cloth, on which were a little bowl of flowers and a plate of homemade cookies. As they sipped and nibbled, the old woman spoke vivaciously of her busy and happy life, her many friends. (She was such a gad-about that many phone calls had been necessary to catch her at home to arrange this visit.) Later that day she was to attend a garden club meeting. She had invited an elderly bachelor in to share her supper, then both of them were going out to sing religious and old-fashioned songs with a group of people their age. Spry and cheerful, she had earned the nickname "Cricket" among her many new acquaintances.

Her skin was freshly washed and lightly powdered, her hair professionally groomed and nicely combed, her clothes carefully pressed. Asked about her health, she laughed and said she had not thought about it.

She spoke of her son with no less warmth than formerly, and of his wife without resentment. Last Sunday she had had dinner with them and the grandchildren; this Sunday they were coming to eat with her. "It does her [her daughter-in-law] good to get out, and you should see the children eat when they're over here! I love to see them come—and I love to see them go home!"

The many daily visits and calls from her son had dwindled to an occasional one: "I must have been a dreadful burden to him, always weeping and wailing. He's a good son, but I'm out so much now, or someone else is here, and he feels like he's in the way."

As she walked to the door with the visitor she said fervently, "Every day I get down on my knees and thank God for the wonderful life I have now. I only wish every person could be as fortunate."

This narrative presents a striking but by no means unique example of the kind of change which took place in the members of a group of older people. What had happened in the interim to account for the dramatic alterations of behavior and outlook?

At the time of first contact "Cricket" was living in one room of an old house in what had once been a fashionable residential district, first encroached upon and now nearly obliterated by the downtown area. After the three-story home was partitioned into one-room "apartments" there was no redecoration. From two walls of this room peeled ornate wallpaper. Unfinished plasterboard constituted the others.

One bathroom was shared by all the people on a floor. Each person was allowed to keep a limited amount of food in the family-sized refrigerator in the ground-floor kitchen, but cooking had to be done on gas plates in the bedrooms. Garbage was carried back downstairs and out to the alley, where malodorous common garbage cans were usually running over. The house crawled with roaches.

Two months later she moved into a clean, attractively decorated apartment, where she had her own bathroom and bedroom, and a kitchen space screened from the living area. Though it was only a few blocks from where she lived before, it seemed a different world. Her apartment was clean, bright, and easy to care for. Also, and perhaps equally important, living under the same roof were many other people of about her age, with whom she found much in common. The second visit occurred one year after this move.

A Common Problem for Older People

Many people over sixty express dissatisfaction with the settings in which they live and feel that their lives generally would become much better if only their housing were improved. Often the possibilities are limited by finances. The depression hit members of this generation at a particularly critical point in their earning years, and inflation diminished what they were able to save.

For some individuals the primary difficulty is physically substandard or inconvenient housing facilities. For others the frustration is primarily social in nature, involving isolation from old friends and contemporaries, or intergeneration conflict and the feeling of imposing or being imposed upon.

The critical question is: if pleasant living quarters are made available, in proximity to those of other people in the same age range, will the later years of these people indeed be better ones?

As Wilner, Walkley, Pinkerton, and Tayback (1962) point out, in the last half century there has been considerable social concern over substandard housing. The resultant programs "have stemmed, no doubt, from both humanitarian beliefs in social justice and the pragmatic belief that housing plays a central role in health and well being" (p. 3).

Wilner *et al.* present a summary of research in the last thirty years investigating the relationship of housing to health and social adjustment. From it they conclude that, while most studies have shown positive associations between housing and health or adjustment, a few have found negative relationships and the reports of others have been ambiguous.

They indicate, further, the difficulty of isolating effects of housing *per se* in such studies and the importance of so doing, and suggest that public-housing occupants provide an excellent source of subjects for experimental or quasi-experimental studies. With them there is possibility of manipulating housing only (or almost only) while controlling other factors such as age, socio-economic status, and health, which are usually correlated with characteristics of housing. Such variables, which also affect satisfaction and well-being, may be similar for groups with different public housing. Even when groups cannot be equated for such characteristics, the range of difference in many of them is probably smaller for public-housing tenants, which tends to minimize the effect of these other variables on measures of morale or adjustment. Also, more information is available on public-housing tenants than is usually the case with private renters. This reduces the probability of attributing to housing an effect actually due to some other difference between groups.

No matter how well-intentioned, a particular program may or may not further progress toward the goal it was designed to realize. A worthwhile social purpose may be abandoned as foolhardy because of inappropriate, but correctible, implementation. On the other hand, a procedure may be outstandingly successful, but for quite different reasons than the obvious ones, with the result that generalizations to similar situations fail.

Objective evaluation of a program's effectiveness relative to its purposes, and assessment of the factors underlying its strengths and weaknesses, are essential as a basis for decision regarding the continuation of any program.

Given the aim of reducing major frustrations of the autumn years, and recognizing that many people in that age span perceive as especially thwarting either the physical or the social situation in which they live, it does not necessarily follow that transplantation to a different environment will achieve the goal. Increase in satisfaction cannot be assumed, even if the new surroundings are designed according to the special needs and desires of the group.

First of all, are people this old able to make the change to modern equipment and to a new social situation? Operating push-button stoves may prove too much of a challenge. Living up to a fine modern apartment may become taxing. Neighbors may prove to be as incompatible as relatives. Availability of other people may be overwhelming. Once in the tailor-made setting, a person advanced in years may look back regretfully at what he left. From an alien land of technical modernity, with consistent standards of cleanliness and beauty, densely populated by strangers, he may perceive his former residence nostalgically as less demanding and more comfortable.

Relative fixity of the older personality and life pattern is commonly assumed, though evidence seems inadequate to attribute this to chronological age, as such. If older people are able to make the adjustment to a new environment, will their enjoyment of life increase, or will more basic dissatisfactions simply take new surface forms? Displeasure with housing may be an expression of a more general frustration at growing old, which cannot be alleviated by changed living quarters. The effort and expense involved in relocating older people may not be justified, if reduction in complaints about residence is matched by increased discontent in other areas.

In addition to expressed pleasure or displeasure with more adequate housing, will there be other changes? Does improving the living situation have a consistent impact on physical and mental health, on attitudes toward others, on self-concept, on patterns of day-to-day living? Both for those who must make plans for aged people, and for those interested in more theoretical aspects of aging, it is important to determine which behavioral characteristics are intrinsic to aging and which are relatively dependent on environmental circumstances. For example, according to one theory, "Aging is an inevitable mutual withdrawal or disengagement, resulting in decreased interaction between the aging person and others in the social systems he belongs to" (Cumming and Henry, 1961, p. 14). Continuity of disengagement rate following improvement in housing, particularly if social contact is facilitated, would support this theory. Declination, or reversal, in rate of disengagement under these circumstances would challenge the equation of aging and disengaging.

A related question is whether some older people adjust to a new, modern living situation more easily and completely than others. Impact of housing my be diluted, in the overall view, by averaging together those affected and those not. Its effect may be obliterated in generalizations about groups which include individuals for whom the change had positive consequences, but others for whom it brought negative results. As factors predictive of favorable change can be identified, this information will assist in the practical matter of selecting tenants when the number of applicants exceeds that of residential units in preferred housing facilities. It should also provide additional insight into the processes of aging.

Some studies support the view that, with advancing age, all personalities tend toward a common state of orientation toward the past, disinterest in people and activities, deterioration in intellect, and resistance to change. However, other research does not justify the tendency to stereotype "old folks" in this way. On the contrary, in his study of superior old people, Bradshaw (1956) found that individual personality was a major factor in the life pattern during old age. The people in his group continued to have outgoing philosophies of life, orientation toward the future rather than the past, usefulness in some capacity, social contacts, and intellectual curiosity, and to maintain active interests of previous years.

McClusky and Jensen (1959) point out that the traditional picture of childhood and adolescence as a period of "growing up" and that of adulthood as a time for "settling down" provides an inadequate picture of changes people undergo as they move toward the end of life. Sward (1945), who dealt with a group of college professors sixty to eighty years of age and a control group of colleagues twenty-five to thirty-five, reports individual differences more impressive than age differences.

If some people adjust better than others, what factors seem to determine this difference: characteristics of the housing or traits of the individual? It makes a critical difference whether the poorly adjusted and unhappy are similarly located in inaccessible residential units, or whether most of them grew up with no siblings, or whether the common factor is a pathological score on a psychological test.

If variables related to adjustment are determined, can they be used to predict it? Then applicants most likely to fail can be spared that experience, and more of those most likely to succeed can enjoy the new way of life.

The interpersonal aspect of adjustment to a new housing situation merits special consideration. Older people claim to suffer from social deprivation as well as from substandard physical conditions of housing. There is still some question whether, and if so, how, residential units can be designed to alleviate this need. In the first place, are people in this age group really willing—and able—to form new interpersonal contacts, or is there an inevitable shift of balance toward kinship ties (Cumming and Henry, 1961)? Is a homogeneously aged group especially dull or depressing? Are planned social activities too demanding?

Answers to such questions should help to clarify the advisability of moving an older person into housing which is physically more adequate, if the change necessitates separation from friends and acquaintances, or of providing him a residence away from his family, even if he wants it. They might also be of interest to future planners making decisions regarding supplementation of residential units with "senior centers," or considering whether to construct facilities for segregated or integrated age groups.

If older people seem capable of developing new relationships, what determines the formation of friendships or of accomplishment groups? Is it primarily a matter of proximity? Or do people come together because they have common backgrounds? Or are present interests the social catalysts? Such information would either indicate to management personnel that it makes no difference where residents are assigned living space within that which is available, or it would suggest some principles for assignment, which would foster development of interpersonal relationships.

Do leaders emerge to play dominant roles in the group as with people at other ages? Is this role assumption determined by characteristics of the situation or by personality variables? If management considers it helpful to foster leadership from within the resident group, perhaps this is best obtained by selecting some applicants with outstanding proclivity for leadership, and distributing them among the other residents. On the other hand, assignment to an apartment in a commanding location, or appointment to a role generally perceived as one of leadership (such as committee chairman), may be the overriding determinant. The relative concentration of leaders among followers may be important to the happiness of all, regardless of how leadership is determined.

Background of the Study

An opportunity to answer some of these questions became available when the San Antonio Housing Authority decided to erect a residential facility limited to the aged. During the 1950's attention was turning, nationwide, to the problem of housing the burgeoning population of people past retirement age. Studying the applicants on its rolls, the San Antonio Housing Authority developed a plan for an apartment-style unit, available only to senior members of the community who qualified for public housing.

The staff recommended also that a Senior Center, to serve all members of that age group in the community, be included under the same roof. At this point the Community Welfare Council was invited to help in the planning. Its executive director appointed a committee, made up of individuals from agencies or organizations already concerned with older people, which worked closely with the Housing Authority personnel involved.

This joint committee called upon the Hogg Foundation for Mental Health, which, in addition to various consulting services, agreed to provide support for a demonstration project in the Senior Center under the direction of a social worker on the Community Welfare Council staff. In addition the Foundation recognized the possibility of research, and in 1959 called together a group of people in the behavioral sciences to consider it. One recommendation of the group was to attempt collection of descriptive material concerning aged applicants for housing, prior to any change in their way of life.

A common weakness in studies appraising programs of housing, nutrition, occupation, and recreation is the unavailability of preliminary data from which to assess the direction, extent, and quality of change in people, consequent upon altered circumstances. The usual impossibility of obtaining comprehensive descriptions of subjects prior to the environmental changes under evaluation obscures conclusions regarding cause. Some programs for the aged may be judged to have improved happiness or competence even though a process of selectivity rather than one of change was operating. Others, potentially more effective, may have been discounted and discarded because selection counter balanced other effects.

Long after ground had been broken for construction of Victoria Plaza, the task of obtaining relevant information about the people who wanted to move into it was undertaken. From the first, data collection was a race against completion of the building and announcement of the names of successful applicants for apartments. The Hogg Foundation financed planning and collection of this material and made available a working paper, summarizing it, to people interested in developing plans for research with members of the applicant group (Carp and Carp, 1961).

The Foundation also approved plans, in 1960, for the studies reported here and agreed to finance the necessary additional interviewing and testing to be carried out in 1961, and the subsequent analysis of data. A grant from the Social Security Administration, with the cooperation of Trinity University, provided a twelve-month period in 1962–1963 for data interpretation and report writing.

A Preview of This Research

This is a study of older people in regard to changed housing and recreation facilities. The research opportunity came when Victoria Plaza, a nine-story building with a community center on the ground floor and eight identical residential floors, was constructed by the San Antonio Housing Authority.

Departing from local custom, Victoria Plaza was high-rise rather than cottage-style construction, it was available only to people within a limited age group, and it was designed with a view to the special problems of their safety and convenience.

To assist future planning of residential units for aged people, reactions of residents to specifics such as location and type of building, special features designed for their security and comfort, and inclusion of a county-wide recreation center, as well as to the age homogeneity and personal characteristics of other tenants, were obtained from them.

One major purpose of the study was assessment of the impact of changed housing on older people. Physically and socially, housing changes were planned to meet the expressed needs of people who were to live in Victoria Plaza. The study attempted to ascertain whether the plan was successful in providing a more satisfying living situation. It also evaluated more general changes in attitudes, life style, and mental health consequent upon alleviation of undesirable living conditions. As a means of assessing the impact of housing change, people who had lived in the new facility for a year or more were compared, in 1961, with a similar group of people who had applied unsuccessfully for apartments there. Comparison of changes in these groups minimized mistaking initial differences for results of improved living and recreation conditions.

A second major purpose was to identify background and personality characteristics associated with differences in adjustment to life in Victoria Plaza. It is important to develop predictors of adaptation to such settings. Basic requirements for admission were determined by the Housing Authority. However, there were in this instance, and probably will be in most, a surplus of qualified applicants. Admission of people who will not make a good adjustment is detrimental to the individuals, their neighbors, and the success of such programs. For maximum social usefulness, those qualified applicants most likely to adjust should be selected for admission.

Evaluation of factors related to individual differences in adjustment to the new situation was, then, a second aim. The extremely modern style of the building, its high-rise construction, the very newness and cleanness of the surroundings, were joltingly different from the homes in which many of the residents of Victoria Plaza had formerly lived. Not only the physical environment but also the social situation was radically changed. From isolation and social poverty, those applicants who moved into the Plaza were suddenly thrust into proximity with many others. For people who were to live in the new building, predictions regarding adjustment were made on the basis of background and psychological test data prior to admission. These predictions were checked against several criteria of adjustment obtained after a year or more of residence in the Plaza.

A third major purpose was investigation of the processes of interpersonal contact, group formation, and leadership emergence. This seemed an excellent opportunity for study of social relationships in a relatively stable group of older people over a period of time. When these people were uprooted, did they have the resilience to make new friends? If friendships formed, were they based primarily on commonality of background, similarity or complementarity of personality traits, or physical propinquity? What accounted for the emergence of certain individuals as leaders? Development of these interpersonal and group processes was followed in interviews at three-month intervals during the first year the new building was occupied. Results may offer suggestions for optimal assignment of residents within such buildings.

The Organization of the Book

One main purpose of this project was to assess the impact of change in residence on approximately half the subjects. All had expressed dissatisfaction with their living situations by applying for apartments in Victoria Plaza, and it would be easy to assume that acceptance there would meet important needs and improve individual and social adjustment. However, complaints about housing could be displaced expressions of other frustrations and therefore unrelieved by improved living quarters; people in this age range may find it difficult to make such a drastic change, if flexibility is related to age; and the type of construction may not be pleasing, if older people are conservative in their tastes. Extent and direction of changes in behavior patterns and attitudes, as well as satisfactions, are important in evaluating this type of residence for older people.

As a setting for this assessment of the impact of residential change, the first chapters describe the people studied, their housing conditions and costs, and the reasons they gave for wanting to move. Next follows a description of the new building, then an account of Housing Authority procedures for selecting tenants, and an analysis of initial similarities and differences between the group selected for residency and those who did not become residents. Successive chapters give selectees' initial reactions to the building on their first tour of it, and their evaluations of it after living there a year, as well as changes in their life style, outlook, and adjustment over that period of time.

Chapter 8 discusses the development of interpersonal contacts, group formation, and leadership emergence during the first year. The following three chapters describe differences in adjustment to the new situations among members of the first group to move into the Plaza, and an effort to predict those differences, with a view to improving selection of tenants in the future. Chapter 12 is a summary.

CHAPTER 2

How the People Were Selected

THE HOUSING AUTHORITY furnished names and addresses of all aged applicants who were not obviously ineligible for public housing under legal restrictions.[1] Some applications were recent, while others had been on file for several years. Many had been made before Victoria Plaza was even a gleam in Marie McGuire's eye, and therefore were requests for cottage-type public housing which was not age-restricted. The research team was delighted to be of some use to Housing Authority personnel by helping to bring application information up to date.

Of the 518 people whose names were supplied by the Housing Authority, research interviewers determined the whereabouts of all but 18. Usually their applications bore the older dates. They were not in the city directory or on public assistance rolls. Social Security information regarding their deaths or present addresses could not be obtained.

Several of the remaining 126 whose applications were removed from the "active" file at this time had died or become handicapped or ill. Others had moved out of the city. However, most of this group

[1] Housing Authority standards for admission to public housing are presented in Chapter 5.

withdrew their applications because they were "No longer interested." One woman's letter to her interviewer is typical:

Dear Mrs. ———,

I'm sorry but I don't think I want a place like this to live. As I told you, I don't like to live upstairs, and I would probly [sic] have to pay just as much rent there as I would any other small place. I'm going to find a small place downstairs where there is a yard and I know I will be much happier.

I thank you kindly,

Mrs. ———

As more information had become available regarding the new construction, some people developed reservations about certain of its features, such as the height, limitation to one age group, absence of private yards, or the possibility of having an apartment next to a "Mescan." Several applications had been filed by one spouse, unknown to the other, and the husband or wife was unwilling to go along with it. Some people chose to withdraw their applications because they had seen, in the case of others, that Housing personnel managed to discover camouflaged excess income. Generally, those already in public housing who lost interest had done so when they learned that rent in the new building would be five to ten dollars a month more than they were paying.

Of the recorded applicants for public housing, 374 wanted to live in Victoria Plaza (which some heard about, for the first time, during this check of application information). These people were potential subjects for the study.

How They Were Contacted

Each of the 374 active applicants was asked, in person if possible or else by phone, whether he was willing to take part in the research. Great effort was made to have him understand that participation was voluntary and had no bearing on admission to Victoria Plaza or other public housing facilities. Nevertheless, it is probable that many applicants believed cooperation would improve their chances. When there was initial reluctance, it usually vanished at mention of the opportunity to assist in increasing knowledge and possibly benefitting others, though not oneself.

If the applicant was willing, an appointment was made, at his convenience, almost always in his own home, and with no one else present. This consideration of the person and regard for privacy during the interviewing were routine procedures from a research point of view, to obtain full and frank responses. A few respondents insisted on interview arrangements which went beyond confidentiality, to the point of furtiveness. Though paranoid tendencies were strongly suspected, further investigation showed that every such individual was reacting reasonably to his situation.

The first person interviewed can serve as an example. She was a beguiling little old lady who was living in the servant's quarters over the garage of a home she had given her daughter. The son-in-law had turned her out of the house because she "got in the way of the family." She was allowed to keep the maid's room only because she did a servant's work every day. Dreadfully afraid of her son-in-law, she was desperately eager to find another place to live, but terrified of what he might do if he should find out about her efforts—unless or until they succeeded. All of her interviewing and testing was done in a drug store booth with an old-fashioned high back, behind which she felt safe from observation.

This woman later kept secret the knowledge of her acceptance into the building, suddenly moved one day while her son-in-law was at work, and phoned the daughter to let her know. His reaction, as reported by his wife to the interviewer, fully justified her mother's apprehension. The older woman's unusually good social adjustment in Victoria Plaza further vidicated her mental health. At the end of a year everyone in Victoria Plaza knew her, and common descriptions were, "Everybody loves her" and "She's a little eager-beaver." The only "oddity" anyone mentioned was her habit of visiting around the apartments and even the lobby with her hair on rollers and tied up in a red bandana. This lowered the "tone" of the Plaza, some residents felt.

More usual than fear, as causes of secretiveness, were reluctance to hurt children's feelings by the attempt to move away from them, and apprehension lest a landlord take the opportunity to deprive the applicant of what housing he had. In such cases, the commonest ploy was to let the child or landlady assume that the interviewer was a case worker.

In one instance this backfired when the landlady phoned the Old Age Assistance office to complain about the "case worker" who would not admit her to the room while the "worker" and "client" talked, nor tell her about it afterward. This landlady not only habitually waylaid renters' visitors in the hall to cross-examine them; in order not to miss anything, she also opened their mail when it appeared interesting.

How Information Was Obtained from Them

Biographic, demographic, attitudinal, intellectual, and other personality-trait information was collected in two series of interview and testing contacts at an interval of twelve to fifteen months. Normally the interviewer spent four to five hours with each person during each series, though some of the old people were so delighted to have someone listen to them that double or triple that time was necessary to obtain the information without rebuffing the respondent.

Most simply refused to be hurried and, if they felt it necessary, would remind the interviewer that there was no compulsion upon them other than the desire to cooperate and be helpful.

Some insisted on perceiving this as an ordinary social situation, requiring the usual give-and-take, which unduly extended the interview time and yet which was necessary to maintain cooperation. One woman considered it only polite, for example, to turn most questions back to the interviewer: if asked how many children she had, she would conclude her answer with the question, "And you?" Another, a former schoolteacher, insisted on writing down questions she could not answer or about which she was not sure, so she could think about them and let the interviewer know. (She did, too.)

Normally each series of contacts numbered about four, two for interviewing and two for testing, depending always on the respondent's fatigue and interest. A considerable number of the people phoned or wrote requesting appointments additional to those considered sufficient by the interviewer. Earlier discussion had reminded the older person of something important he wanted to add, or he decided he had not been completely straightforward, and wanted to rectify his responses. Some of these people only had good advice for the interviewer, urging her to benefit from their own accumulation of wisdom based on experience.

One recalled her interviewer, of whom she had become especially fond, because of, "Something very important I forgot to tell you." After the sessions of interviews and tests, during a period of reminiscing about her past life which had been stimulated by them, the older woman concluded that she had not enjoyed adequately the physical aspects of marriage. Her husband was gone, and for her it was too late, but it became urgently important for her to make sure that this fine young woman did not waste her opportunity in the same way.

Since, in order to assess change, two sets of contacts were necessary, at the end of the first the interviewer tried to find out each subject's reaction to the research program, his willingness to participate again later, and whether any sections of the interviews or tests were particularly distasteful. Only a handful said they disliked the proceedings and probably would not cooperate in something similar in the future. Negative comments centered on questions regarding marriages and those on attitudes, particularly attitudes toward oneself, as being unduly personal and lengthy. A few people said they would take part again only if the same interviewer came back.

The small number of negative comments was not surprising, since the person gave this evaluation to his own interviewer, and a derogatory statement might be taken personally. Also there is little doubt that many felt the interview might influence their chances of getting into the new building, no matter what anyone said, and they wanted to make as good an impression as possible on everyone connected in any way with the Plaza.

Most, "didn't mind," giving the interview and taking the tests, and a third of the number said they enjoyed it very much and looked forward eagerly to the possibility of similar sessions. Generally their pleasure was in having someone with whom to talk. Often, during discussion of their lives, they had been pleasantly reminded of incidents they had not thought about in years. A few individuals expressed appreciation for the opportunity to talk with someone else about a personal problem which, as a consequence, seemed easier to face.

Most applicants expressed satisfaction over the opportunity to give information which might be helpful to later generations of older people. ("You tell me this won't help me get in the building—and I believe you. But maybe what you're doing will make life a little better for people your age, when they get to mine. I'm proud to think I might have helped in that." "*Someone* should benefit from all my living, even if it's not me!" "This is the only useful thing I've been able to do since I retired. You can't know what it means to me—so come back whenever you can!")

Only one person actively objected to the proceedings after having cooperated in them. It was never clear how much this reaction was due to the interviewer, how much to the operator of the home where the applicant lived, and how much to the woman's own suspiciousness. Prior to the contact the interviewer had been warned to avoid giving the home manager any information about the public housing application, since she was known to guard her clientele zealously. The operator of the residence phoned the principal investigator demanding to know the connection between the interview and public housing application, and later mailed a memorandum written by the applicant in which she disclaimed her application for housing.

On the other hand, about one interviewee in five took the initiative in contacting his interviewer, adding information or correcting or justifying his earlier responses. Some of these contacts were made by phone, but the commonest way was by a letter or note accompanying the seven-day diary, when it was returned to the interviewer by mail. For example:

San Antonio 1, Texas
April 23, 1960

Interviewer for the New Golden Age Center
400 Labor St.
San Antonio 3, Texas

Dear Mrs. ———:

In regard to the Questionaire you filled out on Saturday for me—The "Yes" opposite "Alert" should be crossed out and placed opposite "Stupid" instead.

In regard to my claim to being a San Antonian—we paid taxes here from 1887 to 1925—38 years. My mother was Mrs. ——. I do not remember if the taxes were listed in her name or in the name of the —— Estate.

My father came to San Antonio in 1885. He died in 1888. He left a store, thirty acres of land south of the city with a house on it, all paid for, and considerable insurance. My mother bought property. Besides our home she had a number of rent houses. She was not a good business woman. They did not seem to bring in revenue, only taxes. I took after Mother.

In June 1901 when I received an appointment to teach in the Public School she had only one place left, 321 Lavaca St., a two story house we occupied as a home. I taught until 1915. But I furnished the money for the taxes from 1901 to 1925. My mother had a long last illness. I was forced to sell it to defray the expenses.

I do not belong to any organization, but I forgot to tell you I am a "Registered Democrat" of which I am quite proud. Hoping this is satisfactory, I am

Yours most sincerely,

Kinds of Information Obtained from Applicants

The main purpose of the first contact with applicants was a description of these people as they were before any change was made in their housing. This was important, not only to provide a basis for estimating the effect of the environmental change and to provide predictors of subsequent adjustment, but also to clarify generalization of the findings to other applicant groups and comparison of the results with those of other studies.

A comparison of the people admitted to superior housing with those not admitted may reflect initial differences which purposely or inadvertently influenced assignment of individuals to the two groups. After a period of time those in improved circumstances may look better than those not, according to any criterion of success, and the environmental manipulation may thus be credited with an effect it did not produce. On the other hand, if selection is based on need, or if selectors try to help the most severely deprived, absence of any difference between the two groups, after a period of time in an improved environment, may represent a newly achieved equality between them. In that case an effective environmental change may be abandoned as useless. Collection of baseline (prehousing change), demographic, attitudinal, and personality-test data on all applicants precluded such confusion of selection and housing effects.

Similarly, predictors of adjustment to such a situation, in order to be most useful in selection of tenants, should be measured while the people are applicants. Future use of these findings in the selection of tenants for this or a similar housing situation will involve decision making about other applicants, and it is possible that the same human being's reaction as a resident may be different from that he made earlier.

Study of the effects of changed housing on this particular group of applicants would be of very limited value, even though interesting, unless it had implication for other groups of people. There will never be another situation identical to this one, even at Victoria Plaza itself, much less possibly in any other place. However, generalizations can be made to the extent that those other situations and the people involved in them are similar to those of this study. The comprehensive preliminary description of the people should assist in attempts to apply the results to other applicants for housing. In regard to gerontological theory, the basic data should clarify similarities and differences in results between this study and others.

It seems obvious that these findings cannot be applied to people much younger, or more prosperous, or more seriously handicapped physically. They may also be inapplicable to people who have not experienced such intense social deprivation, or who have very different backgrounds of education and socio-economic status. Possibly attitudinal differences are also relevant. At least until much more is known about the processes of aging, as well as the effects of environmental change, generalizing from one group of people to another should be done most carefully, and only where it is justified in terms of demonstrated similarities among the people and the environmental variables.

This problem is accentuated by the fact that studies of older people tend to use groups somehow biased or selected in such a way that they are not representative of most people in their age group. As Lorge (1956) and others have pointed out, conceptions regarding older people tend to be based on research using individuals either in institutions or among the socially or occupationally elite. It is difficult to obtain a truly representative sample of any age group, but particularly so as people advance in years. The visibility and availability of the socially dependent and outstandingly successful are almost irresistible.

However, concepts regarding the aging segment of our society which are based upon the responses of such restricted samples are questionable. In the absence of data on representative elder groups, results should be interpreted in the context of complete descriptions of the people studied. Their divergence from norms such as census figures should be taken into account when stating conclusions which may be accepted as generalizations about "people in general." The similarity between subjects of any study and other people to whom the findings might be applied should indicate the suitability of such application. Apparently divergent and even conflicting findings of various studies might be resolved by fuller pictures of the people involved. Effects may differ meaningfully according to physical and mental health, intelligence level, proportion of men to women in the group, or any one of a number of characteristics of the subject sample.

The goal of the first research contact with the Victoria Plaza applicants was to obtain a sufficiently comprehensive view of their histories and backgrounds, their patterns of living and of viewing themselves and the rest of the world, that people charged with the responsibility of subsequent admissions to Victoria Plaza, or to another residence, can compare new applicants with the original group in order to decide whether these findings are likely to be applicable. Furthermore, the same data enable comparison of these subjects with subjects of other studies, in interpreting coincidence or conflict of results. Moreover, they demonstrate the similarity of this group to "old people in general," or their difference from them, and in this way objectively determine the breadth of justifiable generalization.

The Interview

Obviously, much of the information could best be obtained during an interview. To avoid the influence of preconceptions held by the researchers, and to maximize the breadth of response obtained from applicants, the interview was to be informal; yet for certainty that full information would be obtained, it had to be given some direction. A National Opinion Research Center interview schedule for use with older persons[2] and "Your Activities and Attitudes" (Burgess, Cavan, and Havighurst, 1948) were helpful in suggesting content.

After several revisions, the questionnaire[3] evolved as a guide to the interviewer. It includes sections on parents and siblings, childhood histories and backgrounds, and youth, education, religion, employment history and status, past and current financial situations, leisure activities, friends, marriage(s), family, health, housing and services, problems and wishes, and plans for the future.

The interview schedule served only as an outline for the interviewers, indicating information they were to obtain. The questions posed were not usually phrased as they appear on the interview form, nor were they asked in the written order. The interviewer led an informal conversation to collect the information. If, for example, questions about the father led to a discussion of the husband, the conversation was allowed to follow its natural course, and the interviewer simply flipped through to the proper page for recording, or wrote the material wherever he could and copied it later. He had only to be sure that at the end of the interview he had all the in-

[2] Secured in a private communication from Ethel Shanas, National Opinion Research Center.

[3] Appendix A gives an abbreviated form. Dr. Abraham Carp and Sister Frances Jerome participated in its development.

formation covered by the items. Two hours was the length of the typical interview. Women's tended to be longer than men's.

Responses were recorded verbatim, insofar as possible, and categorizing was done after the interviewing of all applicants was finished. The response categories reflect, then, the reactions of the applicants to open-ended questions, and were not limited to the possibilities which occurred to the research people ahead of time.

ATTITUDE SURVEY

To obtain expressions of attitudes in important areas (about one's own health, financial situation, usefulness, and happiness; toward one's friends and family; and about religion) the attitude scales from Burgess *et al.* (1948) were used. In this case questioning was verbatim. It was anticipated that many applicants could answer these questions—and perhaps would prefer to do so—as a paper-and-pencil task without intervention of the interviewer. This method was preferable also because the authors used the written instrument. However, as it quickly became apparent that the form of some questions presented difficulties, all items were presented orally to minimize ambiguity of responses.

For example, consider the item: "I don't rely on prayer to help me." Almost uniformly if a person responded, "Agree," he did not actually agree with the question as stated but, quite the opposite, he did rely on prayer. The response recorded was not necessarily the first "Agree" or "Disagree," but rather the interviewer's interpretation of a discussion with the respondent about the intent of his answer. This inevitably raises the question whether direct comparisons are tenable between data collected on this instrument in written form and those obtained by interviewers. Cavan *et al.* (1949) pointed out the ambiguity of "Yes," "No," and "?" response categories for statements in negative form. It did not seem to disappear, in this study, with the response words they proposed as alternates.

ADJECTIVE CHECK LIST

For self-description, an adjective check list was adapted from Gough's (1952; Appendix A). Some subjects checked the list themselves. Others preferred to have it read to them and to have the recording done by their interviewer, either because they liked the company and attention, or because poor vision, crippling, or palsy made paper-and-pencil tasks difficult. The interviewer read off each word of the Adjective Check List and the applicant answered "Yes," if he thought it fit him or "No," if he thought it did not. A "Don't know" category was not offered, but sometimes a subject could not decide, or did not know the meaning of the word.

PECK'S SENTENCE COMPLETION TEST

To afford another opportunity for expression of attitudes toward the self, as well as toward other people, the current revision of Peck's Sentence Completion Test,[4] was included (Appendix A). This was also administered either orally or in written form, at the will of the applicant. Some wanted the privacy of reading the sentence stems and writing the completions without assistance. Others preferred to have their interviewers do the work, or to perform the task in a sociable way.

SEVEN-DAY DIARY

It seemed that one richly descriptive piece of information, as well as an important index on which to judge effects of a changed living situation, was the way in which these people usually spent their time. Though the interview included questions on patterns of living and various activities, it seemed desirable to try to get a less subjective record. It is important to find out how people think they spend their time, but this may be quite different from how they actually spend it. Therefore the interviewer filled in a one-day time sheet according to the applicant's account of his activities during each quarter-hour of the preceding day, making sure that the respondent saw how the filling-in was done.

The subject was then asked if he would take a one-week time sheet (Appendix A), fill it in daily and return it to the interviewer by mail. In some instances none was left because the person did not see well enough to complete it, because he did not care to, or because he protested that his life was too routine. Particularly toward the end of the interviewing period, many were too busy getting their things together preparatory to moving into Victoria Plaza if they should be accepted. The high rate of return (over 60%) was a surprise. Not only did a large number of subjects cooperate in the trying task of recording the week's activities hour by hour and returning

[4] Secured in private communication from Dr. Robert Peck, Department of Educational Psychology, The University of Texas.

this material, but a number also phoned or wrote the interviewers subsequently to make some alteration or add a piece of information they felt to be important.

Several people who did not complete and return the time-sheet did take the trouble to explain the default and apologize for it. One woman wrote:

Monday, March 28th, 1960

Dear Mrs. ———,

I am sorry. I could not write a dairy [sic] last week, after I went to see my Dr. I am feeling better and have the shoe bags made for you. Hope you can forgive me.

Sincerely,
Mrs. ———

The one person who was to move out of the Plaza voluntarily during the first year of its occupancy accounted for about half an hour for each of the seven days; she wrote shakily across the back of the form in explanation: "I am so nervous I can't write," and mailed it to her interviewer.

INTERVIEWER REMARKS AND REACTIONS

To provide information regarding observable handicaps, alertness and clarity of thought during the interview contacts, and general appearance and manner, the interviewer filled out a rating sheet immediately after completion of the first series of contacts with each applicant (Appendix A).

Degree of senility and of disengagement seemed important to an adequate description of older people. As a means of providing these data, Cavan *et al.'s* Senility Index was included (1949, p. 182) and a Disengagement Index was devised (Appendix A). Both were filled out by the interviewer as soon as he had completed interviewing and testing the applicant.

PSYCHOLOGICAL TESTS

As it became increasingly obvious that before all applicants could be tested, the building would be completed and announcement made of the names of those to be given apartments in it, it was decided to test those applicants most likely to become residents. Since they would undergo a definite and consistent change in living situation, their psychological test data were more imperative to subsequent studies evaluating the impact of such change. Their location in the building furthermore, would make them likelier subjects for any later study, since they would be easier to contact. The Housing Authority proved invaluable here again by furnishing, from day to day, names of those most likely to be admitted.

It was decided not to take time from testing to interview fifteen people who made application after interviewing had ceased. The assumption that the date of application would prevent their obtaining apartments proved false. Most of them were admitted to the Plaza among the first group of occupants.[5]

More standard information regarding intelligence was secured through administration of the Wechsler-Bellevue Form I (Wechsler, 1946). Usual instructions and procedures were followed except that the Arithmetic Sub-Test was omitted because it was so heartily disliked, and the Vocabulary Sub-Test was substituted.

To supply descriptive material in the areas of personality variables and mental health, the Multiphasic Personality Inventory (MMPI, Hathaway and McKinley, 1949) and three cards of the Thematic Apperception Test (TAT, Murray, 1943) were administered to as many as possible before selection of tenants was announced. The card-sort form of the MMPI was used, for variety of procedure and privacy of the subject and, frankly, because the data collectors were by that time madly racing against the construction crew.

Interviewers were less willing to take the time to read questions and write answers than they had been earlier, and applicants, who by now knew them fairly well and were aware of the pressure, generally agreed to do their own secretarial work. Actually the number of those tested with the MMPI was limited by the number of boxes of test material, and the necessity to make a trip to pick up a box, record one person's responses, shuffle the cards, and take the box to the next applicant. For a few people the task was impossible because of visual or motor problems, or distasteful because they felt it was too personal or "foolish."

The plan to prepare some special TAT-type picture material did not materialize, again because of time pressure, and it was necessary to limit the number of cards to three (1, 6BM and 10) of the standard set. Even then it was possible to obtain responses from only about a third of the applicants before announcement of the Housing Au-

[5] Date of application was only one of many criteria for admission (see Chapter 5).

thority's decisions terminated the existence of an applicant group and effected its division into "ins" and "outs," even though no one had moved physically. No more information could be obtained on an applicant group which no longer existed, and all interviewing and testing ended with the Housing Authority's announcement.

Test administration required, on the average, about three hours per person. This was usually accomplished in several sessions, since no session was allowed to run longer than an hour, in order not to fatigue the respondent, and many were terminated far more quickly than that. With applicants scattered all over the city, testing was costly in terms of time and money.

The next chapter describes the applicant group as it appeared immediately prior to the opening of Victoria Plaza, by summarizing the information obtained from the members of that group in their interview and testing sessions, and from their interviewers and testers in judgments about them which were recorded after the face-to-face contacts.

CHAPTER 3

What They Were Like

THIS CHAPTER DESCRIBES the 352 people who were originally interviewed and tested, as of the time of that first contact. Of this group 204 were later selected to live in Victoria Plaza. Effects of living in the new building were assessed by comparing changes in residents with changes in the remainder of the group, over the period of about one year, with consideration also of initial similarity or dissimilarity of selectees and nonselectees. Individual differences in adjustment to Victoria Plaza and variables related to these differences, as well as the development of social processes, were studied, of course, only in the resident group, and are reported in later sections of this account.

One limitation of much research with aging people is bias in subject samples because of visibility and availability of those in institutions, of eminent individuals, or of members of elite groups. Results of such studies may or may not be relevant to old people who are normal members of communities. Subjects of this study were living in their own homes and directing their own lives, and they wanted to maintain that status.

However, they were not selected on the basis of representativeness but on that of application for public housing. While this automatically makes the results particularly applicable to other public-housing situations, it also means that generalization concerning more privileged older people on the basis of conclusions concerning this group must be made only when such extension is demonstrably appropriate, or with careful reservations.

For this reason, the description of the people studied is divided into two sections. The first part of this chapter deals with variables suspect of bias and variables on which the group were found to be nonrepresentative of "people in general." The latter part of the chapter completes the description of the group with discussion of characteristics on which these people seemed to be much like most others of their age.

For simplicity, all information about one topic is presented together. Therefore many nonbiased characteristics of the group are discussed in the first part of the chapter. For example, religion is there because the applicant group did not represent the local population in regard to religious affiliation. However, there is no reason to believe that religious beliefs, attitudes, and behavior diverged from the normal. Indeed, the very discrepancy from local membership patterns is in the direction of greater similarity to national norms.

Some Sources of Bias in Sampling

DISEQUALITIES FROM PUBLIC HOUSING APPLICATION

All of the 352 applicants desired housing, a situation which reflected not only economic need and housing problems but also awareness of community affairs plus willingness and ability to apply. While information about Victoria Plaza had been disseminated in the community through newspaper articles and speeches, there had been no publicity campaign. Application had to be made in person at the Housing Authority office. Alertness, initiative, and physical wellbeing were required to achieve applicant status. The seriously unwell and institutionalized were not represented proportionately. The marginally intelligent, as well as the passive, were less likely to be included.

Housing Authority personnel screened applicants for financial status before their names were turned over to the research team. The well-to-do or even those financially comfortable were not eligible but, on the other hand, an applicant must be able to pay the minimum rent. All were within a restricted economic range, including neither the financially comfortable nor the acutely impoverished.

INCOMPLETE DATA

Another possible source of bias, though probably a much less important one, was the failure to collect data on one hundred per cent of the applicants. When the Housing Authority made public the names of people to whom apartments had been assigned, interviews had not yet been held with twenty-two of the 374 applicants. (The spouses of ten of them had been interviewed.) To avoid what seemed the greater bias introduced by knowledge of selection, data collection stopped. Though this reduced the coverage of applicants, it avoided influencing responses by knowledge of acceptance or rejection at Victoria Plaza. All first-contact data were collected before the applicant knew whether he would be assigned living space in the Plaza.

People eliminated from the study by the announcement of assignment of apartments tended to be the less accessible. However, in different people this may reflect evasiveness, illness, instability, or activity. On days of downpouring rain, interviewers made efforts to contact those who had previously been away from home. Even in the most inclement weather, many had gone out for their various activities.

One interviewee, who was extremely difficult to locate, belonged to five service and social clubs, played bridge several times each week, and had a wide circle of friends and acquaintances whom she saw often. She drove her own car and took friends on their errands or shopping tours. Even after she was contacted, and though she seemed eager to take part in the study, it was difficult for her to find time.

On the other hand, one woman who was easily located, and readily agreed to be interviewed, refused to answer almost every question. She was an eccentric person. A militant vegetarian who had eaten no meat since 1919, she did not believe in "regular doctors," but made numerous emergency calls to chiropractors, not uncommonly in the middle of the night.

Characteristics of Applicants Studied—with Known or Possible Bias

AGE OF APPLICANTS

Obviously the results are primarily relevant to people in one age group. The average age of the applicants was 72; the youngest person was a woman 52, the oldest a man 92 (Table 1). One woman preferred not to tell her age. Though the Housing Authority's mini-

TABLE 1

Age Distribution of the 352 Applicants (by Percentages)

Age in Years	*% Men*	*% Women*	*% Applicants*
50–54	00	02	01
55–59	00	01	01
60–64	08	06	06
65–69	24	28	27
70–74	30	31	30
75–79	25	20	21
80–84	07	09	09
85–89	05	03	04
90–94	01	00	01
Total	100	100	100
Number	75	277	352
Mean	72.97	72.05	72.27
σ (Standard Deviation)			6.6

mum age requirement was 65 for men but 62 for women, the sex difference in age was not statistically significant. The few below the minimum age were qualified by the total disability clause of Social Security or as spouses or children of qualified applicants.

One man was receiving full disability payments as the result of an automobile accident which occurred while he was at work, crushing his chest, already damaged by emphysema. He and his wife had spent all their savings and sold all their property to pay for his medical care over the four years of his hospitalization. They had crowded, with their son and daughter-in-law and four grandchildren, into a small two-bedroom cottage, after his release. He had always worked hard and well, and wanted to, but there was no task he could now perform.

An eighty-year-old mother tried desperately to secure an apartment for herself and her sixty-year-old daughter, badly handicapped with muscular dystrophy. (She was successful, but died five days after they moved in. She had, however, obtained the best living situation possible for her child.)

It cannot be assumed that these subjects, though neither institutionalized nor eminent, were representative of their age group.

DISSATISFACTION WITH RESIDENCE

Everyone was unhappy with the situation in which he lived, or he would not have been an applicant. Such unanimity is probably not characteristic of all people in this age range. Since this biasing factor is germane to evaluation of consequences of change in residence, characteristics of applicants' housing and their reactions to it are given in Chapter 4, where a description of Victoria Plaza is also presented. Housing Authority standards for selection of tenants are outlined in Chapter 5. Residents' reactions, with changes in their life style a year or more after moving there, are described in Chapters 6 and 7.

SEX[1]

Of the 352 subjects, 21 per cent were men and 79 per cent were women. This inequality was in the direction usually reported, but extreme. For Texas in the 1950 Census there were ten women to nine men sixty-five and over; and in the 1960 Census there were ten women for eight men in this age group (Shore, 1961). The White House Conference on Aging in 1961 reported that "the number of women 65 years of age and over exceeds the number of men by a ratio of 100 to 82" (p. 40). This group of applicants had a ratio of about 100 to 27.

Several factors probably contributed to this high predominance of women over men. Women were eligible for public housing at 62, men at 65, though, as mentioned earlier, women applicants were, on the average, no younger than men who applied. Men interviewees expressed less concern about their living conditions. Some who were living in extremely unpleasant circumstances commented that it did not matter since they could go to the pool hall or somewhere else to see their friends.

Some husbands admitted that they had applied to Victoria Plaza, "Only to please the wife," to secure a little freedom from her ("I won't be afraid to leave my wife alone any more when I go off on my fishing trips") or to provide security should she be widowed ("The figures all show I'll go first, and I wouldn't want her to be alone—especially not in a place like this"). Several male applicants were openly apprehensive that Victoria Plaza would be "an old ladies'

[1] All sex differences reported are statistically significant and are summarized in Appendix D, Tables 1 through 7.

home." This preconception may have kept others from applying. Some men living alone were reluctant to undertake cooking and housekeeping, and this may have reduced the number of male applicants further. Housing Authority personnel were aware of the problem and made every effort to include as many men as possible.

MARITAL STATUS

Table 2 gives the marital status of these subjects and of the similar age group in the United States in 1950 (Sheldon, 1958). Comparatively few of those studied were married and living with their spouses, and the absence of husbands and wives was due to high divorce and separation rate, not death.

TABLE 2

*Marital Status of Applicants Compared to That of the United States Population**
(Percentage Distributions)

Marital Status	*% Women* U.S.	*% Women* Applicants	*% Men* U.S.	*% Men* Applicants
Widowed	54.3	58.5	24.1	25.4
Married: spouse present	33.2	14.5**	62.1	46.7**
Married: spouse absent	3.6	16.5**	5.5	14.6**
Single	8.9	8.0	8.4	12.0
Separated	0.0	2.5	0.0	1.3
Total	100.0	100.0	100.0***	100.0

* From Sheldon, H. D., *The Older Population of the United States*, p. 90.
** The per cent of Victoria Plaza applicants in these categories is significantly different at the .01 level from that in the U.S. population.
*** Sheldon does not round figures to make totals of even 100%.

Married couples are probably more self-sufficient than single individuals, both financially and socially, because they are company for each other; therefore they would be less likely to apply for public housing. Possibly, to people living alone, the apartment situation offered in Victoria Plaza was more attractive than the cottage style available in other public housing. These factors, however, would seem to be relevant for the widowed as well.

Unfortunately, figures on marital status of local public housing applicants were not available in a form which would allow testing of these possibilities regarding cause. It is clear that applicants to Victoria Plaza included a disproportionate number of people whose marriages had been terminated by divorce or separation, though not an excess number of the widowed.

NATIONALITY AND ETHNIC BACKGROUND

This group did not represent the aged population of San Antonio in racial or ethnic origin. According to approximate 1960 Census figures, 7 per cent of the San Antonio's population was 65 and over. For the 45 per cent classified as white, 9 per cent were 65 and over. Seven per cent were Negro and Oriental, with 7 per cent of this group 65 and over. Of the 49 per cent of the population with Latin American surnames, 4 per cent were 65 and over. The group being studied contained only 3 per cent of Latin Americans and included no Negroes.

Since, in general, families of both Negroes and Latin Americans use public housing facilities in proportion to their numbers in San Antonio, the small number of elderly applicants to Victoria Plaza from these groups may reflect the tendency of both subcultures to take care of the elderly within their families.

It is not possible to rule out racial prejudice, which might have operated in several ways. Immediately prior to development of plans for Victoria Plaza a motel-type housing project of thirty-six units was built for elderly Negroes. Applications for residence and for admission to the two facilities were completely separate. Timing of the construction of the two public housing facilities for the elderly may have been interpreted by Negroes as a segregation indicator.

Some applicants refused to be interviewed by a charming and well-trained young woman of Latin American name and appearance, but readily agreed to cooperate with a blonde, English-named interviewer. A few interviewees volunteered that they had not appreciated the attempt at intrusion by "Mescans," or inquired whether any were applying, or expressed concern over moving to Victoria Plaza if it was going to be "that kind of place."

Whatever the cause, the fact that people of Latin American ancestry were underrepresented for San Antonio made the group more similar to "old people in general" in the nation as a whole.

English was the mother tongue of 90 per cent. More men than women had another language as mother tongue, German most frequently. Eighty per cent had use of the English language only; a few people could communicate in three or four tongues. Languages spoken in addition to English were primarily German and Spanish. Five who spoke and read English, but did not write it, grew up in Mexican or German-speaking homes.

One woman who said (in Spanish) that she could write English did even this in a limited way. She did not speak or understand English, and her writing was limited to such things as her name, address, and phone number. However, she spoke, read, and wrote Spanish fluently. Another woman who spoke English but did not read or write it was an American-born citizen holding a part-time job in a drug store who was able to carry on her life in such a way that no one would know of this language deficiency.

Ninety-nine per cent of the subjects were citizens of the United States and 92 per cent were born in this country. A third of their parents were foreign-born (Table 3).

TABLE 3

Country of Birth of the 352 Applicants and Their Parents (Percentage Distributions)

Country of Birth	*% Applicants*	*% Fathers*	*% Mothers*
United States	92	76	83
Germany	2	8	6
British Isles	1	5	4
Russia	1	2	1
Mexico-Latin America	2	2	2
Scandinavia	.5	2	1
Canada	.5	1	1
Balkans	.5	1	1
Other European	.5	3	1
Total	100	100	100

RELIGION

The group included far too few Roman Catholics (15%) to be representative for the geographic area, due probably to the under-representation of Latin Americans. Both the local archdiocese and the Chamber of Commerce estimated that 50 per cent of the population of this area was Roman Catholic.

Of the Protestant group (80%), most claimed formal membership in a major denomination, predominantly Baptist and Methodist. A few attended Pentecostal, Jehovahs' Witness, Bible Students, or

Spiritualist meetings regularly. For these groups formal membership was apparently not a normal procedure. Some in the more traditional denominations, who had left letters of membership in churches no longer accessible and attended others, less preferred, did not consider themselves "members" of either. Therefore, 85 per cent to 90 per cent of the subjects were regularly associated with some church. Surprisingly, all eight who actively disclaimed church affiliation and religious belief were women.

Although religion is often considered a sensitive area, the only person who avoided the question about religious preference was the woman who refused almost every item in the interview. Other questions, particularly regarding finances, may have been more sensitive, since it probably was not possible to divorce research from admission procedures in the eyes of applicants. They talked readily about religion, which was obviously of major importance to most of them.

The most popular pattern of church attendance was once-a-week-on-the-Sabbath, though a third of the people went less than once a month, and 20 per cent "never." Infrequency of religious-service participation was an index of poverty and lack of transportation as well as of disinterest. Probably half the people were frustrated by inability to attend services more often or were dissatisfied because the accessible house of worship was not the one of choice. Women attended church more regularly than men.

In view of the generally held belief that religion becomes increasingly important to people as they grow older, the interviewers asked whether they attended church more or less often than at age fifty-five. Half went less frequently, only 15 per cent more often. A handful of those who reported decreased attendance said it was due to diminished interest. The most common reason, given by two-thirds of the people, was inability to get there. They were too old to make the long bus rides, perhaps with many transfers, necessary to attend the church of their choice or perhaps any church at all. In addition, some "can't afford" responses (20%) indicated inability to pay for transportation to church, and others expressed unwillingness to attend without making some contribution. Sharp dissatisfaction was spontaneously voiced by many about the inaccessibility of religious activities. This was not only a matter of church services. They were eager to have hymn singing, Bible classes, and other religious instruction as well.

Religious programs on radio and television were popular. Half the group listened more than once a week, fewer than 15 per cent "never" did. Particularly well liked was a local radio program in which various ministers took turns giving devotionals. Some applicants listened regularly. Many more made sure to tune in when the minister of their church, or one of their denomination, was speaking.

It was rather impressive that half read their Bibles once or twice every day, fewer than 15 per cent "never." Interviewers thought this was no exaggeration. Ordinarily the Bible was out in a place of honor and close at hand, and showed use. Those with failing eyesight saved what little they had for religious reading. Five percent of the group read nothing else. Those who "never" read the Bible were almost exactly the same people with no Church affiliation. Women read their Bibles with greater frequency than men.

Sure belief in after life was expressed by nearly 90 per cent, definite disbelief by only one per cent. Most considered religion "Fairly important in my life," or "A great comfort," and relied on prayer to help them. For two-thirds of the applicants, religion was "The most important thing in my life"; while only 10 per cent said that, "Religion doesn't mean much to me," and 5 per cent had "No use for religion." Women consistently expressed greater interest in religion and dependence upon it.

Despite their overwhelming interest in religion, the interviewees had little personal contact with church representatives or members. Fewer than half the applicants went to even one social event at church a year. The relatively large number (5%) who avoided responding to the question "Does anyone from your church call on you?" probably indicated embarrassment to admit that no one took the trouble. This lack was brought out as a source of distress by those who reported no visits (over half), and the infrequency was taken as a slight even by those who did receive a visitor occasionally. Church calls were made even more infrequently to men than to women.

HEALTH

The seriously ill and handicapped were eliminated by Housing Authority requirements and initial screening, and probably the group as a whole was above average in regard to health. No physical examination or medical report could be obtained, and only self-report and interviewer observations were available.

Attitudes. Over half of the applicants thought their health was good or excellent, and nearly two-thirds considered it better than that of most people their age, showing some difference when the reference group was specified for them, but not much. Particularly in regard to physical conditions, most of the group used their age group as a standard, without special instruction. This served as an effective buffer against frustration over sensory-motor changes and development of chronic ailments.

Though 80 per cent agreed, "When I was younger, I felt a little better than I do now," over half were "Perfectly satisfied" with their health and 20 per cent "Never felt better in my life." Only a handful felt "Just miserable most of the time" and said, "If I can't feel better soon, I would just as soon die."

Problems. Interviewers were asked to report physical conditions which interfered with interview or test performance. No handicapping physical condition was noticed for two-thirds, difficulty with movement was noted with 15 per cent, hearing loss in 10 per cent, and visual deficit with 9 per cent. Nearly everyone had glasses (97%), most wore dentures (82%), and some had canes or crutches (10%).

Many expressed themselves as "satisfied" with dentures and eyeglasses only because they believed the appliances were as good as possible within the limits of their physical condition and ability to pay. Some wore ill-fitting plates, but the dentist had convinced them improvement was impossible; others wore eyeglasses which gave less than optimal vision, but they realized no glasses could restore perfect sight. However, one person in five was incensed because he believed that more adequate dental or visual professional attention could improve his comfort and effectiveness. Inadequate funds and transportation were the major deterrents mentioned.

Generally people had found the money for eyeglasses or dentures. Fewer than 1 per cent who did not have glasses, and 5 per cent without dentures, said they needed them. However, those who needed hearing aids usually felt they could not afford them. One person in every four mentioned a hearing problem, 15 per cent admitted they needed hearing aids, but only 8 per cent had them. A frequently mentioned reason was that the initial cost was only the beginning. Monthly upkeep was something they did not feel capable of undertaking. ("My budget won't stand the batteries.")

Crippling and stiffness handicapped a third of the applicants. Many more, who were not "bothered," commented that of course they experienced some difficulty in moving, as would anyone their age.

Many more than the one quarter who were "troubled" about shortness of breath experienced it when they climbed stairs or walked rapidly, but they expected this and had learned to make allowances for it. ("Now I just stop on each landing and watch the people.")

Some mentioned sleeplessness as a problem. Thirty per cent took naps during the day and went to bed at an early hour, yet complained because they awoke early in the morning. Others suffered from inability to sleep. Here again, many commented that insomnia was natural at their age. The woman who was admitted to the building but moved out during the first year, for reasons of her own, provides an example. The day preceding that on which she had her first interview, she woke up at 7:00, "rested and napped" three hours during the day, "did nothing" for four additional hours, and went to bed at 9:00. Yet she worried a great deal about being unable to get any sleep or rest.

One person in three said he noticed tiring more easily now than in former years but usually he did not consider it upsetting in any way.

Despite the physical infirmities and ailments acknowledged (Table 4), only one in twelve worried about his physical health; but of those (one in every three or four) who mentioned being blue and lonely, forgetful, nervous, or sensitive to noise, nearly all expressed concern about these experiences.

Restrictions. An overwhelming majority (90%) reported no restriction of activities because of health problems during the month preceding the interview. Most of the remainder were restricted "every day" by a chronic health problem such as a heart disorder, high blood pressure, or arthritis. Very few changed their plans because of a cold or other minor ailment.

Over half reported no days in bed during the last year; 8 per cent, a month or more, and 2 per cent almost all the time. Many insisted vehemently that they had never spent a day in bed in their lives and would never "give in" to sickness. Others were living alone or with others as old as themselves and had to get up to prepare meals and take care of the other necessities of life, whether they felt like it or not. Reasons for being bedridden during the last year were infections (26%), chronic conditions such as heart trouble, high blood pressure, arthritis (12%), operations (4%), and accidents (3%).

Accidents. Three-quarters of the applicants reported no serious accidents during the last five years. Falls during that time were reported by 14 per cent. Though fewer women reported accidents, more women reported falls. This is consistent with Droller's (1955) finding

TABLE 4

Health Problems of the 352 Applicants
(Percentage Distribution)

Problem	*% of Applicants*
Backache	19
Belching	6
Blood pressure (high or low)	13
Constipation	25
Cough	9
Crippling or stiffness	36
Depressed spirits (blue and lonely)	27
Diabetes	4
Diarrhea	1
Dizziness	18
Dreams (bad)	7
Fatigue	33
Forgetfulness	29
Gas pains	14
Headache	10
Health worry	9
Heaving	24
Heartburn	4
Heart trouble	24
Irritation from noise	24
Little relish for food	6
Nervousness	32
Piles	6
Poor vision	36
Shortness of breath	24
Sinus trouble	29
Sleeplessness	30
Stomach trouble	16
Swelling	20
Varicose veins	13

Note: Per cents in this table add to more than 100 because some applicants mentioned more than one disability.

regarding sex differences in falling; and the fact that the women subjects reported more dizziness but no more visual problems supports his attribution of cause.

Medical-Dental Care. Two-thirds had seen a physician during the last year and about a quarter had seen "someone else in the health line," usually a chiropractor, "eye doctor," or "foot doctor." One relied heavily upon a "reducing doctor" and another preferred a naturopath. Half had been to the doctor's office, 15 per cent had seen a doctor at the hospital, and only 4 per cent had received a house call.

One in five had seen a dentist during the previous year. Many laughed and commented, "What would I see a dentist for? I don't have any teeth!" Most had dentures which were as satisfactory as they could afford and saw the dentist only if one broke.

In considering the future, 5 per cent said they would like to see a physician and 12 per cent indicated need for a dentist. Only 2 per cent wanted to see both, while 81 per cent expressed no desire for seeing either. The small number who wanted to see a physician, relative to the number who wanted to see a dentist, bears some explanation, particularly in view of the tendency of most of them to see a physician rather than a dentist. They were answering here in terms of what they would "like to do," unlimited by finances and dental capabilities. This attitude leads to responses inconsistent with realistic expectations (Carp, 1949). Not all 12 per cent would make any effort to see a dentist. Most only wished they could have more satisfactory chewing equipment.

Hospitalization had been experienced once during the past five years by 31 per cent, and more than once, typically for a period of between one and two weeks, by 11 per cent. Three-quarters of the hospitalized group had been in private institutions. Of the men hospitalized, 68 per cent had been in private hospitals, and 32 per cent in military or V. A. institutions. Of the women, 83 per cent had been in private hospitals, 13 per cent in military or V. A. institutions, and 4 per cent in community-supported hospitals.

Half of those hospitalized had insurance policies which helped, though they did not cover the cost. Many mentioned as a serious source of grievance the public-housing limitation on savings. This lack of financial security caused concern in case of a future hospitalization or terminal illness.

To pay for medical-dental care current income was used by 44 per cent, V. A. or military benefits by 5 per cent, community funds by 4 per cent, and savings by 2 per cent. Three per cent were "still paying." They continued to feel responsible for the debt, but had exhausted their savings and each month failed to squeeze it out of income. Seven per cent received either free care or money for the bill from relatives. The remainder had incurred no medical or dental bills during the past year.

MENTAL HEALTH

Old, lonely, poor, dependent to a considerable extent on public money, these people might be assumed to have made relatively inadequate life adjustments. From the type of ailments which "bothered" them, they might be termed neurotic. However, psychological tests found them in astonishingly robust mental health.

There was not one bizarre response to the TAT pictures or any consistent abnormality in completing the sentence stems; there were no deviant scores on the MMPI. Clinicians found all of the material so "normal" that they despaired over instructions to sort the various types of protocols, even on a five-point scale. Using numerical score systems standardized on younger adults, or using clinical judgments probably based on the same reference group, pathology simply did not occur. It must be remembered that test results are available on samples only, not the entire applicant group.[2]

INTELLECTUAL COMPETENCE

On the Wechsler-Bellevue (Form I) the mean IQ of the 93 people who took the entire test was 109 ($\sigma = 13$), and their performance score was 105 ($v = 13$). The mean verbal score for a sample of 103 applicants was 112 ($\sigma = 11$). These IQ's were taken from the table for the 35–40-year age group, since this was the oldest for which norms were available on both verbal and performance sections.[3] With 55–59-year norms the mean verbal IQ was 113. No norms were available, even on the verbal scale of this test, for a group with mean age 72. Obviously the sample was unusual in regard to mental ability.

Unfortunately time did not allow testing of a larger number before the Housing Authority announced admission decisions. Representativeness of the subsample is questionable, since effort was made to test those applicants whom Housing Authority personnel considered most likely to be admitted. Extreme unrepresentativeness of the subsample seems unlikely in view of the similarity, in many ways, of those who moved into Victoria Plaza and those who did not. (See Chapter 5.) Unless the sample tested was markedly biased, the applicant group was well above average in general intelligence.

Intellectual competence of the group as a whole was supported by

[2] Reports on the psychological test results are in preparation.

[3] Materials for the WAIS, which has more adequate norms for older people, did not arrive in time to be used.

interviewer ratings on clarity of memory regarding dates, places, and names. Only about 10 per cent of the subjects showed confusion. Furthermore, less than 15 per cent of the people had difficulty focusing on any part of the interview, and interviewers rated few persons as seeming dull, showing poor recent memory, being unobservant, finding it difficult to learn, or having diminished interest in mental stimulation. However, ratings on alertness and clarity of thought were generally more favorable for those applicants who were to move into the Plaza. (See Chapter 5.) This suggests that, while IQ scores on the entire group would be above average, they would not be so high as those for the sample tested.

No doubt these people made special efforts to document their ability to think and remember clearly, in view of their positions as applicants for much improved housing. Though every effort was taken to assure them of the confidential treatment of research data, it is questionable that all were convinced. They must have been aware that if research material was made available to the Housing Authority's selection committee, intellectual competence would be considered. Also there may be rater overcompensation in view of the advanced age of respondents. On the other hand, their ratings were consistent with intelligence-test scores, which were obtained later.

Other Characteristics of Applicants Studied

The preceding section has described applicants for apartments in Victoria Plaza as they were at first-research contact, in respect to certain characteristics on which the group probably was not representative of "people in general." In some cases the discrepancy from local or national norms was documented; in others it was assumed, generally because of factors related to membership in the applicant group. Though the distinction, in some cases, may seem to be simply hair-splitting, it is important, in trying to make any broad generalization from this study, to keep in mind the ways in which this group was like or unlike older people in this country in general.

Furthermore, for comparison of these results with those obtained using other groups of people, or application of them in new housing situations, similarities and differences should be kept in mind. The same divergence from "averageness" which limits breadth of generalization may insure applicability of these results to certain other situations and groups of people.

Following sections continue the description of applicants, while the building was under construction and before anyone knew who would take up residence when Victoria Plaza was completed, this time in terms of variables on which this group was probably reasonably similar to the rest of their age group, or at least not biased as a sample of it.

FINANCIAL STATUS

Though incomes were small, the average was fairly representative of this age group in the United States (Table 5). The median, $94.40 per month, was similar to the national figure for single retired workers sixty years old and over with Social Security (U. S. Bureau of the Census, 1958). The modal income of $70.00 was typical for those who

TABLE 5

Monthly Income of the 352 Applicants
(Percentage Distribution)

Amount	*% of Applicants*
$210 and above	8
$170–$209	7
$130–$169	16
$ 90–$129	23
$ 50–$ 89	42
Below $50	4
Total	100

TABLE 6

Savings Accounts of the 352 Applicants
(Percentage Distribution According to Amount)

Dollars Saved	*Percentage*
3000 and over	10
1000–2999	11
500– 999	10
300– 499	5
100– 299	10
1– 100	6
None	48
Total	100

received Texas Old Age Assistance (average $52.07 in the state) plus some small medical or other allowance. Mean income was $114.00.

Nearly half the applicants reported no savings account (Table 6). Census figures show 31 per cent in that age bracket with no assets, but "assets" in census terms includes not only savings accounts but also bonds, insurance, and money in checking accounts. For the 50 per cent of Victoria Plaza applicants who reported any savings, the modal amount was $1,000 and the median was $750.

While not biased consistently upward or downward from national figures, this sample was restricted in the range of financial status, since Housing Authority regulations set a ceiling for income and savings, and the rent scale for Victoria Plaza provided a floor.

The means of financial support common to the greatest number of applicants was income from Social Security (Table 7). The figures in Table 7 add up to more than 100 per cent because many applicants received income from more than one source, each "primary" in the eyes of the respondents, since they could not make ends meet if any one source, no matter how small, were lost. This is clearer, perhaps, when it is realized that most Social Security payments were at the minimum ($20.00). The majority of men had Social Security and their payments tended to be somewhat larger, so that fewer than one-fifth of them were dependent on public assistance while nearly half the women were. About a third of the men and a quarter of the women were receiving pension money. In nearly every case the woman's was a widow's protection.

Attempts were made to locate additional indirect or nonmonetary

TABLE 7

Sources of Income for the 352 Applicants
(Percentage Distribution)

Income Source	*% Men*	*% Women*	*% Applicants*
Social Security	91	59	65
Public Assistance	17	42	37
Pensions	35	24	27
Annuities	17	19	19
Earnings			
Own	22	17	18
Spouse's	6	3	4

Note: Per cents add to more than 100 because many applicants received money from more than one source.

support, but little was found. Fewer than one in five of the applicants said that they had received anything for which they did not have to pay, either from an organization or a person, during the past month; and the gifts or donations were not impressive. Perhaps children had paid for a bottle of medicine or sent a birthday present, or food or groceries or old clothes had been given by friends or relatives. Men were less likely to receive such gifts or donations.

In view of their small incomes and savings it is amazing that as many as one in ten described his financial situation as "Comfortable," while only one in four felt "Unable to make ends meet," and very few said they "Hadn't a cent in the world." "Enough to get by if I watch how I spend every penny," was the typical attitude. Women expressed more strongly the need to "Watch every penny," though they had no less income or savings than men.

Two-thirds considered their financial situation worse than at age fifty-five, and only 15 per cent, better. Asked what they had given up because of reduced income, they most frequently mentioned reduction in quality and quantity of what are generally considered the necessities of life—food, shelter, and clothing (Table 8). This was due partly to the fact that their standard of living at age fifty-five did not allow for many frills which could be eliminated, and partly to the

TABLE 8

Effects of Reduced Income of the 352 Applicants since Age 55

	Per Cent of the 352 Applicants
Given Up:	
Vacations	43
Furnishings and repair	31
Car	25
Clubs	25
Hobbies	18
Church	11
Radio or TV	8
Reduced Amount Spent On:	
Clothing	72
Housing	64
Food	48
Car	4

Note: Per cents add to more than 100 because many applicants reported more than one effect of reduced income.

determination of these people to retain some social contact even at the sacrifice of a physical need.

To the question "Do you feel that your present source of income gives you permanent security?" about a third said, "No," another third, "Yes," and the others gave some kind of qualified answer: they had adequate income but were insecure about its continuing, or felt financially secure only until they should become ill, or they could get along now but would not be able to when they retired from full or part-time work, or their income would be adequate if they could obtain a residence for cheaper rent.

Without doubt, the section of the interview on finances was the most painful. For people in this income bracket, at their age, public housing seemed the only possibility for a decent place to live. Their financial resources would have to be doubled or trebled in order to secure comparable private housing, and they dared not add to their incomes, even if they had been capable, for fear of losing Social Security and Old Age Assistance.

For the 50 per cent who had no savings, the waiting period to re-establish Social Securiy or Old Age payment was impossible. Most of those with savings had accumulated them slowly and painfully so that a last illness and death would not make them utterly dependent upon charity. They were most reluctant to jeopardize this safeguard. They detested dependency and wanted, at all costs, to provide for themselves. They were concerned over the possibility of having too little to pay the minimum rent—or an excess in income or savings which would disqualify them. The leeway was small and alternatives not nearly so attractive.

The tension created by concern over money was serious. One woman furnishes a clear-cut example. Having put, over a period of years, a few pennies each month into a savings account, to provide a meager but decent burial, she had amassed thirty dollars above the legal maximum. To be buried in a pauper's plot was such a horrid fate to contemplate that she had consistently chosen, through the years, to go without common necessities in order to be sure of her little savings. Thirty dollars represented considerable self-denial.

When the little hoard came to light, it was necessary for this seventy-five–year–old woman to get the thirty dollars out of the bank or lose her eligibility for an apartment. Then she was faced with the choice of leaving the cash in her room, in an area in which robbery was a way of life, or of squandering it, which was entirely contrary to her discipline of years. Failure to "eliminate" the thirty dollars would have resulted in termination of her Old Age benefits which would automatically have made her ineligible for Victoria Plaza, because she would have been unable to pay the rent there. Of course, she could not have continued to rent the dirty, dilapidated room she had, either.

Several people told the interviewers they knew they would fail to qualify for Victoria Plaza if Housing personnel discovered a similar, usually very small, sum they had saved, in excess of allowable assets. They could not even keep it to buy something for the new apartment, should they get in. They gave it away, bought something they did not need, used a subterfuge such as putting it in traveler's checks, or simply hoped their second savings account would not be discovered.

A few of the applicants had owned property which, on paper, would have disqualified them, but which they could neither sell nor rent, nor use, nor maintain on their tiny incomes. Their only recourse had been to assign it to relatives,[4] losing thereby a measure of self-esteem and independence.

One applicant in five had a car. Most were in the low-price bracket and over six years old. Men were more likely to own automobiles, and their cars tended to be more expensive and newer.

TABLE 9

Education of the 352 Applicants
(Percentage Distribution)

Extent of Education	% Applicants
Attendance in graduate school	1
College degree	3
Attendance in college	10
Graduation from high school	12
Vocational training	13
Attendance in high school	14
Termination after 3rd but before 9th grade	40
Termination before 4th grade	5
No school attendance	2
Total	100

[4] Marilynn Wacker, assistant executive director, San Antonio Housing Authority, points out that such assignment of property is easily identified and is cause of disqualification for assistance by the State Department of Public Welfare and other agencies.

EDUCATION

Though bright (see "Intellectual Competence," above, this chapter) the group was not unusually well educated. Median highest grade attended, the eighth, was that of their age group in the 1950 Census (von Mering and Weniger, 1959). Fourteen per cent had some high school training, 12 per cent a high school diploma, 10 per cent some college training, and 3 per cent a college degree (Table 9).

Seven never had attended school. One man with no education except tutoring was the child of great wealth and no doubt had had an excellent education. One woman who lived on a ranch where no school was available had received tutoring, which was probably very good. In other cases where families lived far from school facilities,

TABLE 10

Occupations of the 352 Applicants and of Their Fathers and Sons (Percentage Distribution)

	% Men Applicants	*% Women Applicants*	*% Applicants' Fathers*	*% Applicants' Sons*
Professions, gentleman farmers	4	0	9	11
Teachers, registered nurses, architects, ministers	4	3	9	15
Pharmacists, superintendents, grade-school teachers	16	5	25	25
Small farmers, bookkeepers, clerks, railroad engineers	38	15	31	30
Dressmakers, practical nurses, policemen	25	31	17	15
Taxidrivers, cooks, sharecroppers	12	4	4	3
Laborers, miners, servants, aides to housewives	1	3	1	1
Those without working experience		39		
Total	100	100	96*	100

* Information in this category was lacking with 4 per cent of the applicants.

parents passed on to their youngsters what they could and the "tutoring" was informal and not extensive or skilled.

EMPLOYMENT HISTORY

Typically the men had been small farmers, bookkeepers, clerks, or railroad engineers. One in five had been self-employed during most of their working years, and nearly half had run their own farms or businesses at one time or another. Many had lost them during depression years. Few had been professional men, and even fewer, common laborers (Table 10).

There was no difference in job levels (McGuire, 1949) between the male applicants and the husbands of female subjects. Both tended to be slightly lower than those of the preceding and following generations.

The influence of the form of a question on respondents' answers was indicated clearly in women's responses on employment history. Though 40 per cent of the women "Never held a job," only a third of that number had "Never earned money." Those who had supplemented family income by doing housework or sewing when times were hard did not feel that they had "worked" or "held a job."

Of these women who "Never held a job," two-thirds reported themselves "housewives" and the rest said they "Never worked." This apparently reflected another difference in viewpoint, since it was not related to marital status, and every woman in the group had kept house most of her adult life. Strangely, no woman said that she was presently a housewife. Except for the very few jobholders, everyone was "Not working." Apparently the housewife role had lost its meaning, not only with the departure of children and death of spouse, but even for women who still cared for a husband or child.

In round numbers only 5 per cent of the men reported that their first wives ever worked, and 20 per cent reported a working wife in any subsequent marriage; while 60 per cent of the women reported they had "held a job" and 85 per cent that they had earned money. Though part of this discrepancy must be due to premarital jobs for women, it may also reflect a difference in viewpoint between men and women, particularly in the applicants' generation.

Several women reported more marriages when occupational information was being collected than earlier, when marital data were requested. Perhaps some were reluctant to say how many times they had been married when directly asked, but inadvertently revealed this when discussing jobs of their husbands. A marriage or two had "simply slipped the minds" of others.

USE OF THEIR TIME

The interview included open-ended questions regarding jobs and other duties, as well as leisure pastimes. In addition, to provide perhaps a more objective picture of how these people spent their time, the interviewer led them back through the preceding twenty-four hours and recorded what they had done, and left a seven-day diary for the applicant to fill out. Information from the two sources was by no means always consistent. Since interview responses were available for all applicants and time-diary material was received from only about 60 per cent, the discussion below is based primarily on interview responses.[5]

Work. At the time of the interview, 4 per cent reported full-time jobs and 11 per cent, part-time. An unusually large number (3%) avoided answering. In a few instances the interviewer knew of unreported work, such as selling cars on a commission basis. Probably other applicants were reticent to mention such a secondary source of income. Proportionately as many women as men were employed.

Over half expressed interest in working, should it be possible. Not only could they use the money, but also they felt they would be happier. However, jobs were extremely scarce for people with their ages and backgrounds, even if they had the money for transportation to look for employment. Those with Old Age Assistance did not dare, as a rule, to jeopardize it with work at which they would have no seniority or other tenure assurance.

Some who had checked carefully realized that a little extra income would endanger their application to live in Victoria Plaza, by giving them either a total in excess of the upper limit, or an income inadequate to pay the minimum rent, should the new employment cut off another secondary source of income, such as Old Age benefits, and then prove to be only temporary. The majority of applicants thought that they would be better off personally if they worked, and they felt that they had something to contribute to society; but few could obtain work, and some considered the financial risk too serious.

Jobs of the fifty-four applicants who reported partial or full employment were in lower levels than previously. Men sold cars or real

[5] "The Time Diary as an Index of Life Style," in preparation.

estate, or collected rents in the slum areas where they lived; women were salesladies, cashiers, practical nurses, babysitters, and music teachers.

Favorite Pastimes. As they discussed with the interviewers their use of leisure time, activities mentioned spontaneously were recorded. Reading, watching television, and working around the house were most frequent. Also popular were entertaining and going visiting, writing letters, shopping, taking rides, napping, going to church, talking on the phone, listening to the radio, sewing, taking walks, and playing card and table games.

More women went to church, sewed, talked on the phone, "sat and thought," worked in the home, and wrote letters. More men did shop work, engaged in or watched sports, took naps, and watched television.

READING. Subsequently they were asked direct questions about reading, television, radio and movie habits. According to information from the responses, an hour a day was typically spent reading, though nineteen people reported reading on an average of over four hours daily and three of them for eight hours or more. Those (about 10%) who said that they usually read less than an hour a day—except for one who could not read or write—were able, because of poor vision, only to scan headlines.

Forty per cent said that they regularly read newspapers and magazines and books. Only about 5 per cent reported no regular reading. Again, except for the one who did not know how to read, these were people with vision problems. The 4 per cent who never read anything but the Bible had failing eyesight, which necessitated elimination of all but the most essential reading.

The diaries suggest that the respondents tended to exaggerate the amount of time they spent reading. So little was recorded over the period of seven days that "reading" did not even emerge as a scoring category for diary analysis. Most diaries recorded none during the week following the initial interview.

MOVIES. Half "never" went to movies. This did not imply that they literally never saw a movie, but that they went seldom and perhaps had not seen a movie in years. An additional quarter attended once a year or less. Fewer than 10 per cent usually went once a month, and fewer than 5 per cent once a week. Lack of money and transportation were deterrents but, more important, having television, they felt no particular desire to go to movies.

RADIO AND TELEVISION. These seemed very important. Generally people who "never" listened to radio or watched television (nearly 15%) did not have a set available. For those who did, the modal time reported was 12 hours a week, with 15 per cent reporting 22 hours and 10 per cent, 40 or more. According to the diaries, the modal time was twenty-eight hours a week, and a few people averaged nine hours a day.

For some, radio and/or television was a full-time occupation. Others turned on the set when they got up in the morning and left it running while they went about other activities.

In view of their very limited financial circumstances, radio and television equipment was surprisingly new and expensive. Apparently these aged people were willing to go without other things in order to have good sets. The "frills" (clothing, housing, food) were sacrificed as income fell (Table 8), in order to maintain the "necessities" of radio or television. For many, radio or television was one of their few contacts with the outside world. Some commented that the people on radio or television were their friends and almost the only people who "came to see them" in their homes.

SOCIAL ACTIVITIES. Fewer than half of the applicants said that they had taken part in any organized group activity during the past six months. Church-related activities were most frequent, being mentioned by one person in four. Church-sponsored old-age groups involved both men and women, and women belonged to church guilds, circles, and societies. Secular clubs and fraternities, which ran a close second in popularity, were largely Rebekahs, Eastern Star, and Hermann Sons. Rebekahs and Hermann Sons are insurance organizations which provide social activities such as bridge clubs, dances, and parties, as well as old-age homes and decent burials for the insured. For every person who had held office in any organization during the previous six months thirty-three had not.

Diaries were consistent with interview responses regarding participation in formal organizations, and indicated that in the week of record 20 per cent of the diarists had no social contact of any sort.

PUBLIC AFFAIRS. Men past the sixty-fifth birthday and women past the sixty-second were not required to pay the Texas poll tax, but only to present themselves with proof of age in order to obtain an exemption certificate. Among Victoria Plaza applicants, three-fourths of the men voted in the most recent national election, and about 80 per cent had poll-tax receipts or exemption certificates; half of the women voted, and about 60 per cent had poll tax receipts or exemption certificates.

Differentials for both sexes are significant. Some women commented that not only had they failed to vote in the last election, they had never voted in their lives and had no intention of doing so. They were adults when women were given the vote, and many considered voting not only unladylike but also daring and even dangerous.

During final stages of the 1960 national campaign, interest was at fever pitch, discussions waxed fast and furious, and friendships were made and broken over political agreements and differences. Interviewers were harangued and cajoled in regard to their votes, and campaign buttons and literature were pressed upon them. These people felt very strongly about the election and seemed as well informed and as vocal as any citizens.

FREE TIME. A very few who held full-time jobs or were taking care of sick relatives felt they had almost no free time, but two-thirds usually had "All day free." They did not loaf all day every day, but had no required activities to be performed at a given time. If the housework did not get done or an errand run today, it could be done tomorrow. Their lives were not structured by any regular commitment of time. Over a third had "More free time than I know how to use." Women tended to have more free time, but to have less difficulty finding things to do in it.

Over half estimated that they spent less time on leisure activities than they did at age fifty-five, and the remainder were evenly divided between those who felt they spent more now and those who thought there had been no change. Most of those who had increased time spent on leisure pursuits were no longer working and had more leisure time. A few mentioned decreased responsibilities, usually due to the death or recovery of a spouse or other member of the family, freeing time for recreation. Reasons given for reduced leisure activity were smaller income, greater difficulty of transportation, poorer physical condition, and loss of contact with friends and acquaintances.

ATTITUDES REGARDING THEMSELVES

Happiness. Looking back over their lives as a whole, most considered them happier than the average person's. Though nearly a third mentioned a time between the ages of twenty and forty as the happiest of their lives, an even greater number reported that all of life had been equally happy, and only one per cent said that they had never had a happy period. Those who chose a period during childhood, (10%), the teen years (15%) or later life (over age 60, 2%) usually mentioned freedom from responsibility as the reason. Some period between twenty and forty was selected as the happiest because of the responsibilities and pleasures of raising a family, being happy with spouse and children, or not having money worries.

When the applicants were asked about the least happy period of life, the number of optimists remained high, with a third insisting they had never had an unhappy period, and only 2 per cent asserting that their entire lives were unhappy. Unhappiest periods had occurred between twenty and sixty, with a fairly even distribution through this age span. Loss of loved ones, unhappy family relationships, illness, loneliness, and economic depression were the primary causes. Of the 120 people who were seventy-five or over at the time of the interview, 5 per cent specified "over seventy-five" as their unhappiest period.

When asked to look back over their lives for the things hardest to bear, more than one person in every ten insisted that he had never had anything really difficult. ("The Lord never sends you things you cannot bear.") Loss of loved ones was by far most frequently mentioned.

Concerning the present, half said, "I am just as happy as when I was younger," a third, "My life is so enjoyable that I almost wish it would go on forever," and a quarter, "These are the best years of my life." On the other hand, the majority thought, "My life could be happier than it is now," one in five found this, "The dreariest time of my life," or said, "My life is full of worry," and one in fifteen found "Less and less reason to live."

Accomplishment and Usefulness. The large majority endorsed the statements, "I am some use to those around me" and "My life is still busy and useful." But one in four could not "help feeling now that my life is not very useful," and some admitted, "Sometimes I feel there is no point in living," or "My life is meaningless now."

Evaluating their present ability to work in comparison with that at age fifty-five, only 10 per cent considered it worse. Nearly half said their effort was slower but as good in quality, or even better—if they were not flustered by having to hurry. Two-thirds were satisfied with their capacity to perform at the present time, though 20 per cent felt they could "No longer do any kind of useful work."

More women than men were satisfied with their present competence. Men were using, as reference, hypothetical return to a job probably changed in the interim, and at which they would be, at best, out of practice. They tended to feel in the way if others performed household tasks and inept if they took them on; while women continued their long-practiced role of homeworker, at which they felt competent, but which was nothing to "look forward to."

Most were well satisfied, in general, with the way they had lived their lives, and fewer than 15 per cent expressed regrets. Those only fairly content with their accomplishments often said that when they were younger they were better pleased with what they were doing, but now realized they could have made much wiser choices. However, they had done the best they could as life moved along and, though they later realized it could have been better, they did not berate themselves.

The much smaller number dissatisfied with what they had accomplished in life felt that if they could do it over again they would do a much better job, with the wisdom and understanding they had acquired subsequently. Generally they considered themselves wiser than at any earlier age, and more competent to make important decisions. Many added, bitterly or humorously, that they no longer had decision-making opportunities. ("Now that seventy years of living have taught me how to do it, the most earth-shaking thing I have to make my mind up about is whether to fix tea or coffee for supper.")

Half said they had done about as well financially as close relatives of the same generation. If the unusually large number (10%) who gave no answer were being modest, that would about equalize the group who felt they had done not as well (25%) with those who felt they had done better (15%). However, it was the interviewers' impression that most who avoided responding considered their financial accomplishment inferior to that of relatives.

Age-Group Identification. The majority perceived themselves as "middle-aged" compared to those who were "aged," "old," or "elderly," all taken together. This is consistent with the responses of Tuckman and Lorge's (1954) noninstitutionalized elderly people, and with those of a representative sample of people sixty years old and over in Elmira, New York (Blau, 1956). In justification of this age placement, some Victoria Plaza applicants mentioned that they enjoyed being with young people. To them, this indicated that they were young, at least in spirit, and they wanted to continue being with young people because it kept them young.

More considered themselves middle-aged because they were still physically and mentally alert. ("I still feel young and full of spirit.") Loss of these abilities would indicate to them being "aged," "old," or "elderly." Most looked astonished when asked why they felt they were in the age group they had mentioned and said, "Well, that's the way I feel!" or "That's where I belong!" and seemed unable to give any clearer explanation. To them, it was self-evident.

This age identification is not inconsistent with interviewers' ratings on the Index of Senility (Burgess, et al, 1948, p. 182). No one was considered by his interviewer to be suspicious of change, and few to have poor recent memory or regrets over their lives, to talk about the past "in glowing terms," or about "how hard it was." Few wanted to be alone, were unobservant, found it hard to learn or change plans, were very shy and timid, or collectors and hoarders. However, half were rated by their interviewers as nervous under time pressure, one-third being made nervous by noise, a quarter seemed concerned with their own feelings, and a fifth were self-centered. In every case the senile characteristic was attributed more often to men than to women.

Age identification was consistent also with ratings on the Disengagement Index (Appendix A) devised for this study.[6] Though most showed decreasing interest in controlling the lives of their families, few seemed to have diminished interest in activities, material belongings, people, or mental stimulation.

These people did not consider the terms "old," "aged," and "elderly" to be appropriate because of the accumulation of years. Chronological age was not a good index of one's "age group." In no instance was their application for residence in Victoria Plaza taken as a confession of being old and helpless. During the period just before completion of the building, when it was to be named, prospective residents were considerably agitated at such suggestions as Golden Age Center and Sunset Manor, because of the implication of agedness. Applicants were in favor of the noncommittal "Victoria Plaza" since it could apply to any apartment building and carried no suggestion of an "old folks' home."

Self-Description. In selecting adjectives which did and did not describe themselves, applicants presented a stereotype of social desirability. Over 90 per cent were affectionate, cheerful, cooperative, generous, good-natured, helpful, kind, and tolerant—without being bitter, disorderly, gloomy, nagging, whiny, or quarrelsome.

[6] "An Index of Disengagement," in preparation.

In regard to independence, they were nearly unanimous. Only one per cent said they were not independent. The ability to get along on one's own seemed to be a consistently dominant need. It was related to applicant status: living in Victoria Plaza should extend the period of independence. It probably underlay the tendency to identification with middle age.

There were about even splits in regard to "clever" and "wise." Those who considered themselves clever or wise generally justified it by saying that, with the wisdom they have acquired from years of living, they could now do much better with their lives. Those who did not consider themselves clever or wise pointed to the poor decisions they had made in the past and their lowly financial level at present to document their lack of wisdom and cleverness.

Assignments of "sensitive" and "talkative" were also divided, probably because of ambiguity of meaning of the first and ambivalence regarding desirability of the second. They wondered whether "sensitive" means responsive to others or thin-skinned; whether "talkative" people were friendly or boring.

More women attributed to themselves the terms active, affectionate, and busy; more men, brave, clear-thinking, easy-going, sociable, tactful and unselfish. Fewer men considered themselves bitter, sarcastic, self-centered, self-pitying, sensitive, nervous, and tense.

For most adjectives, only four or five people said they did not know whether they applied to them. However, 15 per cent could not say whether they were "weak." Many asked whether it meant weak in mind and spirit or weak in body, and when they were left to choose for themselves, usually decided not to give an answer.

Positive self-attitude was reflected also in responses to incomplete sentences. Half of those who filled out Peck's Sentence Completion Test answered "happy" to the stem "I am———," and said, "My mind is (good, clear, normal)." Over a third said, "People think of me as (good, friendly)."

PROBLEMS AND PLANS FOR THE FUTURE

Toward the end of the interview, when they were asked an open-ended question about major problems without reference to any special area of their lives, finances and housing were most frequently mentioned, with health running third. Other problems were personal adjustment, companionship, recreation, and transportation.

Asked about services or programs they needed, recreational programs were most frequently mentioned, and housekeeping aids (stoves, refrigerators, washing machines, and vacuum cleaners) were important. Others were instructional programs, cafeteria, elevator, medical services, transportation, barber or beauty shop, and religious services. Women were more eager for services and programs.

The interviewer asked what activities the respondent would like to take part in if he had the opportunity. Appendix D shows those named. Card games were most desired. Sex differences revealed by the statistical analysis were the expected ones, with men wanting to watch baseball and football games and to participate in bowling, dominoes, pool, horseshoes, washer tossing, hunting, fishing, and shop work, and with women wanting book reviews and monologues, crafts, and modeling. In regard to the last it must be made clear, as it was not initially even to the interviewers, that these women did not want to make pottery but to wear beautiful clothes for others to see!

About half wanted to join one or more organizations. Men felt this need more than women. Among those who protested they did not want to join any groups were people who were already members of at least as many as they could manage. For example, one woman belonged to the Eastern Star, Veterans Auxiliary, Spanish American War Widows, a bridge club, and a garden club, and had no days into which she could fit any more meetings without giving up informal visits with her friends. On the other hand, eagerness for memberships did not always indicate lack of social participation. An active member of every old-age group in the city, who already had a meeting most days and many evenings, said she would be delighted to join more if they were formed. She would "make" the time, and even help new units get organized. Church-related groups, some instructional and others social, were most desired.

Regarding motivation for joining organizations, pleasure in social contact and enjoyment of the activity involved were certainly expected, but it was surprising that only one per cent seemed motivated by need to pass the time. Some wanted to join an organization in order to help others or to improve themselves.

Over half had no specific plans for the next year or so except to move if possible. Most who planned to travel were looking forward to visiting relatives. Others intended to take up some specific hobby, look for work, take care of their health, study, or do civic work. One had a fairly definite plan to write a book, a quite reasonable aim, since she had already published several.

Generally they considered "making wishes" ridiculous, commenting, "We're too old to make wishes that way," and indicating that it was pretty foolish to wish in this fashion since it was clear that their wishes would not come true. In most instances the interviewer had to encourage a great deal in order to get any response. Even with urging 15 per cent did not express one wish, and only 40 per cent stated as many as the three that were requested. This is consistent with the findings of Shelton and Kastenbaum (1961), who reported that with their group of subjects sixty-five years old and over the mean number of responses was 1.68. However, it is not significantly lower than the number given by a group of college students.[7]

The most frequent wishes were for good health, financial security, and cheaper or independent housing. The three were interrelated; generally the idea was expressed that if they had one, the others would come naturally. For example, if they had good health, they could work and this could bring them increased security. Then housing would not be a problem. In addition they would fulfill their less critical wishes: they would be able to do things for others, they would never be a burden to others, and they would have peace of mind. Or if they had cheaper rent they would feel secure and their health would improve.

Travel and recreation were next in importance. Very few wished to be younger, though some wanted to have loved ones back. More wished for a better world situation or for wisdom and strength to live life as God wanted them to live it.

Summary

These people probably were quite similar in general background and current characteristics to the majority of those in their age range. Careful generalization seems justified, not only to elder applicants for public housing, but to other groups as well.

The people studied were old by the calendar but "middle aged" in their own eyes. They were poor, but probably no more so than most people in their age group. Though perhaps above average in intelligence, they were no better educated than was typical for their generation. Forced into dependency, they were reluctant to be social burdens and had strong needs to stand on their own.

They accepted inevitable physical and sensory losses and com-

[7] "Age-Related Traits," in preparation.

plained little of ailments, though they resented the inaccessibility of the little medical attention they needed and the appliances which could make life more comfortable. Though neurotic-type ailments "bothered" them somewhat more, all indexes showed them to be in unusually sound mental health. Overwhelmingly interested in religion, they regretted the meagerness of attention received from religious institutions and people.

Common to everyone in the group was the desire to find a better place to live, one which he could pay for himself, and in which he could live life as he wanted. The next chapter pictures typical living situations of applicants for apartments in Victoria Plaza and reasons people gave for wanting to move there. Additional background material on the people, related to family members and friends, is in Chapter 8, to which some readers may prefer to turn before reading Chapter 4.

CHAPTER 4

The Housing They Had and the Housing They Wanted

The Settings for Applicants' Lives

THOUGH MANY of the applicants had grown up on farms, less than one per cent of them were rural residents when they became associated with the study. The majority lived in "apartments," most of which consisted of one room in an old residence which had been divided up for maximum rental income.

Forty per cent had lived in San Antonio thirty-six years or more, though a third had been in the present residence less than a year. They had spent their lives, or at least their adult years, in the same town. Even the transiency shown in moving from room to room had begun only in recent years. Once they had been forced to move from the relatively comfortable homes of their working years, the dreary succession began.

Some kept themselves constantly depleted, financially and physically, searching for a new place, moving, being disappointed, and starting all over again, never losing hope of improvement. Others had made a series of moves unwillingly, as the old buildings in which they could afford to live were torn down, one after another.

Nearly all were well satisfied with San Antonio as a place to live. (God's country," "It's home," "I came here as a bride and would never want to leave.") The parts of town in which they lived, however, they considered somewhat inferior to those in which they had lived at age fifty-five. No one wanted to move out of San Antonio—only to a better part of it.

CONDITIONS OF HOUSING

In evaluating their present housing, not one person said it was "Very good" or even "Good." The most common judgment was "OK," by which they meant that they were doing as well as they, or anyone else, could do in the situation. Some of those who rated present housing as better than at age fifty-five (one in five) had meanwhile moved into public housing facilities, which were more conveniently located and easier to keep clean, with modern conveniences such as indoor toilets and hot and cold running water. Others, by moving in with relatives, had improved physical housing, but had undertaken difficult interpersonal relationships or brought on themselves increased isolation from friends and others their own age.

Nearly 60 per cent lived alone (most of them women). Most of the others lived with their spouses or children, a few with brothers or sisters or people not related to them. Two women lived in households of more than ten people.

About half of the applicants, most of them women, customarily did their own cooking and ate alone, and a few others (mostly men) usually bought their meals and ate alone, so that over half these people had solitary mealtimes. Typically those who ate together were husbands and wives, though a few (again mostly men) habitually ate with others in boardinghouses or cheap restaurants.

Most were provided with heat, though it was not always adequate or safe; an inside commode, often shared with several others; hot and cold water; an ice box or refrigerator and a cook stove, again often shared. Nearly everyone had access to a phone and radio, and three-fourths had a television set or could watch one. Washing machines were available where they lived to only one applicant in five, four out of five had no provision for repairs or maintenance of property or appliances, and half did not have a satisfactory means of garbage disposal.

COSTS OF LIVING

For this style of living, modal monthly costs for rent and utilities, and for food, were $24.50 each (Table 11). There was a highly significant sex difference in regard to food costs. Women tended to spend

TABLE 11

Basic Monthly Living Costs of the 352 Applicants
(Percentage Distribution)

Cost	*% of Applicants* Rent and Utilities	Food
$90–	3	1
$80–$89	1	3
$70–$79	6	2
$60–$69	7	10
$50–$59	11	10
$40–$49	11	14
$30–$39	17	20
$20–$29	24	25
$10–$19	9	4
$ 0–$ 9	11	10
Total	100	100
Mean	$37.30	$38.80
Median	$34.50	$36.00
Mode	$24.50	$24.50

less on food, probably because they had more experience in shopping and preparation, and ate more meals at home, and also because more women were living with relatives. Included in food costs were some medicines as well as diet supplements. For example, diabetics typically included insulin in their food budgets.

In the interpretation of these living costs, it is important to keep in mind the modal monthly income of $70.00 and to realize what a large proportion was expended for rent, utilities, and food. Many of those in the $20–$29 rent-and-utility bracket were already in public housing facilities.

Though the median income ($94.40) was higher than the modal value, so were median costs for rent and utilities ($34.50) and food ($36.00). Using means to express the average, income went up to $114.50, rent and utilities to $37.30, and food to $38.80. By any method of report, little was left after these people paid for food and shelter, though these essentials were not enjoyed in a grand style. Those who had neither food nor rent payments were living, of course, with relatives or friends. Probably because of their limited means, most knew immediately, to the penny, what they spent for food during the previous month.

About half felt that, for what they were getting, rent was "about right." A quarter thought that even though the payment was low, it was "highway robbery." Those in public housing facilities generally considered that, relative to its value, the charge was low, as did those housed adequately but unhappily with relatives.

WHY THEY WANTED TO MOVE

Reasons for applying for space in Victoria Plaza varied. Most wanted to get "something a little cheaper" or "a little better" or to be with people. Some said the primary need was lower rent. Often they were poorly housed, but the greatest pressure was financial. In order to pay for shelter they were forced to cut food to bare essentials, and little was left for clothes, church, transportation, and entertainment, or medical and hospital costs in case of illness.

Many of those who wanted to move in order to obtain "better housing" lived in slum areas. Buildings had inadequate plumbing. They were very old and could not be kept clean and free of bugs. ("I've lived in a hundred-year-old house for thirteen years and I'm tired of it. I'd be glad to get over there where things are clean and modern." "I never thought *I* would have roaches, but I've tried everything!") An interviewer arrived for one appointment just in time to help extricate the interviewee, who had fallen through the floor where it had been weakened by leakage from the refrigerator.

In some instances there was inadequate privacy. ("That's what I'm interested in—a bathroom to myself, not shared with bums and drunks, and dirty, inconsiderate people." "When I can't sleep at night I just have to lie there—can't turn on the light to read and wake up my grandson. He has school tomorrow.")

Ventilation often was poor in this climate of intense summer heat, sometimes as a result of the partitioning of big, old-fashioned rooms into several. Heating facilities might be inadequate even for the mild winters. ("My son says it's because I'm getting old, but I notice he keeps his coat on when he comes to see me." An interviewer became faint during one September session in a tiny third-floor "apartment" with only one small, high window which could be opened.)

For other applicants, the location of their place of residence and consequent lack of companionship were the most irksome factors. Because of the kind of dwelling available to the older person, and its location within the city, he was isolated from stores, friends, and activities with other people. Some lived on upper floors where the only access was by old, steep, and dark stairways, and they knew that the new building would have elevators. As a rather extreme example, one woman lived up three dark rickety flights of stairs in the slum district and, "Until you came, I had spoken to no one for three months but the Chinese groceryman. He's so kind, but his English is not real good and he has to hurry." She had broken her hip once and did not dare attempt the stairs alone.

For others in substandard housing the need most urgently felt was for security. Since they lived in an area where many buildings were being torn down to be replaced by office buildings, parking lots, and expressways, these people feared most greatly the loss of even the housing they had. ("The building next door has been sold . . .," "If the expressway comes through here . . .," "I've already had to move twice this year . . .")

About one in five had housing which was adequate or even very comfortable, but which isolated them from friends and activities or involved them in unsatisfactory interpersonal relationships. Some named independence as their greatest need in regard to housing. Often they were renting rooms or apartments with money given them by their children, or living with the children, and felt that they were imposing on the younger generation or being imposed upon by it. ("Teen agers shouldn't have to share a room with me," or, "I can't even have a *thought* of my own," or, "I could afford to pay for an apartment [in Victoria Plaza] out of my own money, and my children can't say it isn't a nice place.")

SUMMARY

Need for improved living conditions was unquestionable. People in the applicant group suffered either substandard housing, social isolation, or interpersonal stress. However, they had not lost initiative. Much of the high rate of mobility was due to efforts to improve matters. As one man said in relation to his application for an apartment: "I'm a fellow who likes to improve himself, and when I see a chance come along, I grab it!"

The letter from one applicant to her interviewer states her case and speaks for others:

April 7, 1960

Dear Mrs. ———,

I couldn't talk very freely here yesterday as to *why* I wish to live in the new building as both the man and his wife here are in and out of my kitchen frequently throughout the day and it is very easy to hear conversation there as there is so much open space under and around the door.

A private bath is one *very* great reason, for the bathroom situation here is *most* unsatisfactory for many reasons that I won't take your time to go into.

Lack of privacy is another reason. With two people in and out of your kitchen all day from *very* early in the morning which usually wakes me and in the past few years all hours of the night that always wakened me when the big ice-box door was closed, you don't have much privacy, and my kitchen door into this room needs to be open all day for ventilation, especially in warm weather, so I have very little privacy all told.

The heat is terrific in this west room in summer as the ceiling is low with a *flat tin* roof over it that receives *no* protection whatever from the hot sun all day long, and the sun beats in the two west windows wholly unprotected also, so I have to keep the shades down *all* the time from noon until after six P.M.—which of course makes the room dark. The house shuts off *all* the breeze from the southeast so *all* the breeze I ever get in summer comes from the south outside door. I feel the heat more and more each summer. I never have a headache except from the heat in here. It ached all yesterday P.M.—when so hot and we are not used to such heat after the winter's cold. We need *some* gradation in the matter. My head still aches tonight from today's heat. (Over one-hundred degrees).

Excessive dampness that I mentioned is of course another reason. I've never lived in any dampness before. My things—good things—smell of mildew, and my bed has been too damp to sleep between sheets this year for the *first* time.

Wholesomeness, privacy and independence are the three great essentials for the elderly. Proper diet for *me* keeps me out of serious trouble so I wish to prepare my own meals and do for myself just as long as is possible and feel that the new building with all its conveniences will give me the best possible chance to do so. It was a real pleasure to talk to you yesterday. You are beautifully suited for such activity. With my very best wishes,

—— ——

Victoria Plaza[1]

GENERAL ARRANGEMENT

While the first set of interviews and tests was being done, the new building was under construction. Nine stories high and shaped in the form of a modified T, it is oriented to the prevailing breeze and per-

[1] For a more detailed description see Wacker, Marilynn, ed., *Victoria Plaza Apartments*.

mits cross-ventilation in each apartment. There are 184 dwelling units on eight residential floors, 16 two-bedroom, 16 efficiency, and 152 one-bedroom apartments. The ground floor contains the Senior Community Center, administrative offices, and a public health clinic.

Victoria Plaza is located on a two–and–one–half–acre site seven-tenths of a mile from the center of the city and adjacent to neighborhood stores and churches. There is a regularly scheduled bus stop in front of the building.

This high-rise dwelling offers many advantages for the safety and comfort of its residents. There are two self-service elevators with special features. Continuous handrails throughout the building and grounds provide for ease and safety of movement. Galleries with four footrailings extend across the building and provide each apartment with an outside entrance. Decorative panels give protection from wind and rain and provide an added sense of security to persons using the open galleries.

THE SENIOR CENTER

The main entrance of the building opens into the lobby and Senior Center. This area is furnished with gay and comfortable furniture. The pool table, combination hi-fi and television set, and conversational groupings of furniture offer an atmosphere of rest and recreation to any senior citizen of San Antonio.

A large veranda closed on three sides leads off the lobby and to a shady garden patio. An eight-foot brick wall surrounds the patio and gives privacy from traffic.

The ground floor of the north wing of the building contains the management offices of the Housing Authority and the Senior Center director's office. Adjoining these offices is a hobby room with equipment for various crafts. Next is the library. At the end of the wing is an eight-room clinic with a nurses' station and examining rooms for use by the Public Health Department. Just outside is a public patio with benches and play area for neighborhood children waiting to use the clinic.

In the west wing are a small post office, two counseling offices, and a three-bedroom custodian's apartment.

A community kitchen, where food can be prepared for parties, banquets, or group meetings, adjoins the recreation room. Here there are card tables and a piano, available at all times to resident and non-resident senior citizens. For special events, such as plays or more formal entertainment, there is a movable stage and a stage curtain. Beyond the recreation room is a large area available for later addition of equipment for other activities. In one corner of the room is a small self-service beauty shop, the contribution of a generous San Antonian.

APARTMENTS

Unusual conveniences are provided in each apartment unit. Shelves and light fixtures are low. Refrigerators are set on fourteen-inch platforms. Doors have levers instead of knobs and are wide enough for wheel chairs. Showers have Alaskan cedar seats and tempered doors rather than curtains. Pushing a button in the bathroom rings an emergency bell on the gallery when help is needed. There are electric ranges and central heating. Lines of 220 volts for air-conditioning and telephone jacks are standard equipment. Each resident must provide his own furniture, and may add an air conditioner and telephone.

Of particular interest is the space flexibility. Apartments can be turned into one big room or separated through use of three movable closet units. The kitchen area is separated from the living room by a screen covered with light vinyl fabric for easy cleaning, and the dining area is by a window opening on the gallery.

There is a laundry room on each floor, with coin-operated washer and dryer, and tubs and lines for handwashing. Each floor also has an incinerator chute for waste disposal, centrally located by the elevator.

APPLICANTS' OPINIONS OF THE BUILDING

During the first interview they were asked their opinions of the type of building Victoria Plaza was to be. Though it seemed important to get this information for comparison with reactions after a period of residence there, a few applicants did not even know where Victoria Plaza was being erected, and others said they did not know about the type of structure. Of the 85 per cent who were somewhat familiar with the plans, the large majority responded in a very favorable fashion. Some gave a neutral response. They were not the least bit interested in what type of building it was to be, because it was bound to be better than what they had. One person liked no feature of the projected building. She definitely wanted to move in, but just as surely could improve on every detail of the plans! There was no evidence of "conservative" resistance to the novel high-rise construction and "modern" style.

Those who were acquainted with the building were then asked whether, if they should live there, they had a preference or aversion for any part of the building and why. Each residential floor was an exact copy of the other. The only difference was in elevation.

As would be expected, lower floors were preferred by people who were concerned about height (25%). ("I'll take any place, just so it's not too high up!") The building has outside halls, which furnish the only access to apartments. The necessity to walk along these open balconies at a considerable height was at least as important as having residential space on a high floor. (To a friend: "Don't you choose the ninth floor—I'd never have the nerve to come visit you.")

Ventilation was pre-eminent in importance to some. ("Most of all, I want good fresh air.") Each residential floor had its proponents, who considered it to be superior in this regard. Among those whose preference was influenced by ventilation, choice of the top floor (30%) is not surprising, but there is no obvious explanation for the equally large number who selected the fourth floor because of its superior ventilation.

One in every nine indicated that his preference would be determined by the amount of noise. Though the top floor was most favorably regarded in this respect, each floor, with the exception of the lowest residential floor, was chosen for quietness.

A few applicants specified particular (different) floors, "to be with younger people." They had to be guessing about where the "younger" people would live since, at the time of the interview, no one knew.

Generally, whether applicants knew much, very little, or nothing about what Victoria Plaza was to be, they were eager to be in it. These choices were only preferences and did not imply reservations about acceptance of apartments.[2]

[2] The Housing Authority staff adds the interesting footnote that the two top floors were the first to be fully selected.

CHAPTER 5

Selection of Tenants by the Housing Authority[1]

As a basis for the assessment of change in people attributable to the impact of living in Victoria Plaza, it was planned to compare, over the period of about a year, those members of the original group who had lived in the Plaza with those who had not. To insure against perceiving, as housing effect, some difference which existed between the groups originally, it was important to compare them on the basis of the 1960 data. If there were important differences, they would most likely be reflected in characteristics taken into consideration by the Housing Authority.

Application of these criteria conjointly to determine eligibility for public housing requires special training in housing management operations. Here each was used separately in an effort to test the initial similarity of applicants who were to live in Victoria Plaza and those who were not. Differences between groups would be more likely to occur in regard to characteristics which were considered during admission procedures, even though every individual in both groups qualified for admission.

All 352 subjects had cleared preliminary screening for eligibility

[1] Lola G. Netter contributed much to analysis of the data in this section and reported some of them in "The Use of Housing Authority Criteria in Tenant Selection for Victoria Plaza, an Apartment Building for the Elderly," unpublished master's thesis, Trinity University, 1962.

by the Housing Authority. After the initial interviewing and testing, 204 were accepted as tenants, 120 were refused and 28 became "no longer interested." It was not clear how many of this 8 per cent simply changed their minds and how many scored low on admission standards and were subtly influenced by Housing Authority personnel to decide against the move before they might have to be rejected. The latter seemed likely in many cases.

For purposes of this study, applicants were divided into two groups: those who moved into Victoria Plaza and those who did not. The next section compares the two groups in relation to Housing Authority's admission standards,[2] using research data which seem to be relevant.

Legally Defined Admission Criteria[3]

AGE

According to law, admission was limited to women sixty-two and over, and men sixty-five and over, as family heads. The eighteen residents who were younger were spouses or children of qualified applicants. There was not a significant difference in age between those admitted and those not.

INCOME

Housing Authority criteria gave figures for maximum income ($2,500 a year for one or two persons) and assets ($2,000), but the minimum was only implied. Applicants were advised of approximate costs of living in Victoria Plaza and knew that expenses were slightly more than in other public housing.

For construction of Victoria Plaza funds were borrowed through the Public Housing Administration from the federal government. Operating costs were to be met with income from rent. The average income of state pensioners in Texas was $52 a month and it was impossible to operate housing facilities on a monthly rent of $10.40, which would be 20 per cent of this average pension. Therefore in San

[2] According to "A Discussion of Admission Criteria: Apartments for the Elderly," 1959, an unpublished document of the San Antonio Housing Authority, which was made available in personal communication. To avoid confusion between Housing Authority requirements and research data, and to make the former easily available to every reader, they are reproduced in Appendix B.

[3] Tests of significance of difference between groups on items relevant to legally defined admission standards are summarized in Table 12.

TABLE 12

Differences on the Legally Defined Admission Criteria Between the 204 Applicants Who Were To Become Residents and the 148 Who Were Not

Criterion	*Chi-square*	*df*
Age	13.06	8
Income	.13	1
Savings	19.47*↓	8
Length of Residence	9.42	8
Date of Application	22.05	14
Veteran Status	3.05	1
Need		
Condition of Present Housing	1.62	2
Worth of Present Housing Relative to Cost	8.36	4
Housing a Major Problem	8.27**↑	1

* Significant at the .05 level.
** Significant at the .01 level.
↑Higher scores for applicants who were to become residents.
↓ Lower scores for applicants who were to become residents.

Antonio the public-housing minimum rent was $16.00 a month. The 20-per-cent formula applied only above that minimum.

It was necessary to set the minimum rent for Victoria Plaza apartments even higher, because of the greater projected operating costs. Rentals began at $24.00 a month and increased by one dollar for each $60 annual income over the minimum, following the usual public-housing formula. There was a monthly utility surcharge of $1.20. If the individual had an air conditioner, there was a $5.00 fee for each of the five months during which its use was most likely. Actually, well over 20 per cent of income was paid as rent in many cases.

Income distributions, both for applicants who were to move into Victoria Plaza and for those who were not, were quite similar, except that the few highest incomes tended to be more frequent among the latter.

Twelve applicants who had reported, to the research interviewer, monthly incomes apparently in excess of the maximum stated in the admissions criteria were assigned apartments. Housing Authority staff members point out that monthly income is only one factor in determining eligibility, and that these individuals may have had special exemptions. Personnel on the Housing Authority staff had verified income carefully, within sixty days of each person's admission to the building. It is possible that these few applicants enjoyed increases in income after the final eligibility screening. However, it is also possible that, because of the firm assurance that no information given during the research interview would be made available to the Housing Authority, the income reported for research purposes is more truthful.

To enable further investigation into this possible discrepancy, the Housing Authority made available their records of monthly income of applicants. A spot check for agreement between figures recorded in Housing Authority files and those reported to interviewers showed that the number reported higher to research workers was exactly balanced by the number reported lower. Consistently, those applicants in upper brackets gave larger figures to research people than to the Housing Authority, and those in lower brackets, smaller. These response trends seem beyond coincidence. They suggest the possibility that a few individuals managed to hide, from the most careful search of Housing Authority personnel, the exact amounts of their incomes, in eagerness for admission. If this is true, and the figures given the research interviewer are more realistic, it is equally true that as many applicants exaggerated the amount of their incomes as diminished it. This is reasonable in view of the fact that admission depended upon both economic need and ability to pay the rent.

The majority of applicants received Social Security, Old Age Assistance, disability insurance, or pension checks. Their incomes remained fairly stable and open to examination by Housing Authority personnel. Some, however, did odd jobs and added to their incomes in varying amounts difficult to confirm. There was no statistically significant difference in source of income for those admitted and those not. A few more of those who remained outside the Plaza were receiving public assistance.

SAVINGS

Differences between the groups in regard to savings were not impressive. Approximately half of those admitted, and the same proportion of those not admitted, reported no savings to research interviewers. With applicants who had saved, there was a tendency for those with smaller savings to be admitted, and for those with larger savings to remain outside Victoria Plaza. Six people who had reported savings in excess of $5,000 were admitted. They may have had no other source of income being forced to live on this capital, or they may have included insurance policies when reporting savings. Ownership of an automobile was not significantly related to admittance. Seventy-five per cent of those who were to become residents, and 80 per cent of those who were not, owned no car.

LENGTH OF RESIDENCE

A residence requirement of six months within a five-mile radius of San Antonio (which could be waived in case of hardship) was the eligibility standard. No difference was found between the groups for length of residence.

DATE OF APPLICATION

Admission standards stated that when all else was equal the date of application should be considered. No difference was found in date of application for those admitted and those not. Twelve applications were filed prior to 1950; seven of these were approved. Fifty-three applications were dated 1950 through 1957, of which thirty-two were accepted. The majority were received from July, 1958, through June, 1960, while plans for Victoria Plaza were made public and the building constructed. Application dates for those admitted and those not admitted were evenly distributed through this two-year period.

VETERAN STATUS

Though the admission criterion gave veterans and veterans' families preference for public housing, they were no more likely to be admitted to Victoria Plaza than were nonveterans. Again, it must be remembered that, in the Housing Authority's determination of eligibility, all factors were considered. However, at the time of admission to Victoria Plaza it was mandatory under the law that preference be given to veterans and families of veterans or servicemen. Veteran status was to take precedence, for example, over date of application. Nevertheless, admission rates for the two groups were identical: 15 per cent of the applicant group and 15 per cent of the residents claimed veteran status.

NEED

"Need for decent housing," was no longer a legal requirement for housing the elderly, but the stated policy of the Housing Authority was to give it consideration. Definition of need did not limit it to substandard housing and hazardous physical conditions, but included unsatisfactory living arrangements due to interpersonal relationships and family dynamics.

There was no significant difference between the groups in their own direct judgments of their present housing or in their evaluations of its worth, relative to what they paid for it. Neither were there differences in availability of such conveniences as heat, hot and cold water, refrigerator and washing machine, or in the number of persons living in the household. No difference appeared in reasons for wanting to change housing.

More applicants who spontaneously mentioned housing when interviewers asked what was their major problem were subsequently assigned apartments. Housing was a major problem to about 40 per cent of those who were to move into the Plaza when it was completed, but it was uppermost in the minds of less than a quarter of those who were not.

Criteria for Measuring Ability to Adjust to Close Community Life

Because of the structural characteristics of Victoria Plaza, the Housing Authority tried to select applicants with good "ability for adjustment to close community life."[4] In addition to legal requirements, discussed in the preceding section of this chapter, admissions personnel were to take into account the individual's physical and mental health as appropriate to such an environment.

ALERTNESS

In selecting apartment occupants, the Housing Authority was concerned with applicants' comprehension, understanding, and general alertness.[5] According to the research data there was no difference between the two groups in education level, as indicated either by age when schooling terminated or by highest grade completed. Nor was there difference between them in self-description as "alert," "clever," or "clear-thinking" and "wise."

However, interviewers' ratings showed consistent differences throughout, with the acceptees manifesting a higher degree of the Housing Authority desideratum—general alertness in the tenants.

[4] According to "Supplement to Application and CO's for Elderly Persons," a mimeograph of the Housing Authority received in a private communication and reproduced in Appendix B.

[5] Tests of statistical significance of difference are summarized in Table 13.

TABLE 13

Differences between the 204 Acceptees and the 148 Nonacceptees
Alertness

Index of Alertness	*Chi-square*	*df*
Education		
Age when schooling was completed	6.18	8
Highest grade completed	4.78	8
Self-Evaluation		
Alert	3.78	2
Clever	.34	2
Clear-thinking	1.60	2
Wise	1.26	2
Activities		
Hours read per day	8.56	8
Types of reading material	11.66	7
Correspondence	12.56*↑	4
Phone contacts	13.01	8
Interviewers' Ratings		
Observantness	15.66**↑	2
Alertness	10.44* ↑	3
Memory for dates	16.80**↑	4
Memory for places	15.75**↑	4
Memory for names	14.23* ↑	4
Ability to learn new ways	12.22**↑	2
Negative talk about the past	14.79**↑	2
Interest in mental stimulation	14.28**↑	2
Interest in interview	15.50**↑	4

*Significant at the .05 level.
** Significant at the .01 level.
↑ Higher scores for applicants who were to become residents.
↓ Lower scores for applicants who were to become residents.

Though differences were not great, interviewers tended to perceive those applicants who were to become the first residents of the Plaza as more alert, more capable of new learning, and clearer in memory.

In regard to measured intelligence, it is interesting to look at the Wechsler-Bellevue scores of a sample of 93 (Mean $= 109$, $\sigma = 13$, using the 35–49 year old norms). Unfortunately, because of time pressure, the test was administered to those most likely to be admitted, so comparisons of accepted with rejected applicants cannot be made. However, it appears that the Housing Authority was successful in selecting an intelligent and alert group.

Comparisons made through other possible indicators of "alertness" indicate that people selected by the Housing Authority were better correspondents, though they had no more contacts with others by phone than did the applicants who did not get apartments, but that there were no differences in amount of time spent reading, or in the type of material read.

HEALTH

For a check on another aspect of ability to adjust to community life Housing Authority personnel were to observe the general health of applicants, especially in regard to their ability to keep house and look after themselves. In the research material no differences were found between those admitted and those not, in regard to history of hospitalization, illness, and medical-dental contacts; or present type or number of health problems; or use of aids and appliances; or attitudes regarding health. Insofar as these are indexes of health, Housing Authority did not select from among the applicants those in better condition.

It is possible that every applicant was capable of the kind of independent living necessary in Victoria Plaza. The group in general apparently enjoyed such homogeneously good health that differentiation would have been difficult, at least without information based on a physical examination, which neither the Housing Authority staff nor the research group had. Few health problems were reported in research contacts—so few that statistical test of sex or residence difference was questionable in some cases and impossible in others (Table 4). This is not unreasonable in view of the fact that physical handicaps or records of illness which might limit an applicant's ability to look after himself were considered in the preliminary Housing Authority screening, so the entire applicant group should have been in better than average physical condition. Also, applicants may have been hesitant to reveal health problems, even in the research interview, through fear of endangering their chances of admittance to the apartment building.

Generally these people accepted gracefully the physical problems attendant upon advancing age as "What one must expect." Stiffness and aching in joints, failing eyesight, breathlessness, and similar indicators of physical decline were regrettable, yet normal, and should be allowed to interfere as little as possible with enjoyment of life. In the kind of housing they had been able to obtain, any health problem was a more serious handicap. Victoria Plaza attracted them because there they could be financially self-supporting and at the same time able to enter into life more fully, despite some infirmity or impairment.

When a member of the Housing Authority staff explained to a ninety-year-old man that because of his palsy they felt he could not care for himself in the new building he retorted: "You take my folder out of that 'feeble file' and if you still entertain any ideas that I can't

TABLE 14

Differences between the 204 Acceptees and the 148 Nonacceptees Other Abilities for Adjustment to Close Community Life:

Index of Adjustment	*Chi-square*	*df*
Cleanliness		
Interviewers' ratings	1.01	1
Acceptance of reduced income		
Own evaluation of present financial situation	2.93	2
Own evaluation of present finances compared to age 55	2.06	2
Things given up because of reduced income	11.72	9
Own evaluation of life's accomplishments	2.22	2
Reduced interest in material things	16.87**↓	2
Acceptance of reduced activity		
Age identification	4.38	3
Time spent in activities (present)	3.57	1
Time spent in activities (compared to age 55)	3.56	2
Reduced interest in previous activities	14.28**↓	2
Reduced interest in personal contacts	14.28**↓	2
Participation in Community Activities		
Membership in organizations	11.59	7
Office-holding	1.90	1
Desire for membership	1.61	1
Motive for membership	3.50	4
Desire for group activities	8.98**↑	1
Cooperativeness in data collection	13.62**↑	3
Selection to Round Out Community		
Sex	.51	1
Marital Status	.47	1

* Significant at the .05 level.
** Significant at the .01 level.
↑ Higher scores for applicants who were to become residents.
↓ Lower scores for applicants who were to become residents.

get around, why you just come to the Hermann Sons dance with me Saturday night and I'll show you how feeble I am!"

CLEANLINESS

Admission criteria pointed to good "general appearance" with reference to personal grooming and cleanliness, and also to housekeeping, since these would be related to acceptance in such a community as that anticipated for Victoria Plaza. The overall ratings on desirability as tenants made by research interviewers who called on applicants in their homes more than once and had opportunity to see them under informal circumstances, generally agreed with Housing personnel's decisions which were based, so far as personal contact with applicants was concerned, on more formal interviews in Housing Authority offices (Chi-square = 17.79**, df = 3).

However, it was not people the research interviewers rated as dirty or uncouth (Table 14), but those rated antisocial and eccentric, who were not assigned apartments, while there was a tendency to admit those perceived by the research interviewers as having unusual concern for others and being socially adept. Perhaps some subjects could clean up and put on good manners when trying to make a favorable impression at their formal interview in the Housing Administration offices, but found it more difficult to conceal an attitude of social disinterest or negativism. Probably a genuine concern for others shows in any face-to-face situation. Also Housing Authority personnel may have been more concerned with interpersonal attitudes than with externals, despite inclusion of "general appearance" among the criteria they were to use.

Unfortunately, the interviewer for the one man who was forced to leave the Plaza before the end of the year did not record any ratings for him. Later, his neighbors in the Plaza commented that perhaps that contact was what precipitated his interviewer's sudden move to another state.[6] During this resident's stay in Victoria Plaza he seemed to go out of his way to shock and displease the other tenants.

ACCEPTANCE OF REDUCED INCOME

The Housing Authority supplement proposed healthy acceptance

[6] A male social worker had been employed to collect data from male subjects, particularly those whose places of residence were not considered suitable for female interviewers. He left, after conducting a few interviews, to continue his education.

of the limitations imposed by age as one criterion for good adjustment, and made particular reference to reactions to financial resources. Research data show no significant difference between those accepted and those not accepted in their own evaluations of their present financial situation. Neither was there a difference in number or kind of possessions or activities given up because of reduced income since age fifty-five nor in evaluation of their own accomplishments in life.

Acceptance of reduced income should be reflected in diminished concern with material possessions. There was a significant difference in interviewer ratings on this characteristic between successful and unsuccessful applicants, but in the direction opposite to that predicted on the basis of Housing Authority admission standards. Applicants who had been rated as showing sustained interest in material things were more likely to become tenants. Over 70 per cent of the applicants admitted to Victoria Plaza had been rated, in their first interview, as showing no evidence of loss of interest in material possessions; while half of the unsuccessful applicants had been rated as showing diminished interest. This may be related to alertness and awareness of modern changes or it may reflect an envious attitude due to reduced circumstances.

In selecting tenants for a beautiful new building, it is not surprising that the type of person who would be interested in material things was shown preference.[7] However, selection procedure here seemed to reverse stated policy. On the basis of the supplemental Housing Authority policy statement to the effect that ability for adjustment should be considered and that acceptance of the limitations of age was probably a favorable indication, it was predicted that applicants rated by research interviewers as less interested than formerly in material possessions would be more likely to be assigned apartments. Not only was this assumption not true; the opposite was true.

ACCEPTANCE OF REDUCED ACTIVITY

The Housing Authority was looking for tenants who, according to its policy statement, accepted physical limitations rather than resenting them, as indicative of a happy attitude and acceptance of aging.

[7] There is no implication that Housing Authority staff members purposefully used this characteristic in tenant selection. Visits were not made to the homes of applicants by members of the Authority staff, and they had no way of knowing about the material possessions of an applicant.

The majority of applicants considered themselves "middle-aged" and there was no significant difference between those admitted and those not admitted, in age identification.

Amount of time spent in leisure activities at present, or compared with the amount spent at age fifty-five, was similar for acceptees and non-acceptees. However, fewer of those who subsequently moved to Victoria Plaza had been rated by interviewers as seeming to have less interest in activities, and in people, than they had formerly. Three-quarters of the applicants later admitted to Victoria Plaza had impressed their interviewers as people who were maintaining interest in activities, while only a little over half of those not admitted had. Eighty per cent of successful applicants, as opposed to two-thirds of unsuccessful, seemed to show no loss of interest in other people.

While there was an initial difference between members of the resident group and of the nonresident group, it does not appear due to a bias of the residents toward acceptance of reduced activity. Rather, fewer of those who moved to the new building had revealed, in the research contacts, disengagement from activities and people.

POSSIBLE PARTICIPATION IN COMMUNITY ACTIVITIES

The Housing Authority recognized that in any close-knit community, where residents are more or less dependent on each other for recreation and social participation, a variety of activities is necessary. Potential for contribution to community activities was considered in admission.

In regard to past activities in clubs, associations, or organizations, no difference was found between those admitted and those not admitted, either in membership or office holding. Neither was there a difference in desire to belong to an organization, if circumstances permitted, or in motive for wanting to join. However, a significant difference appeared in desire to participate in activities with other people. Half of those who became residents, but only a third of those who did not, wanted to join a group to "do something" (play cards or pool or do ceramic or leather work) though they were no more interested in formally organized clubs.

Consistent with this was the correlation of interviewer ratings of applicants' cooperativeness in interview and testing procedures with likelihood of admission. Those applicants who impressed their interviewers as more cooperative in the face-to-face data collection situation were more likely to become residents of Victoria Plaza than were those applicants who cooperated less fully in research procedures.

Housing Authority personnel seemed successful in selecting people who maintained interest in participation and in other people, both of which are favorable characteristics for group living. Selection was related to expressed interest in activities and people, but not to enumeration of past activities, or to membership or desired membership in organizations.

HUMOR

The Housing Authority considered a sense of humor an asset for adjustment to community life. In describing themselves by means of an adjective check list, almost all of those interviewed saw themselves as having no undesirable traits and readily admitted they were good-natured, cheerful, pleasant, and jolly. Interviewers' descriptions, being somewhat less socially perfect, allowed for testing of differences between groups. Among those admitted to Victoria Plaza, there were fewer who were judged by research interviewers to be bitter, complaining, dissatisfied, or fault-finding, and more who were described as cheerful (Table 15).

MARITAL STATUS AND SEX

In order to normalize, insofar as possible, the neighborhood being

TABLE 15

Humor as Judged by Interviewers
Differences between the 204 Acceptees and the 148 Nonacceptees

Adjective	*Chi-square*	*df*
Cheerful	7.61**↑	1
Bitter	6.50* ↓	1
Complaining	11.50**↓	1
Dissatisfied	43.77**↓	1
Fault-finding	30.56**↓	1
Fussy	7.12**↓	1
Gloomy	18.16**↓	1
Irritable	7.89**↓	1
Moody	17.05**↓	1
Worrying	17.43**↓	1

* Significant at the .05 level.
** Significant at the .01 level.
↑ Adjective used to describe more applicants who were to become residents.
↓ Adjective used to describe fewer applicants who were to become residents.

constructed by tenant selection, the Housing Authority recommended that male applicants and married couples be given preference. It was mentioned (Chapter 3) that single men and married couples living together were underrepresented in the applicant group. Despite the efforts of the Housing Authority staff in regard to single men, the proportion of acceptees to non-acceptees was practically identical for men and women applicants. Similarly, among the group of applicants studied members of husband-and-wife teams were no more likely to become tenants than were any other individuals.

Effect of Religious Affiliation on Admissions

According to the supplemental admission form, religious preference was to be recorded, but for "interest only and has no bearing on eligibility or selection." Since it seemed that Housing Authority staff members would have data in this category on all applicants,[8] and in the realization that, when discrimination among members of a relatively homogeneous group is required, selections may, quite inadvertently, be made on the basis of "halo effect," one source of which is religious affiliation (Flyer and Carp, 1961), a test of difference was made. It was statistically significant (Chi-square 10.04, df 4).

Protestant applicants were more likely to move to Victoria Plaza than were Roman Catholic applicants. In describing the entire group of applicants (see Chapter 3) it was remarked that the proportion of Roman Catholics was far below that expected on the basis of census figures for this geographic area. There is no way to determine whether this was related to the nonrepresentative ethnic distribution, whether it was entirely due to lack of desire on the part of Roman Catholic individuals, or whether it may have been in part a function of preliminary Housing Authority screening.

All (nine) Jewish applicants were admitted. This may be due to the small number of applicants, a strict effort to avoid even the appearance of anti-Semitism, or the happenstance that all nine were well qualified.

In view of the fact that religious affiliation was not recorded until after selection proceedings, these results are impossible to interpret.

[8] Housing Authority staff members recently advised that, at that time, this information was collected only on those selected for residency. However, it is now, apparently, a standard item on application forms (personal communication from Marilynn Wacker, assistant executive director, the Housing Authority of the city of San Antonio, December 4, 1964).

However, it is necessary to report them, because they demonstrate an initial difference between the resident and nonresident groups. They do at least suggest some, probably unconscious, source of bias in the selection procedure which caused statistically significant differences when the information was not even consistently collected and recorded. Assessment of its effect when religious affiliation is routinely recorded, as apparently is the current practice, is clearly needed.

No doubt there are valid reasons for religious affiliation to appear in the records of people living in public housing facilities, but one might wonder at its inclusion in an application, if it is irrelevant to eligibility, as it was explicitly labelled on these forms. The requirement that staff members collect such information, which may be highly ego-involving for them, and then disregard it in making such wholistic, subjective judgments as are required on some of the admission standards, may set them an impossible task.

Summary

Though plans for statistical treatment of data provided for initial differences between the groups, so that their similarity was not crucial to the experimental design of the study on impact of housing change (Appendix C), the infrequency of differences, in the variables where they would most be expected, was satisfactory from a research point of view. The small number and modest size of these differences indicated considerable similarity between the group which was about to undergo dramatic change in living conditions and that which was not. Even with a less sophisticated statistical approach, there would be little danger of attributing to the environmental change differences based on selective factors and inherent in the groups from the beginning.

Items in the Housing Authority standard were used quite differently for research purposes than for eligibility determination. However, intergroup differences in research data which seemed relevant to individual admission standards suggest that further refinement of selection from among the original group of qualified applicants proved difficult, on the basis of the legally defined criteria. The group which was to move into the Plaza was almost identical with that which was not, on items of research data selected as relevant.

Research results generally support the Authority personnel's selections on the basis of ability for adjustment to close community life.

The data indicate that the Housing Authority selection generally followed the clearly stated criteria and were quite successful in the areas where global impression and subjectivity were necessary. This was particularly difficult since preliminary screening left a fairly homogeneous group of applicants from which to select residents. However, it would seem that, instead of choosing applicants who had gracefully accepted limitations of activity and possession, selectors favored those with unabated interest in material things and desire for informal social participation.

CHAPTER 6

Reactions to Victoria Plaza and the Senior Center

Prospective Residents' Comments at First Sight[1]

WHILE FINISHING TOUCHES were still being put on the building, applicants selected for first admission were taken on tours to indicate their preference regarding apartments. They were asked to come in groups of eight, for a two-hour period during which they were shown two apartments, were given opportunity to express preferences regarding apartments, and were assigned times (day and hour) for moving in.

Invitations to attend were received with relief and enthusiasm. A ninety-year-old woman who had been ill got up and dressed for the first time in weeks to keep her appointment for the tour. One man announced victoriously: "When I made my application at Victoria Courts over a year ago, they didn't have a vacancy and suggested I apply for this new building. I said 'Hell, I won't live that long.' But here I am!"

THE BUILDING IN GENERAL

Initial reactions to the new structure were of delight: "This is a miracle! It shows someone has a heart for the old folks." "I never dreamed it would be like this!" "Anyone who wouldn't be pleased

[1] Many of the quotations in this section were recorded by Elna Gill, a member of the Housing Authority staff, and were made available through the courtesy of that Authority.

with this would just be hard to please" "This building certainly improved the neighborhood." "Truly a paradise for old people." "We knew it was going to be nice, but it is even better than our expectations." "I have lived here sixty-three years and this is a page in history for San Antonio." "This is a big feather in San Antonio's cap. The whole world will be looking at this." "Well, I think the whole thing is just mighty darned awful nice."

Their gratitude extended to people who had been instrumental in obtaining the building. Overheard during a heated argument about what the building was to be called: "There is only one obvious name for this building and that is McGuire Spire!" "Oh, yes, yes, that would be perfect! Think how hard she has worked for this. If it hadn't been for her, we wouldn't be here."[2] Many expressed concern over the hard work for the staff which the tours involved: "Too bad you had to come up again for us. You must be awfully tired."

IMPORTANT DETAILS

Spontaneous favorable comments were elicited by many specifics of the construction: "Look at the nice woodwork." "Such a lot of shelves and closet space." "Oh, look we have a place for our name outside the door." "A doorbell! How wonderful! Look at the doorbell!" "I like the laundry room." "I like the bathroom best of all!" "Look, we will have some privacy!" "Look at these beautiful cabinets." "Praise the Lord! No yard to care for!" "These apartments are larger than I thought they would be." "Look at the deep-freeze space in this refrigerator. Boy, I mean that's larger than the one I have!" "I wouldn't have any trouble keeping this place clean." "Can you imagine the moonlight coming through that sunscreen? It will be nice at night."

"I grew up on a farm and loved it when I was young. But when you get this age, you want to be where things are convenient." "I'm pleased with all the storage space." "Does each apartment really have a private bath?" "This is out of the world. What I want so bad is a shower. I can't get in and out of the bathtub." "I know what you mean. I have arthritis so bad I fell last year in the bathtub." "Did you notice the tile bath?" "I see that it's completely fireproof. I can't see any part of the building that would burn." "I like the covered patio, so that we can still sit out, even when the weather is

[2] Reference was to Marie McGuire, then director of the San Antonio Housing Authority, now commissioner of the U.S. Public Housing Administration.

bad." "I can't get around too much, but I will enjoy sitting up here on the balcony watching all the activity below."

There was incredulity: "Does the incinerator really take cans and bottles?" and there were some questions: "Will there be chairs on the patio?" "Can we have our own chair on the balcony?" "May we have potted plants?"

Immediately, people began visualizing cherished belongings in the new setting. One man commented: "I'm a retired architect and I collect antiques and paintings. I hate to give up my crystal chandeliers; but I am thankful the maintenance man can hang my oil paintings. I got the measurements of these apartments months ago and I drew it to scale and I have all my furniture already arranged on paper. True, there won't be much space for walking, but I'll be happy among my treasures."

A woman remarked, "I have a beautiful redbird plant that will look fine behind this sunscreen. I'll just make that space a miniature solarium." A man said, "I know this divider can be moved. I would like to move it farther back, because I only have a cot and this would give me more living space to entertain my cronies."

Some realized that they would have to get rid of belongings: "I don't know what I'm going to do with all this stuff I have." "I'll have to sell my two cabinets. I guess I'll have to sell my wardrobe, too." "I'll have to get rid of my big bedroom suite." "I'll have to get rid of my old dresser. It would take up too much space." Reluctance to let go of belongings was rarely shown during the tour. When one woman commented to a friend, "You sure are going to have to sell a bunch of stuff," the response was, "Well, that old dresser I'll be glad to get rid of anyway."

A few applicants showed they would experience a painful wrench at letting go of furniture and other possessions which had, for so long, been part of their lives. One couple at last faced, during the tour, what they had tried not to think about, for as long as possible—the obvious fact that the apartment could not accommodate their huge and ornate furniture and the collection of dishes, silver, pictures, and curios which dated from their courtship and recorded their fifty-odd years of marriage.

Stiff and white-faced at the end of the tour, they confided to their interviewer that, had they been able to locate any place they could afford, in which they could live with their "own things," they would have chosen it without hesitation and let someone else have the beautiful new apartment. However, they had exhausted all possibilities and had no option. Heartbroken, they would part with their beautiful beloved things and buy small, inexpensive, strange pieces.

OTHER RESIDENTS

Women immediately manifested their interest in the opposite sex. A little eighty-three–year–old woman who arrived late for her tour slipped up to a staff member and whispered, "Aren't there going to be any men in this building?" One woman not even considered as a tenant, but who somehow got in on a tour, explained that her gentleman friend was going to live in Victoria Plaza, and she was now applying to Victoria Courts so she could be near him (but for propriety's sake across the street).

When one of the staff mentioned to a group of ladies that there would be a number of eligible bachelors, they laughed loudly and applauded. Several women who happened to be going up in the elevator together discovered that they were all retired nurses. A staff member suggested they start a nurses' club. "Oh, we will," they agreed, "We might even go back in the business." The building administrator commented, "Why, every old gentleman in the building will come up with a sore toe or something if you ladies make it known you are willing to nurse them!" One replied, "Well, I'm an old maid, but that doesn't make me averse to nursing the men!" and they all nodded agreement.

One couple, explaining to their research interviewer that they had been assigned a one-bedroom apartment instead of the two-bedroom unit they had expected, giggled like youngsters and said the one-bedroom apartment was so nice they just went ahead and took it.[3] Another couple carefully explained that they needed, not a two-bedroom apartment, but a one-bedroom apartment, "Because, after all, we are only sixty-five."

Even during this exciting inspection tour of the building, when sixty-five prospective residents a day were being shown through it, nearly all of them for the first time, there was much evidence of efforts to get acquainted. When people were introduced they tried to find a common bond: "I know some ———'s. Are you any relation to them?" or "My mother had a cousin named ———. They came from ———, too. Did you know them?" Groups of women formed, trying

[3] The one-bedroom apartments were intended for two-person occupancy.

to outdo each other in regard to the number and achievements of children, grandchildren, and great-grandchildren.

When two friends were asked if they wanted to live next door to one another, one answered, "Heavens no! Put us as far apart as you can. We need an excuse to get out and move around." On the other hand, one woman paid a deposit on the apartment next to hers, to insure that her best friend would have it. Some reassured themselves, "I already know five people who are moving in," but others could not wait, "to get to know all these people."

Men who had never met before challenged each other to a pool tournament or a game of dominoes to be played as soon as they moved in. One said to another, "Aren't you my neighbor on the ninth floor?" When the other responded in the affirmative, the first speaker grinned, raised his hand and said, "Howdy, neighbor!" Another remarked, "I'm living over the patio. When I see someone I might want to know, I will just go down and get acquainted."

One of eight women who happened to ride up in an elevator together announced, "I'm practically blind so I won't recognize you ladies when I see you again. But my name is Miss ——— and as soon as we are all in I want to have a welcome party for all you ladies in this elevator." Everyone agreed to come.

Mood was euphoric and humor abounded: "Is Mrs. Youngblood here?" "No, but there are plenty of Old Bloods!"

PREFERENCE FOR APARTMENTS

Generally people were not at all difficult to please in their selection of apartments. When asked, "What apartment do you want?" a common response was " I just don't know. I can't decide. I would like any of them!" One man grinned, "Put me anywhere. I'm not hard to please, honey!"

People viewed only two apartments on the tour. At the end, when they were asked where they wanted to live in the building, most answered, "The first apartment we were shown." One man said, "Give me any apartment. I don't care, just as long as I have plenty of sun. You can't live without sun;" but another, "I want the fifth floor on the shady side. I've lived in the sun too long."

A woman announced, "I don't know where 713 is, but I want it. That's my lucky number;" and another, "I don't care where I live just so long as it's on the ninth floor, the south wing, and it's a green apartment." One preferred "the north wing with its pretty view," to which a second standing by said, "Oh, I don't know. I want the south view overlooking the driveway to see who's coming and going." One lady requested the top floor corner so she could shake her dust cloth out the window where the wind would be the strongest to blow away the dirt. "Put us on the second floor so we can walk up," two women requested, adding, "We need the exercise."

DISINCLINATIONS

Some reservations were voiced during the tour: "Is there any chance of backing out after I'm all signed up?" "I'll need help in using this here stove." "My daughter will sure have to be careful when she brings the children on this balcony." "I don't know if I can learn to take a shower." "This is a real safe building, isn't it?"

After looking over Victoria Plaza two women decided they preferred to stay in Victoria Courts, but the decision was close and they consoled themselves over and over again, "At least we will still be neighbors" (to Victoria Plaza). Another said, "I don't think I'll move. I'm happy at Victoria Courts." And a fourth, "I have a nice apartment over at Victoria Courts. I'd feel too hemmed in here."

The additional expense was a problem, insurmountable to some ("I can't afford to pay $8.00 more for rent. This beautiful building is going to make us dissatisfied over at the Courts." "I wish I could move over, but I don't have the extra money.") but not to all ("It will be worth going without one meal a day to be able to live here.").

Very few negative reactions were heard. The most frequent was, "The medicine chest is too high." At the time of the tours the elevators were not yet working properly. Applicants did not appear to be perturbed about this, but waited patiently, laughed and joked about stops between floors, and expressed delight in having any elevator at all. There were several comments about the need of a ventilating fan in the elevator, particularly if it maintained the habit of pausing.

SUMMARY

The most adequate summaries of reactions of people on their first visit to Victoria Plaza were typical responses to the questions: "When do you want to move in?" which were: "As soon as I can!" and "I've been waiting a year and a half for this apartment. I just don't see how I can wait five minutes longer. This is judgment day!" and "How can I wait until the twelfth? Can you tell me? This looks like Shangri

La;" and a wistful comment at the outside door, "I just don't want to leave!"

Evaluation of the Residence a Year Later

OVERWHELMINGLY FAVORABLE REACTION

About nine months after they moved in, apartment occupants were asked to rate, on a five-point scale, their satisfaction with Victoria Plaza as a place to live. Only three women (fewer than 2 per cent of residents) were not "satisfied" or "very satisfied."

Since this might have sampled the "honeymoon" phase, a similar question was put to them three months later. At this later time only one woman reacted unfavorably. (She was the same woman who was consistently negativistic in all research contacts, beginning with the preliminary interview. She insisted on being interviewed, but refused to answer nearly every question, including her current marital status. She was the only person who would not tell her age.)

These favorable ratings seemed reasonably honest reflections of residents' feelings. Their occupancy of living space in the Plaza was secure and there was no longer pressure, as there may have been while they were applicants for housing, to give responses which might improve chances of obtaining apartments. From the beginning it was obvious to any observer that they were delighted at their good luck and appreciative of the many changes brought about in their lives. This first flush of enthusiasm, far from dying down or swinging back toward disillusionment, seemed only to deepen with continuing experience.

They did not feel that the building, their own apartments, the Senior Center, or the other people living in the Plaza, were perfect. However, they did not expect Utopia, and most were wryly aware that they were not without fault, themselves. Even more important in determining the unanimity of their satisfaction with Victoria Plaza was the dramatic improvement it represented over what they had had immediately previous to residence there. They had moved from substandard housing to a freshly completed, totally modern apartment building, and they appreciated and enjoyed the convenience, cleanliness, and beauty. From social isolation or resentment-producing interpersonal situations they had been transported into the midst of a bountiful supply of people, yet with control over their own privacy and choice of associates. They were genuinely pleased and grateful for these marked improvements in the determining realities of their day-to-day living.

Members of the applicant group who had not lived in Victoria Plaza were also asked to evaluate the residence. Many had not been near the building; more had never seen an apartment in it. Of those sufficiently familiar to make judgments, nearly two-thirds gave Victoria Plaza the highest possible rating, while less than 5 per cent were unfavorable. Negative responses probably were "sour grapes" reactions from people badly disappointed at not being included. Though these few people professed to like "nothing" about the building or the people living in it, they carefully kept their applications active.

Since the residents were speaking on the basis of much closer and more extensive experience, only their views, as expressed in an interview a year to fifteen months after they moved into the Plaza, are presented here, in evaluation of it as a place in which to live.

Best Things. For those living in Victoria Plaza the "best things" were its cleanness; modern conveniences such as stoves, refrigerators, private bathrooms and elevators, which they had not had; and the rent, which they felt to be low for what they got (though 50 per cent were paying more than when they were applicants). The most frequent causes for complaints about former housing, which caused them to apply for apartments in Victoria Plaza, apparently were absent in the new homes.

The Plaza had turned out to be even better than expected in many ways. The cleanness of the building and the conveniences in it were even more gratifying than anticipated, as were the comfortable warmth in winter and the cooling summer ventilation. Few had realized that the location would provide such easy access to churches and downtown stores, as well as to public transportation to other points of interest.

Half the group expressed surprise that other residents were so friendly and helpful, and many had not expected that Victoria Plaza would attract such a "good class" of people. Also exceeding expectation was enjoyment of games and other group activities.

Life Impact. As the single most outstanding effect of the new housing on their lives, most residents mentioned security. Others pointed to longer life expectancy, new independence, dignity, and self-respect, and the chance to make friends and join in activities. For nearly one in ten the most remarkable change had been in awareness of the general problems of aging. These people had come to realize that the difficulties they faced were not peculiar to them as individuals, but were widespread in society. Living in Victoria Plaza had had "no effect" on the lives of another 10 per cent.

The Building. Nearly half the residents insisted that "everything" about the type of building was so perfect they were unable to say what about it they liked best. Specific features most often mentioned were its compactness and the "hotel-like living" it afforded. They approved of the compact high-rise design for several reasons. For one thing, it made for easy upkeep. This was not only a matter of such considerations as eight rather than ten- or twelve-foot ceilings, but also one of being able to dispose of garbage in the hall of the same floor of the building as that on which one lived, and of being able to keep food in a refrigerator in the same room in which cooking was done.

Compactness was also mentioned as the "best thing" about Victoria Plaza because of the easy availability of other people. Residents enjoyed the informal social contact that was facilitated by being able to visit with any one of over two hundred people without needing to go outdoors, let alone having to pay for transportation. The closeness of neighbors was also a source of security to many residents. Though most had never called for help, they were reassured by the accessibility of other people, in case of sudden illness or other emergency.

Maintenance by a trained, hired staff was much enjoyed, and most renters applauded the absence of hard work. The elevator was frequently mentioned also as a great boon, relieving them of unpleasant exertion in the performance of necessary household tasks, and providing them effortless access to other people.

Most had no aversion to any particular part of the building. A few disliked the open galleries, which were the only means of access to apartments, the elevators (for fear of getting stuck in them, not completely unjustified in terms of past performance), the lobby (because of the inordinate amount of gossip it encouraged), and the unlocked outer doors (because of the neighborhood).

Other Residents. Asked what they particularly liked about the people living in Victoria Plaza, a few avoided giving an answer, suggesting a certain lack of enthusiasm. The pleasing characteristic most frequently mentioned was friendliness. Other residents were also perceived as representing a "good class of people," as being generally helpful, and as taking pride in the building and in their own appearance.

In answer to an open-ended question, several people mentioned "living with nobody but old people," as a source of dissatisfaction, but when directly asked what they thought about such a dwelling being restricted to one age group, practically everyone was favorable. The majority were definitely not interested in living close to families with children, who create noise, run through yards, and generally disturb life.

However, there was a pervasive feeling that a few residents had not really met self-care admission requirement, which imposed an unfair burden on their neighbors. Those were the "old people" whose presence in the Plaza was resented. Most residents wanted the stimulation of contact with "middle-aged" people, like themselves. Given the choice of homogeneous age grouping such as in Victoria Plaza or the all-purpose public housing they had experienced or observed across the street, nearly all would choose the former.

Friends. Living in Victoria Plaza had stimulated friendships. Only two people complained that moving there had caused them to lose all their old friends, while the majority had kept former friends and added new ones. Generally those people reporting no change in their friendships over a year's residence in Victoria Plaza had moved from Victoria Courts, a neighboring cottage-type public housing development. Some of their friends had moved with them, and others were only as far away as across the street.

SOME NEGATIVE COMMENTS

While residents were almost unanimous in expressing an extremely high opinion of Victoria Plaza as a whole, they were not uncritical of details. Though a quarter of them could suggest no improvement, an equal number said it had not lived up to their expectations in one way or another, and half reported undesirable aspects of living there. The Plaza was still "As near Heaven as I expect to get on this earth," and so far superior to what they had had previously that they praised God daily for their deliverance. Nevertheless, they could see room for improvement.

Neighborhood. Especially disappointing were the unavailability of grocery stores and of "decent" places to buy a meal within easy walking distance. Some, as applicants, had understood that the ground floor "community center" would be a shopping area and were disappointed that it was not. In Central Texas "community center" is a common designation for a suburban complex of stores. They also objected to the appearance and reputation of the neighborhood, and (especially women) continued to wonder why such a beautiful building was not in a safer and more attractive part of town. ("The prettiest, shiny new thing in the city and they put it down here in shanty town." "This really belongs on the north side, where people could take a walk without fear of being knifed.")

Administration. No questions were asked about the administration of the building, but criticisms of it were not infrequently volunteered. Most of the spontaneous comments were to the effect that staff members imposed upon residents and invaded their privacy.

The Plaza was an achievement of which the entire city was proud, and during its first year it was on display. Residents shared in this pride but they also had a proprietary attitude about their homes and wanted the Plaza to be less a public show place. There were numerous complaints about the number of outsiders who made tours of the building, scheduled meetings in it, and used the recreation facilities.

These renters took great pride in paying their own way, and they valued the privacy of their apartments, so they resented both being "shown off" as recipients of charity and being subject to "open house" without notice and with no regard to their convenience. Nevertheless, liking the administrators and appreciating their situation, occupants could not refuse tours of their apartments, and they knew they had no control over use of the recreation area. Some hesitated to risk alienating staff members for fear they would lose their apartments. This conflict was painful for many residents at the end of the first year.[4]

Resentment was expressed to data collectors also over the fact that each one of over two hundred residents was required to take the elevator (which might stick), go through the lobby (with all those old gossips), push open the heavy outer door, walk across a point of land and across the street, to go to the Housing Administration office and pay his monthly rent. They did not see why one member of that staff could not spend a day or a half day each month in the office in

[4] Housing Authority staff members had quite a different view and were impressed by the number of people who eagerly offered their apartments as places to be visited (personal communication from Marilynn Wacker, December 4, 1964).

Victoria Plaza, collecting rent. ("One walk on young legs would do the work of two hundred pairs of old ones." "I think they do it just to keep us in our places.")[5]

Some residents told their interviewers they were irked also by what seemed to them imposition of staff plans on their activity groups and social organizations. In view of their very limited financial resources, they tended to be frightened, as well as resentful, of what seemed to them to be staff efforts to have money collected for flowers, "Every time another resident, or a staff member, or even a relative of one of them, gets sick or dies or gets married." (I can't even afford a present for my own daughter and, by damn, it makes me mad to have to fork over one for her [staff member's] sister. I never even laid eyes on her!" "Did you ever stop to figure out how many funerals you are likely to have in a year, in a place where everybody is this old?" "Maybe I'll be lucky and kick off soon, and leave you fellows to buy the flowers!")[6]

They also resented what seemed to them a staff decision implemented through the organization of apartment occupants, that each resident should "chip in" to buy attractive furniture for the landing by the elevator on each floor. Irritation became particularly acute when floor representatives (officers of the residence organization) began competing, each trying to have his floor outdo all others.

To make the money-raising more palatable for residents of one

[5] Marilynn Wacker suggests it be pointed out that "The move by the Housing Authority to require that the rent be paid other than in the building was deliberate. In the first place, this was an attempt to cut down on the number of staff that would be required to operate the building, but more, it was intended as a way of getting the people out of the building at least once a month. The Authority felt some concern over the fact that if everything were provided in the building, there would be no incentive to remain part of the community." Furthermore, Housing Authority staff members did not perceive much resentment over the practice (personal communication, December 4, 1964).

[6] According to Marilynn Wacker, "There was no person connected with the Housing Authority who was involved in the building at the time of its opening who recalls any money collections for flowers or for any other reason. The resident organization set up its own tin can for collections at meetings of the group where people could put dimes or quarters to be used for remembrances. This was the decision of the group in which the staff was not involved. In fact, the staff attempted to discourage the group from such collections and in two instances when attempts were made by the residents' council to raise money for gifts for the Center director and for the building manager, the drives were actually stopped by members of the staff" (personal communication, December 4, 1964).

floor, someone had the idea of a community supper, to which each was expected to contribute labor, and from which every one was expected to buy. To some people, instead of being a pleasurable joint enterprise and a delicious chicken dinner, this was perceived as an imposition of double jeopardy, and the staff, somehow, was held responsible.[7]

These resentments and irritations should not obscure the widespread good will and gratitude toward staff members. Not infrequently one of them was named in the sociometric data collection as a resident's best friend. Perhaps this affection inhibited freer expression of grievances to members of the staff.

Plan of the Building. One distasteful aspect of living in Victoria Plaza was confrontation with illness and death. This stemmed basically from living in a homogeneously aged group but was emphasized by the necessity to take ill persons or corpses down the central elevator and through the community center, regardless of the hour or the activity underway. Though the resident group was calm when deaths occurred in the building, many of them suggested one elevator in a more secluded area of the ground floor. Probably related to this suggestion were their responses to the question, "Do you ever think about the end of life?" which was asked in a different section of the interview. Over a third of the residents responded to the effect that "I try not to think about it."

Not only the removal of the dying and the dead, but the moving in and out of furniture, and transportation of all service equipment and personnel, had to be handled through the elevators which were clearly visible from much of the ground-floor area, the center of group activities. It was suggested that another elevator giving access to residential units from the service area of the ground floor would be a useful addition to plans for future buildings. Installation of seats and a fan in existing elevators was recommended by some residents, for the assistance of those not feeling well and, perhaps even more important, the convenience of those occasionally stalled in the elevator during repairs.

Each floor (twenty-three apartments) had a laundry room equipped with one home-type washing machine and one dryer. Some

[7] Interestingly, when staff members reviewed this material late in 1964 one administrator challenged the fact that such a dinner ever was held, while another reminisced about it at length, as a well-known example of cordial staff-resident relationships.

residents complained that these were often out of order and that on wash day they might have to chase from floor to floor trying to find an appliance in operation but not in use. Comments were also made to interviewers that apparently repairs to laundry equipment took so much time that the maintenance crew could not always attend to other needs of residents.[8] Many renters suggested that commercial equipment would be more satisfactory and, in the long run, more economical.

Another criticism of the building as one designed for the aged and infirm was that lobby doors should be lighter or automatic. Many people suggested the addition of a mail chute on each floor near the elevator, or at least one in the downstairs post office, to eliminate the necessity of going not only all the way downstairs, but also through the very heavy entrance doors to a drop box some distance from the building.[9]

Plaza Restaurant. Eating facilities in the building were recommended by many residents. A greater proportion of women than of men wanted them, probably because men felt freer to patronize the type of eating places within walking distance, and because more men had cars. Most people did not want to give up cooking, and valued their separate kitchens very much, but would like to buy one hot meal a day or one occasionally.

Apartments. Though the occupants were proud of their apartments, enjoyed them, and were thankful to be in them, at the end of their first year to fifteen months of living in Victoria Plaza they were willing to make critical comments and offer suggestions for improvement of living units in future construction of buildings of this type.

Alteration of the window arrangement was the most common and urgent recommendation. Windows in the living area of apartments open onto the porch, which is also the only hall from one apartment to the next. Heavy traverse drapes were supplied as preferable to window shades or venetian blinds, and renters were requested to

[8] "At the time of the opening of the building and throughout the first several years of operation, the washer and dryer installations were on a contract basis to a private firm and repairs were its responsibility" (personal communication from Marilynn Wacker, December 4, 1964).

[9] "With respect to the mail chute, again perhaps the observation should be made that the location of a mail box at a point away from the building was a deliberate move by the Housing Authority to get people out of doors. The distance from the building is approximately 180 feet" (personal communication from Marilynn Wacker, December 4, 1964).

leave them in place. As a consequence of this arrangement, if drapes were closed to give privacy artificial light must be used all day, according to some apartment dwellers. On the other hand, they commented, if a person tried to enjoy fresh air and a view, he felt that his entire apartment was open to the gaze of everyone who passed by, and some added that at certain times of day his apartment was filled with glaring light reflected from the concrete porch. Venetian blinds or cafe curtains were suggested to give some control over privacy, illumination, and ventilation.[10]

The wish for privacy expressed in comments about the window treatment was probably related also to criticisms of the absence of bedroom doors. Though in each apartment the living room and bedroom are divided by a closet, a few people felt insecure without a closed door. For example, an occasional person could not really relax on his bed in the summer unless he closed the living-room drapes, which cut off the breeze. A small number of deaf residents habitually left their apartment entrance doors unlocked, because they might not hear someone trying to contact them. (In at least one case, it was necessary to touch the resident to get her attention.) These renters would have appreciated bedroom doors, which they could close as an indication of need for privacy.

Residents pointed out that in apartments for more than one person there was additional need of bedroom doors for quiet and privacy, especially in case of illness. Several renters made sketches attempting to show that bedroom privacy could be greatly improved simply by rearrangement, and without using more material.

Related also was the much less frequent complaint about inability to control the central heating. When the furnace was "on" in the building, turning it "off" in apartments was relatively ineffective. If a person felt too warm, he simply had to make the choice between enduring too much heat and giving up his privacy by opening the window and drapes.

Frequently mentioned by residents was need for phones in the bedroom of apartments for people in their age range, phones which could be provided either by adding jacks or by locating the one phone in the bedroom. This relocation was not for the convenience of lolling in bed to enjoy social conversations, but for allaying fear of

[10] "Many of them have, with the assistance of the management, put up glass curtains or other types of curtains" (personal communication from Marilynn Wacker, December 4, 1964).

inability to get to the phone in case of emergency during the night and for use when in bed because of illness. One diabetic, knowing that she might have an emergency situation at any time, did without everything but the barest essentials of food until she could buy a day bed so she could sleep near the phone in the living room.

One "special design feature" of the apartments was installation of clothes rods several inches lower than usual, to eliminate the necessity for these aged people to stretch or lift. However, the rods were so low that women's dresses and some men's clothing swept the floor.[11]

Though kitchens were especially planned for the convenience and safety of older people, residents found them less than ideal, and in some ways perhaps inferior to standard kitchens. Refrigerators were unusually inconvenient. High placement to obviate stooping resulted in unexpected difficulties. Short women could not see into the freezing compartment, and removal of the elevated drip trays was a difficult and messy job. This inevitable untidiness was particularly frustrating to these people, so eager to keep their treasured "modern conveniences" in perfect condition. Several mentioned having been dreadfully embarrassed by apartment tours which caught them in this sloppy mess.

Kitchen ranges had controls at the back, in line with safety recommendations. However, residents pointed out that for their needs, unlike those of families with young children, front controls would be preferable, because of the poor vision and unsteadiness common among the aged.

Bathrooms, again carefully planned for the needs of this age group, presented some perhaps trivial, but very frustrating, situations. Many women could not see even the tops of their heads in the mirror and men might have to stretch to watch themselves shave.[12] Some occupants, even after the period of a year, continued to long for a tub bath, though private bathrooms provided continuing delight, and most residents felt safer using showers. They suggested that such buildings should include at least one or two tubs in each wing. A few put plastic tubs inside their showers so they could sit and soak.

[11] This was such a common problem that after about eighteen months rods were moved to standard height.

[12] "As quickly as possible after the building was occupied, the medicine cabinets were reversed so that the situation would be less difficult" (personal communication from Marilynn Wacker, December 4, 1964).

Another problem arose in connection with bathrooms: Though the door itself was sufficiently wide for a wheel chair, a few residents, who had tried it, said the bathroom was so small that the chair could not then be turned to enable the person to get out of it, except by stepping into the shower stall. They felt that because of this situation a person unable to walk could not use the washstand or commode without assistance.

A source of considerable embarrassment to a small number of renters was the noisy flushing of commodes. At night the sound of their own seemed to them to roar through the building, and a constraint was felt to wait until neighbors were out or asleep or until daytime to push the plunger.

Some occupants were quite perturbed by what they called the "whistling doors." Particularly in winter, the prevailing north wind, blowing down the long outdoor corridors, moaned eerily through front doors of apartments.[13] This and the plumbing noises were especially trying to the relatively large number (about 25 per cent) who admitted, while they were applicants as well as later, that noises made them nervous.

Though the convenience of an incinerator chute from each floor was much appreciated for the disposal of garbage, soot from the smokestack settled on porches and dirtied apartments, frustrating the residents in their intense need to keep everything spotless. A different-type incinerator, or addition of a filter, was urged by some Plaza dwellers.

Many residents felt that future buildings should include service areas, preferably a small one for each apartment or, if that was impossible, a larger one for each wing of the building—space to air and shake mops and rugs, and to store cleaning equipment. The only place in which to clean and dry rags and mops was the bathroom and, when interviewers took up the offer to smell the results, they appreciated the complaint. Apartment occupants suggested that the service area might also provide storage space for such things as luggage, out-of-season clothes, and Christmas decorations, for which they begrudged clothes closet or kitchen space, which was limited.

A year of housekeeping experience in the Plaza also led some people to recommend a different type of flooring material. They said

[13] This was corrected by adjustment of weather stripping (personal communication from Marilynn Wacker, December 4, 1964).

that, no matter how hard they worked, floors marred and seemed to be deteriorating. For appearance, easy care, and durability, they thought a better material could be found.[14]

In line with this view to economy, many renters suggested putting each light on a separate switch. When illumination was wanted in either the kitchen or the living room area, it seemed to them extravagant to burn the bulbs in both.

These people had to manage their own funds solicitously, and they abhorred waste, even when the money did not come out of their pockets. They valued highly the beauty and comfort of their low-cost housing, and wanted to assist the fine efforts of the Housing Authority to provide as much as possible, at as low a cost as possible, to as many people as possible.

Since visitors had commented on the smallness of apartments, it was interesting that only seven residents, all women, volunteered that rooms should be larger in future buildings. Each of the seven had treasured pieces of large, old-fashioned furniture before moving to Victoria Plaza and continued to regret inability to have it with them or to show it off properly, if they had it crammed into the apartment.

The couple mentioned earlier who were known to have had much difficulty in parting with the collection of a life-time continued to long for their possessions. The wife was one of those who recommended larger rooms in such buildings in the future. The husband declined the opportunity to offer suggestions, commenting, as did many others, that anyone critical of such a fine residence was simply ungrateful and should be ashamed. However, neither husband nor wife seemed really happy or at ease in Victoria Plaza. In their case, as perhaps in a few others, the surrender of furniture and other possessions was important, not only because the objects were missed, both as items in themselves and as reminders of the family events associated with them, but also because their absence and the substitution of cheaper and less distinguished furnishings was a continual reminder of general loss of status.

Those people who experienced most difficulty in accepting furni-

[14] "The flooring material in the apartments, except for the kitchen, is asphalt, and in the kitchen, vinyl asbestos. They are a higher grade of flooring than normally permitted in low-rent housing developments and were approved only after insistence by the local housing authority" (personal communication from Marilynn Wacker, December 4, 1964).

ture suitable to the apartment were not necessarily those who had to dispose of the most beautiful, valuable property, but rather those who felt embarrassed and ashamed at having to move into public housing. Had they been able to surround themselves with their "own things," remnants of a period in life when they were more competent and independent, they might have forgotten, sometimes, about their reduced position in life. Surrounding themselves with new belongings kept them continually reminded of their own inadequacy.

Other Residents. Despite the obvious satisfaction of most people with their neighbors, interviewers easily elicted criticisms. Only 20 per cent said there was "nothing" they disliked about the other tenants. A similar number avoided the question, and a majority voiced one or more specific criticisms. Evasion, here, did not indicate lack of negative feeling about other apartment occupants. These people would "rather not say," usually because they thought it would do no good to talk about it. Often, in refusing, they mentioned that "there is already too much gossip in this place."

In sections of the interview dealing with the most intimate details of their own lives, it was unusual for more than one or two to refuse to answer. It was a different matter to criticize others, and particularly so because "gossip" was one of the major problems in Victoria Plaza. Complaints most frequently voiced were that other residents were nosey, gossipy, bossy, bragging "know-it-alls;" less frequently, that they were dirty or complained about their health. The vast majority kept their apartments immaculate, and they deeply resented lack of such care by others.

Negative references to "old people" and those who did not really meet admission standards are relevant here. For example, after their great relief at moving out of slum buildings complete with bugs, tenants were quite dismayed to find roaches invading their new, clean apartments and the furniture they were buying, at great sacrifice, "on time." However, the man in whose residence the infestation had started, and from which it spread, said he was doing as much cleaning as he could manage, in his physical condition. His neighbors felt that he had been incapacitated much earlier, and should not have been given an apartment in the first place.

Similarly, a blind woman, who had been remarkably self-sufficient before she moved into Victoria Plaza, quickly found that she could play on other residents' sympathies and became indignant when others did not do everything for her. There was wide-spread resentment among her neighbors by the end of a year, a general feeling that she took advantage of others' good nature and her handicap, and much questioning of her having met admission requirements.

Though independence and opportunity to be with others were the most important favorable comments about living in Victoria Plaza, a few residents would have preferred a living situation which did not force them to be with others to such an extent, or which did not necessitate their being so independent. Most residents had gone from one extreme to the other during the past year, and a minority had not found a happy medium. From pre-Victoria Plaza social isolation they had moved to concentrated group living, or from constant family contact to infrequent visits with relatives. Generally the change was thoroughly enjoyed and applauded, but a few people either had not become accustomed to it after a year, or found they did not like it.

Some preferred old friends to new acquaintances among the residents. Others (mostly men) said they would like it better if there were more men in Victoria Plaza. In the midst of so many women they were overwhelmingly outnumbered. In any decision they could easily be outvoted, and they were fed and pampered and made to feel uncomfortably indebted, usually not to only one, but to several women more or less competing for their attention and gratitude. To a certain extent they basked in this situation, but most men became uncomfortable in it. One reason for the very disproportionate sex distribution of residents was the reluctance of men both to apply for, and to accept, apartments, for fear they would live out the rest of their lives in an "old ladies' home." Unfortunately the experience of most male Plaza-ites justified this apprehension.

Few individuals were consistently pointed out as undesirable, in addition to the small number who did not keep their apartments clean, either because they were unable physically or because they were careless. About the former, most neighbors felt ambivalent. They could not be hardhearted and refuse help or expect the impossible, but they were resentful of the effect on the Plaza. Basically, they thought that these folks could have been identified, as applicants, and that selectors should have eliminated the problem.

Some occupants simply did not try to keep their apartments clean. Their neighbors were most intolerant of them and again placed most of the blame on the selection system and the building management. ("You can't tell me they didn't know what kind of a housekeeper she is. If her apartment is a pig-sty after such a short time, can you imagine what it was like where she lived before?"[15] "Anyone who doesn't appreciate this wonderful place enough to keep it clean ought to be thrown out.")

One man's behavior was sufficient to arouse indignation widely throughout the building. Proud as they were of the "good class of people" in Victoria Plaza, tenants were highly incensed at one man who brought various girl friends up to his apartment via the fire escape. Since this route is clearly visible from the street, patio, and porches, his surreptitiousness only focussed attention on his escapades. To add insult to injury, he habitually took his evening stroll on the balcony in his undershorts. This again, might have been predicted. Unfortunately he was one of the few applicants not interviewed by one of the primary data collectors, but by one who left after doing only a handful, and those meagerly. However, other applicants reported such unusual pre-Victoria Plaza behavior such as his bicycling through dark side streets in the nude. Actually, moving to the Plaza seemed to have toned down his behavior, to some extent.

SUMMARY

A very few residents liked "nothing" about the building or the other people in it, but taking an apartment there was the best arrangement for a roof over their heads they could manage. One, a farmer all his life and desperately lonely for the country, had a choice of this or sharing a small bedroom with his grandson. He hated every minute of city living, apartment dwelling, and the clusters of, "gossipy old ladies."

However, the Plaza was a splendid success to nearly all who lived in it, and they were delighted and thankful to be there. Criticisms about the building were given freely, but as from any observant householder, and primarily because the residents wanted their experience to improve buildings for other old folks. Complaints about people were rarely bitter and often ended with a good-natured, "Of course, I'm like that too," or a grudging admission that they would miss even the gossip and "doing for" sick neighbors.

Use of the Senior Center

In accord with the general policy of federal granting agencies to require local participation in public projects the Housing Authority, in

[15] Housing Authority staff did not make home visits to applicants.

order to use federal funds for construction of the ground-floor Senior Center, had to obtain a firm promise of community funds for its operation. The Community Fund could not support a center reserved to residents of Victoria Plaza; the Community Welfare Council could assist only by incorporating this as part of a city-wide program.

There is not unanimous agreement on the advisability of incorporating, within residential buildings, community centers designed to serve a wider clientele than the resident population, or even on the need to provide communal facilities for those living under the one roof. During the final interview, both residents of Victoria Plaza and applicants who were not given apartments were asked about their use of the Senior Center on the ground floor of the Plaza, their views on it, and what they would recommend to improve such a facility in planning for subsequent housing developments.

WHO USED IT DURING THE FIRST YEAR?

In the follow-up interview 90 per cent of residents said that they had used the Senior Center, while only about 5 per cent of nonresidents said that they used it. Three-fourths of the residents habitually went to the Center, while the remaining quarter used the ground floor "only as a lobby." True, some of the interviewers lived too far from the Center to use it, and the recreation facilities were enjoyed by folks who had never made application for an apartment and so were not involved in the study. Nevertheless these figures reflect the obvious preponderance of Plaza residents in Center activities during the first year of operation.

Because the possibility of such a situation was anticipated, the staff from the beginning had made every effort to ameliorate it. The Senior Center was publicized as a community resource for all older people. Special invitations were extended to nonresidents, responsibilities were offered them, programs and activities were tailored to their interests. Outside response continued to be poor.

Apparently this was an area of difficult communication, not only to people with other living arrangements who were eligible for Center activities, but also to apartment occupants. Misunderstanding seemed to result partly from the fact that the relationship between the Plaza and the Center was complicated. In the development of plans, and in their implementation, areas of responsibility and lines of authority were sometimes unclear, even to the planners and the professional staffs involved, so it is little wonder that distinctions between the two were hazy in the minds of others.

In addition, special motivational factors probably influenced apartment holders in the Plaza. During that first year the building and its services were given much publicity, not only local but national, and, despite their annoyance with the fish-bowl existence, most people who were admitted as renters enjoyed the attention and their identification with the accomplishment. In addition they were touchingly pleased with their beautiful, clean surroundings and the opportunities for social interaction.

Obviously they continued to perceive the Plaza and the Center as a unity, and their pride and proprietary interest surrounded the whole. The ground floor area usually was perceived as their living room, an important area of their own home, a home they paid for in rent adequate to meet its cost. For the most part, they were immune to explanations of the administrative and financial relationships between the Housing Authority and Community Welfare Council, and the consequent community-wide right of older citizens to use the Senior Center.

On the other hand, the nonresidents studied were disappointed applicants for residence in the Plaza and, as such, were especially sensitive to any intimation of rejection. No one knows how many other old people in the geographic area adjacent to Victoria Plaza would have made application for apartments had they thought they could qualify. For them, as well as for residents, the interaction of Housing Authority and Community Welfare Council proved difficult to explain. Even those who lived across the street, in cottage-type public housing, tended to feel that if they used the Center they were doing so at the sufferance of apartment occupants, and that they had no "right" to use the facilities. Of course, it is not known how many nonresidents would have used a similar facility located under a separate roof.

Questions about the desirability of incorporating into residential buildings facilities for nonresident people was not asked at any time by research interviewers. Since the decision had been made and construction was under way when the first research contacts were made, it was thought best not to probe reactions of applicants. Exploratory questions might lead to misunderstanding and controversy, perhaps stimulating the situation least desired. However, unsolicited opinions were not infrequently given during follow-up contacts, residents almost always strongly in favor, nonresidents equally against. According to most spontaneous statements by people in the apartments they believed "outsiders" should come only as guests, by specific, individual invitation, and not by right. Those who felt otherwise would, of course, be less likely to comment at all.

HOW WAS IT USED?

Over a third of the residents used the Center daily, and two-thirds participated in something there at least every two or three days, though a quarter used it "only as a lobby." These people were involved in no planned recreation programs and did not sit downstairs to visit with others; they simply passed through on their way in and out of the building, and some wished they did not have to do even that. Nearly 10 per cent said they "never" used the lobby. When it was pointed out that, at least, they must use it to go in and out of the building, they replied something like "Well, of course I do, but believe me, I walk through as fast as I can."

Resident Organization. Three-quarters of the residents regularly attended "building meetings." Unfortunately, attendance cannot be equated with interest or favorable attitude. These were meetings about once a month for which residents of the Plaza were organized somewhat like a club, with three officers, president, vice-president, and treasurer, and two representatives from each residential floor. This organization originated in the building administrator's recognition of the need for some channel of communication regarding regulations, ways in which residents annoyed each other, and other matters of general concern.

At these meetings residents were advised against such matters as unlocked doors, unswept porches, use of fire escapes for purposes other than that intended, bringing "girls" into the building for immoral purposes, and putting nails into the walls for any purpose whatever. At these meetings, also, attempts were made to discuss matters of general concern and to resolve specific frictions between residents in regard to cleanliness, noise, and such problems.

At one meeting, according to some residents, money was taken up for beautifying the small lobby by the elevator on each floor. This incident and others similar to it (collecting money for gifts and planning money-raising events) caused considerable irritation.[16] Regular attendance at the meetings indicated for some people genuine interest, desire to participate and perhaps to lead, but for others, quite the reverse, resentment that one must attend to protect one's rights.

As a matter of fact, this entire matter of the "building meetings" is not related to the Senior Center and is reported in this context only because residents consistently talked about them when asked how they used the Senior Center, never when discussing the residence. Simply because of space requirements, building meetings were held in the Senior Center.[17] However, they were sponsored by the director of the residential floors and stemmed from the Housing Authority's management role rather than that of the Community Welfare Council. This points again to the confluence in residents' minds of Plaza and Center, which no doubt also gave rise to their feeling that the Center was their living room[18] in which everyone else, except upon special invitation, was a mannerless intruder.

The "Lobbyists" and "Porch Sitters." Quite a number of residents said they enjoyed just "sitting and thinking," or, "sitting and looking." One in four mostly "just sat" when they were in the Senior Center, and nearly as many more were known as "porch watchers." They passed many enjoyable hours on the open balconies, which afforded an advantageous view of other people's activities. Membership in the two "watcher" groups was fairly constant, and what one member missed, another was happy to supply him.

Clubs and Activities. Twenty per cent, who had no television sets or who preferred companionable viewing, went to the lobby to watch

[16] "It should be observed that no money collections were ever taken at resident council meetings. The memorial or flower fund was voluntary and was in no way a part of the meeting, except that the can for the fund is placed on a table at the door to the meeting room" (personal communication from Marilynn Wacker, December 4, 1964).

[17] "It should be observed that the space on the residents' floors was not adequate for any group meetings; therefore when the Residents Council met it was necessary to request the use of the space in the Senior Center just as would have been done by any other group participating in Center activities" (personal communication from Marilynn Wacker, December 4, 1964).

[18] In regard to feeling that the Center was their living room: "That is the concept—verbalized by staff to residents when Center is not in operation" (personal communication from Dorothy O'Neill, executive director, Senior Community Services, Inc., December, 1964).

favorite programs. Nearly two-thirds had attended one or more special programs such as a touring boys' choir or a dance group. Half considered it their "place of recreation," much as they would a family room or den area in their own home, where they enjoyed a variety of activities. They played cards, pool, dominoes, watched television, or started a discussion with someone, depending on their mood and who else happened to be there. One resident in every three served on a regular schedule as host or hostess at the lobby desk.

Over a third usually attended a weekly bingo session. They played for prizes of canned goods, soap, toothpaste, powder, or any small funny things brought by the previous week's winners. Some, mostly men, said they would enjoy playing bingo, but stayed away because of this prize arrangement. They objected that there was no point in winning, since you had to turn right around and bring something back for a prize next week.

About one in three attended the movie every Wednesday evening. (Before moving into Victoria Plaza, half "never" went to a movie and only one in twenty-five saw a movie as often as once a week.) Fifteen per cent regularly participated in the Sunday evening "sing-song." This was an informal occasion on which folks gathered around the piano and sang old favorite hymns and other songs everyone knew.

Nearly a third belonged to a garden club. This was largely a group of women, though two men were among its most active members. Grounds had been landscaped and maintenance was provided, but these determined "green thumbs" cared for plants in the lobby and took advantage of a small open area in back, where anyone interested could have five feet to do with as he wished. There they cultivated a variety of flowers and vegetables. Few Plazaites would welcome back the responsibility and labor of a yard of their own, but some thoroughly enjoyed gardening on this reduced scale.

Though only one in five, most of these women, used the hobby room, they kept it busy, rarely missing bi-weekly instruction periods, and spending considerable time working there on their own, between visits from the city recreation department instructor. Their ceramics and metal work won prizes in city-wide hobby shows, and brought them some money, as well as supplying gifts for relatives and friends, and much pleasure in accomplishment.

Library. Only 15 per cent used the library at the time of final interviewing. Selection of books for this station collection from the city library was unfortunate. These older people were not interested in "how to" books, but in reading for entertainment. ("What do I want with a cook book? My cooking's kept my husband happy for nearly fifty years." "Why can't we have some light fiction? Maybe a few who-done-it's?" "They never have historical novels." "These books are older than we are!") Resentment was added to disappointment when books given to the Center library did not reappear on its shelves after they went to the central library for processing.[19]

Clinic. A similar number (15 per cent) had used the clinic for the health-maintenance services offered them—having blood pressure or temperature taken. Nearly an equal number said they had to go, on a regular basis, to their doctors' offices or to the community-supported hospital, for routine medical service such as injection of Vitamin B-12.[20]

Beauty Shop. More would have used the beauty shop had there been an operator. As it was, a few used the equipment to do each other's hair. The shampoo bowl and chair, and the dryer, were particularly helpful in the case of slightly crippled women. Those who had been beauty operators washed and set the hair of those who found it difficult to stoop and wash their own hair, or for whom raising the hands to the head was painful because of arthritis. Some did this as a friendly gesture, others for a fee.

Other Uses. Additional activities in the Center, attended by relatively small numbers of Plaza residents, were meetings of church groups and welfare organizations (such as a cancer-bandage-rolling committee), and playing games available in the yard, such as tossing plumbing washers into bottles.

WHAT DID THEY THINK OF IT?

Nonresident members of the applicant group who had participated in activities there tended to be negative toward the Center, although they had no complaints about physical facilities, equipment, or pro-

[19] According to Dorothy O'Neill, executive director, Senior Community Services, Inc., this was not because of San Antonio Public Library rules, but was "Committee of Management of Center policy." The "Library did [the] processing and good and acceptable books were returned to Senior Center shelves" (personal communication, December, 1964).

[20] "This is not so—Visiting Nurse Association provides such services upon referral by Medical Doctor—an RN in residency also performed such service" (personal communication from Dorothy O'Neill, December, 1964).

grams. Typical comments were: "I always feel like an outsider," "I am not welcome," "The people over there are all snobs," or conversely, "The people in Victoria Plaza are poor white trash."

Only 3 per cent of residents liked "nothing" about the Center, while 70 per cent were completely enthusiastic, insisting that they liked "everything" so well that it was impossible for them to single out one "best" feature. Even when the question was turned around and they were asked, "What do you dislike about the Center?" 70 per cent insisted "nothing," with the same 3 per cent disliking "everything." The remaining quarter were those who did not use it and were indifferent to it. ("I've never paid any attention to what they do there." "The only time I'm in it is waiting for the elevator.")

As with the apartments, delight with the Senior Center was not always accompanied by absence of criticism. Even those who "liked everything" and "disliked nothing" tended to go right on and expound on what about it displeased them or suggest improvements for future buildings.

Criticisms. The most heated objection to the Center given by residents was against gossip, which they felt was augmented by having the Center in the building. According to their way of thinking, there are nosey neighbors everywhere, but because of the exposed elevators, open porches, and window treatment in apartments, details of their lives were open books, not only to neighbors and other residents, but to anyone who entered the building. They felt strongly that gossip was fostered by inclusion of the Center, since anyone with nothing to do but "sit and watch" was provided a perfect place, in the lobby or on the galleries, from which to observe in comfort and compare tid-bits with others so inclined. Actually the "lobbyists" and "porch watchers" were almost all residents of the Plaza. Their nosiness was greatly resented, but that of "outsiders" much more.

Another complaint pertained to the clinic. Primarily a well-baby service, it offered minimal assistance to old people of the area. Plaza dwellers felt that if a medical service was to take up space in "their building" it should be for them, or at least for adults, not infants.

There was critical comment also about the pool table. This was really an interpersonal rather than an equipment problem. Some would-be pool players felt that others got down too early in the morning, took over the table and would not "take turns." The early birds felt they earned their rights. In addition, television viewers and hi-fi listeners found the pool game, as well as each other, disturbing to watching and listening. Several ladies considered it "disgraceful" to have their visitors immediately confront a pool table surrounded by "tobacco-chewing old men in their shirt sleeves," and they felt sullied by having to pass through this "pool-hall atmosphere" to go in and out of their own residence.

For some folks, there was "too much dressing" in the Senior Center. These critics tended to be the people who considered the ground floor as an area in their own homes, and they did not want to don their best clothes every time they went downstairs. Everyone had to go through the lobby to get his mail or post a letter, and if a woman went down without girdle and hose, let alone in hair curlers, she felt that the "sitters" had a new topic for gossip. Men resented feminine pressure to put on a coat, or at least a dress shirt and tie, when they went down to play pool or cards, to watch television, or just to visit with their friends. Too, the attitude toward dressing was another reaction to "outsiders," since naturally they were somewhat more dressed up, as well as often wearing coats and sometimes even hats. Special care with appearance was an understandable reaction to their feeling of "differentness" and even rejection, and unfortunately it supplied another basis for resentment on the part of residents.

Suggestions. Residents were asked what they would change in planning the Senior Center for a similar building. Over half could suggest nothing—some because they were well pleased, and others because they used the ground floor only as a lobby and did not know or care enough about it to comment. Some apartment occupants who did not use the Center recommended eliminating such a facility in future buildings or, if one were included, provision of access to living quarters without going into it.

Most frequent suggestions were removal of the elevator from the recreation area and more convenient placement of the mail drop. Addition of a cafeteria or some food service was recommended. The main room should be larger, particularly if nonresidents were to be allowed to use it, as well as residents. Some activities should be moved—the pool table out of the lobby, the hi-fi away from the television, and both of them away from the pool table and the card table space.

Many mentioned again that a "well-baby" clinic should not be in such a building, and some suggested adding a clinic to meet the needs of building occupants, not so much for emergencies as for routine periodic care. For example, those who took shots (insulin, B-12) regularly had to pay bus fare, take the bus ride, and often wait in the hospital as much as an entire day. Money, time, and considerable frustration would be saved if they could receive their shots at the Plaza.

Because of the expense and effort, as well as the general disinclination to "give in" to sickness, medical attention was sought only when an illness was quite serious. ("Mrs. ——— would not be in the hospital now if a doctor could have seen her.") Many residents satisfied with their own arrangements for medical care resented the use of space by a baby clinic. ("They could put their pool tables back there, and everyone would be happy." "Wouldn't it make a perfect card room?")

A few women thought Senior Centers should include gyms, since apartment care was so easy they did not get enough physical activity to keep fit. Another few said such buildings should have bomb shelters. They did not feel that their own lives should be especially safeguarded, but that any such fine, new public building should provide this facility for people in the area.

SUMMARY

Enthusiasm for the Senior Center was not universal. Some residents disdained the ground floor as anything but an entry to their apartments; some who used Center facilities continued to find fault with them and with the others who used them—particularly the "outsiders" and the gossips. Nevertheless, most criticisms were offered in the spirit of suggesting improvements, either for their own or for some future building, and the Center was much used and thoroughly enjoyed by the majority of residents.

Some criticism of the Senior Community Center and the residential facilities of Victoria Plaza is probably an indicator of generally good morale and healthy adjustment among residents. Feelings of security and self-confidence must underlie such freedom to voice complaints and suggestions for improvement.

CHAPTER 7

Changes in Life Style and Adjustment

A YEAR after the first occupants moved into Victoria Plaza, reinterviewing and retesting began in an effort to find out, not only how residents liked the Plaza after having lived in it, but also what impact it might have had on their way of life, their general adjustment, and their attitudes toward themselves and other people.

Procedures for Comparing Change in Residents and Nonresidents

Comparison of changes over this period of time for those who had lived in the Plaza and those who had not, in light of their similarities and differences as applicants, seemed the safest way to assess impact of residence in Victoria Plaza. Of the original group of 352 applicants, 295 were reinterviewed, 190 of whom had lived in Victoria Plaza twelve to fifteen months and 105 of whom had never lived there.

The design followed a traditional analysis of covariance model. For assessing residence effect, a multiple-regression approach developed by Ward and Bottenberg (1963) was used with continuous and ordered variables. The McNemar Change Test (McNemar, 1962, pp. 224–228) was applied to dichotomous variables. A more detailed description of statistical procedures is given in Appendix C, and tables summarizing results of the tests for differential change among residents and nonresidents over the period of about a year are given in Appendix D.

Though many unsuccessful applicants openly expressed bitterness over not having been admitted to Victoria Plaza, none who was contacted refused to participate in the follow-up study, and interviewers' ratings of their cooperativeness were similar to those made for original data collection. Resentment did not generalize beyond Housing and Center personnel. The lack of change in cooperativeness with research people supports the separation of admission and research in subjects' minds and the primacy of motivation to help further knowledge and to benefit others, rather than to influence their own chances of living in the Plaza.

To gain their participation in the 1961 data collection, the interviewers found it necessary to remind some nonresidents that the earlier research had nothing to do with assignment of apartments, but only with an effort to gain information about older people, and that they could make an additional contribution to it by completing the second interview. For example, one couple who had been most gracious at the first data collection, moving furniture for the convenience of the interviewer's note taking and preparing refreshments every time she came, made it clear a year later that they were not even going to let her in. However, after chatting a few minutes at the door, the wife exclaimed, "Well, of course, it was not your fault we didn't get in, and we are being very poor sports about it." With that, they ushered her in and, after unloading all of their bitterness and disappointment, spent several hours in full cooperation.

Not surprisingly, interviewers found residents even more cooperative than they had been at the time of first interview. This reflected not only their generally euphoric mood but also the greater ease with which they could arrange meetings with their interviewers.

All residents of Victoria Plaza, but only 90 per cent of the nonresidents, were accounted for at the time of the final data collection. Naturally, nonresidents were more difficult to contact, simply because they were not all in one place. In addition, nearly a third of them had moved one or more times during the year, usually leaving little or no information about where they were going. Only two persons had moved out of the Plaza. Change in place of residence had, to all intents and purposes, ceased with admission to Victoria Plaza, while it continued for those remaining outside.

A few residents were not interviewed because they were hospitalized or were away on vacations during the interview period. Two women were in Alaska; several others had pooled their resources and were motoring through New England.

Death rates cannot be compared because of the failure of exhaustive efforts to obtain information as to the whereabouts of so many (about 10%) of the nonresidents. Five per cent of the residents died during the first year, and 4 per cent of the nonresidents were known to have died during that time.

All follow-up data were collected by the two research assistants who did the bulk of earlier interviewing and testing. So far as possible, interviewers were assigned the subjects from whom they had collected data previously.

The second interview[1] repeated items from the first, where relevant, to measure changes during the intervening period. Some new items related to people's perceptions of change in themselves were added, and interviewers were asked to make judgments regarding change since the previous contact, as well as to re-evaluate each person on the rating scales used earlier. Tests were readministered to as many as possible who had taken them earlier.

Satisfaction with Housing and Living Arrangements

Housing had practically disappeared as a "major problem" among residents of Victoria Plaza, while it continued to plague those outside it (Figure 1). Direct evaluations of their present housing by residents were drastically different from those they had made in the initial interviews, while evaluations made by nonresidents were not appreciably different from those they had made a year earlier (Figure 2).

Residence in Victoria Plaza had had tremendous impact also on satisfaction with arrangements for eating, sleeping, garbage disposal, and maintenance (Figure 3). Plaza dwellers were unanimously delighted with these conveniences, regardless of their evaluations of such housing and living arrangements at the time of initial data collection. Regardless of how an individual described his living conditions at the time of the initial interview, with only the fact that he was to move into the Plaza one could predict his follow-up evaluation perfectly. Nonresidents' views of their housing and living con-

[1] Questions asked in the first interview but not the second, and those asked in the second but not the first, are so identified on the abbreviated questionnaire in Appendix A.

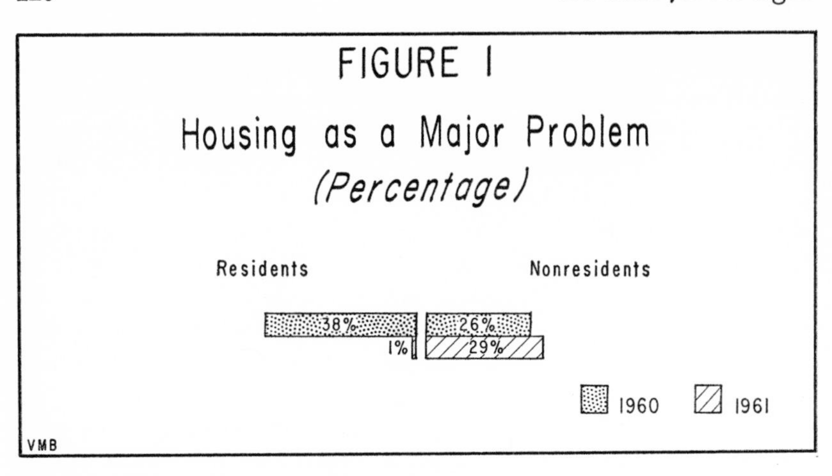

ditions were also predictable, though in a different way: they did not change. These results suggest that the earlier judgments of these older people were realistic, and that they related to the specifics of their environment rather than expressing generalized dissatisfaction which could not be alleviated by improved housing.

Since original expectations were so high (see Chapter 6) and were

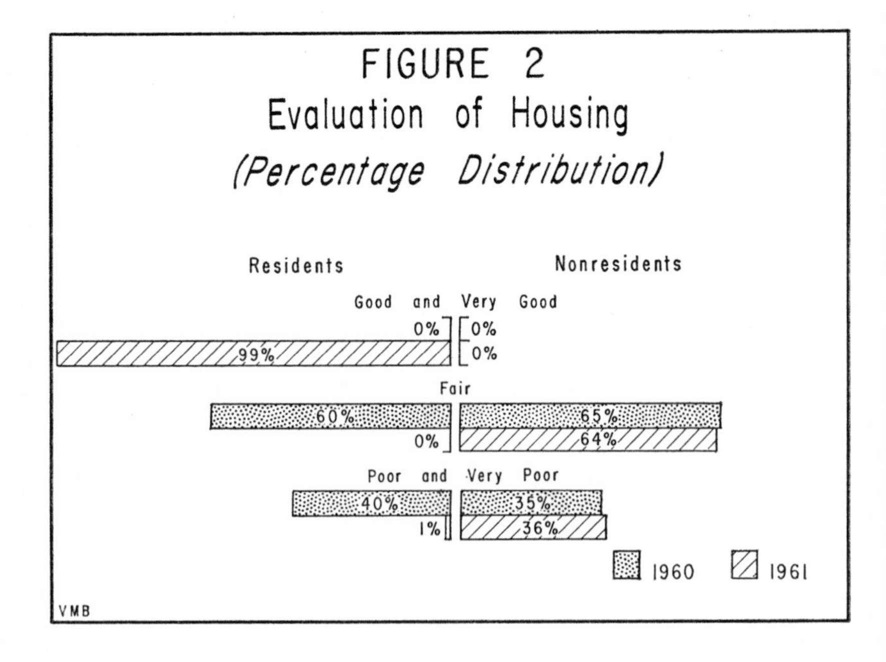

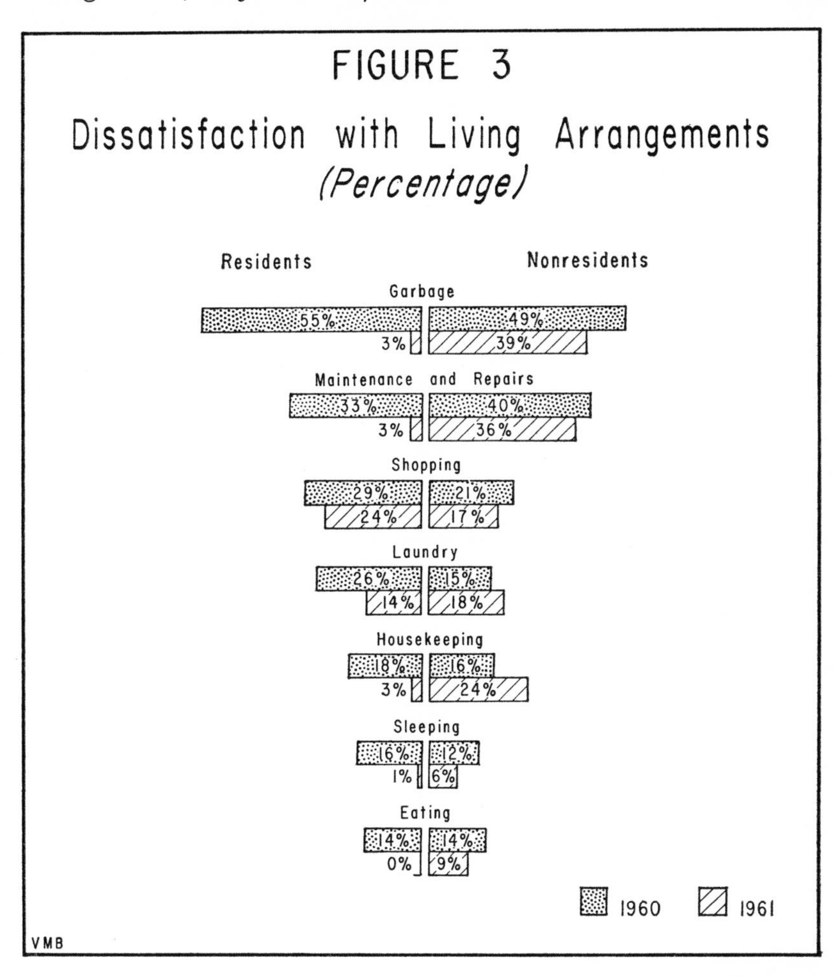

based on such meager information regarding what Victoria Plaza was to be like and since they occurred in the absence of experience with a similar living situation, rather general disillusionment after a "honeymoon" period was anticipated. This would be particularly true if older people find it difficult to change. However, at the time of final interviewing, which was after twelve to fifteen months of residence, the Plaza was consistently "Heaven on earth" and "Even better than I thought it could be." As this is written, in 1964, the honeymoon goes on.

Most of the people who lived in Victoria Plaza rated the neighbor-

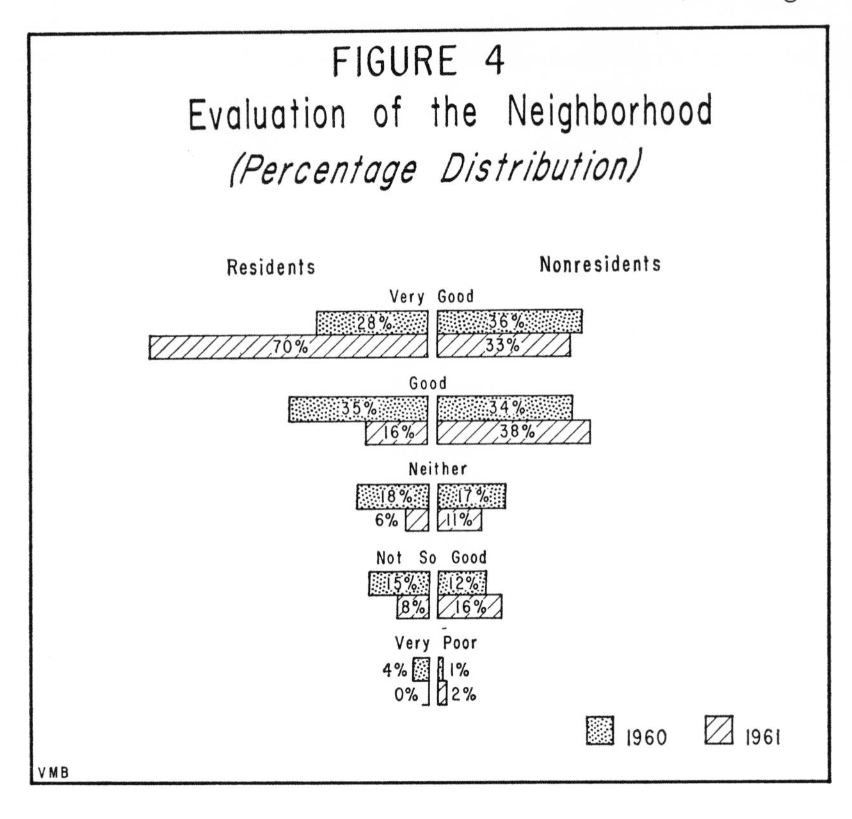

hood a "good" or "very good" one in which to live, an evaluation indicating a consistent change from that of the previous neighborhood (Figure 4). Though some criticized the neighborhood as being in the "slums," unsafe for women to go out alone, lacking in "decent" eating places and stores, still, when asked how good a place it was in which to live, they rated it favorably.

Here, again, the context of the question and the frame of reference selected by the respondents are important. In discussions of the neighborhood as a geographic area most people felt that the beautiful new building should not have been located in this zone of obsolescence. On the other hand, when questioned about the neighborhood as a place in which to live, they thought in terms of "neighbors," and these were the other people in Victoria Plaza. Needs for socializing and recreation were nicely met under that roof; most residents enjoyed their neighbors. Yet when they needed to go to the grocery shop or out for a meal it was necessary to expose themselves to what many considered a slum area surrounding their island. In a different sense, this was also their neighborhood, and they were not delighted with it. Nonresidents' neighborhoods had not changed significantly, and neither had their evaluations of them.

Services Wanted

Residents showed greater satisfaction also by a dramatic decrease in the number of services they felt they needed or would like to have. Here they were responding to the general question: "What services do you think you need or could use?" No further specification was made by the interviewer. In the final interview fewer than 20 per cent of those in Victoria Plaza named one or more "services" as needed, though over three-fourths of the same people, as applicants, had named one or more.

The pattern of change is interesting (Figure 5). From first interview to second, fewer residents mentioned recreational facilities, instructional needs, housekeeping, transportation, and medical services. On the other hand, an increased number of residents wanted a cafeteria or other food service, and more women residents expressed the desire for a beauty shop. The apartments had met their earlier need for a decent place to live, with housekeeping aids and conveniences which they used and appreciated. The Senior Center and the proximity of residential units had satisfied their desires for instruction and recreation.

Transportation had become less of a problem to residents. The geographic location of Victoria Plaza made transportation easier, and it had become less important because of all the people immediately available in the building.

Need for medical services declined among residents. During the period between interviews "65+" health and hospitalization insurance became available in Texas, but this apparently was not the source of relief, since nonresidents showed a significant increase during the same period. Improved housing may have affected physical well-being. Preoccupation with need for medical attention may have decreased with the generally improved morale of people who became residents. The health services available in the Plaza apparently did meet the needs of residents to a considerable degree; and the unsatisfied minority was agitating for very little more. However, residents generally did not think of routine procedures such as blood-

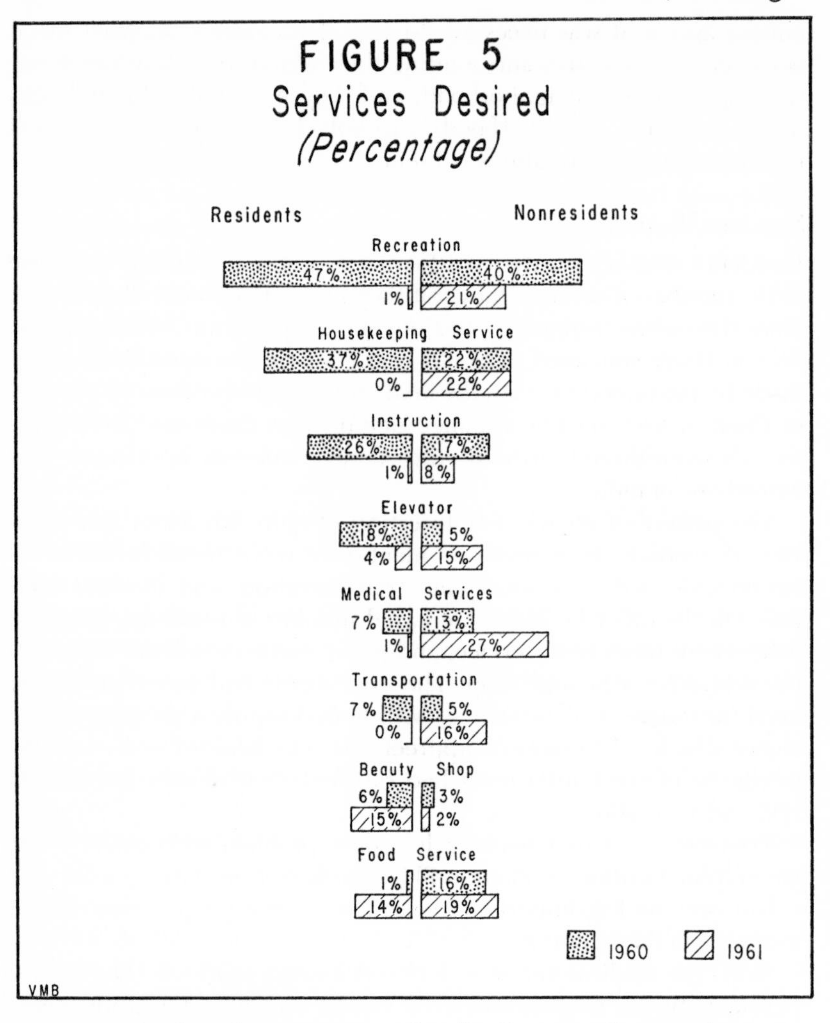

pressure check and injections as "medical service," since they were usually administered by nurses.

In both series of interviews, desires for medical care were minimal, and obviously based on need. These people asked for surprisingly little and looked upon illness as a sort of moral weakness. Here again the need for independence was clear: unless the medical care was requisite to keeping them self-sustaining, they did not want it. A health service which met their every demand would be a small, inexpensive operation.

Increased requests for meal service and, among women, for a beauty shop, no doubt were related to satisfaction of more basic needs for adequate housing and social contact. Though they would not give up their private kitchens for anything, most residents would like to be able to buy a meal a day or a meal occasionally.

The men had another reason to wish for some food service—the excessive zeal of the women around them. These gentlemen would have been more comfortable (and felt a little safer!) had they been able to refuse a home-cooked meal on grounds that they had just been out to eat or had promised to eat out with someone, or had they been able to reciprocate and take the lady for dinner occasionally. Both men and women preferred to eat in the company of other people, and they became bored with preparing three meals a day. Besides, now there were so many interesting things to do that they begrudged the time.

The initial difference between the applicants who were to become residents and those who were not to move into Victoria Plaza was unexpected. Actually, by the end of the first year in the Plaza the residents had grown more similar to the nonresidents in regard to their desire for a food service. Possibly some of the applicants who became "no longer interested" were people who especially wanted food service and learned, after application, that none would be available in Victoria Plaza. However, this was not often offered as a reason for withdrawing. It is also possible that the selection staff, if they knew of a person's strong desire for food service, may have considered this a contraindication for successful adjustment in the Plaza, since there was to be no cafeteria or restaurant in it.

Men did not mind going out to a barber shop. Women residents, however, having become much more interested in their appearance than previously, experienced considerable frustration at the absence of beauty shops in the neighborhood of the Plaza. The dearth was no greater than in their former locations, but the desire for good grooming had been augmented. Ideally, the women would locate a beauty salon in the building, with an access route other than through the lobby.

Living Costs

There was a residence effect in regard to cost of housing, though it was less straightforward. For those who as applicants had been paying about $28.00 per month rent there was no change; for those who had been paying over $28.00 per month the move to Victoria Plaza tended to decrease the rent; while those who had been paying less than $28.00 the move to Victoria Plaza increased the payment, in inverse proportion to the size of the original rent. This, of course, was an artifact of the Public Housing rent formula for the Plaza.

Nearly half of the residents paid more rent in Victoria Plaza than they had paid previously. Some of these had lived rent-free with relatives, so that any payment for independent living space would have involved an increase. All who moved to the Plaza from other public housing facilities had to pay more, since the base rate was higher in order that the program be fiscally sound. They, as well as other applicants living in privately owned housing, had been informed of the Plaza rent scale, and had made the decision in full knowledge of the financial obligation involved.

In addition to a question in the final interview about satisfaction with their housing, the people were asked to evaluate it in terms of what they paid for it. This evaluation of housing in relation to its cost was highly predictable for a resident: regardless of what he had said about his earlier housing, and regardless of any change in rent, the typical resident felt that, for what he was getting, the monthly cost was "low" or "very low." None considered it "high" (Figure 6).

Though one of every three nonresidents had moved in the period between interviews, that group showed no consistent change in cost of housing or in evaluation of it. They had been able to find nothing cheaper or better. One woman had not qualified for admission because she did not have sufficient income to pay the minimum rent. Her pride was so great that she "lived" on $44.00 a month Social Security rather than apply for Old Age benefits. A year later, after several moves, she was paying more rent than the Victoria Plaza minimum, for a dirty little third-floor room and the privilege of sharing a bath with occupants of four other rooms or apartments, and cooking on a hot plate in her room. A refrigerator was "available" on the ground floor, to all tenants of the building. Garbage was collected in the alley.

There was also a residence effect on amount of money spent for food. The period between interviews was one of slightly rising cost of living, and food prices went up. This was reflected in the tendency for nonresidents to increase their food budgets very slightly (by about fifty cents a month). However, residents spent, on the average, $3.65 less per month for food than they had as applicants. (The

Courtesy San Antonio Housing Authority
Photo R. J. Leydon and Associates

1. A Front View of Victoria Plaza

Courtesy San Antonio Housing Authority
Staff Photo

2. The Patio

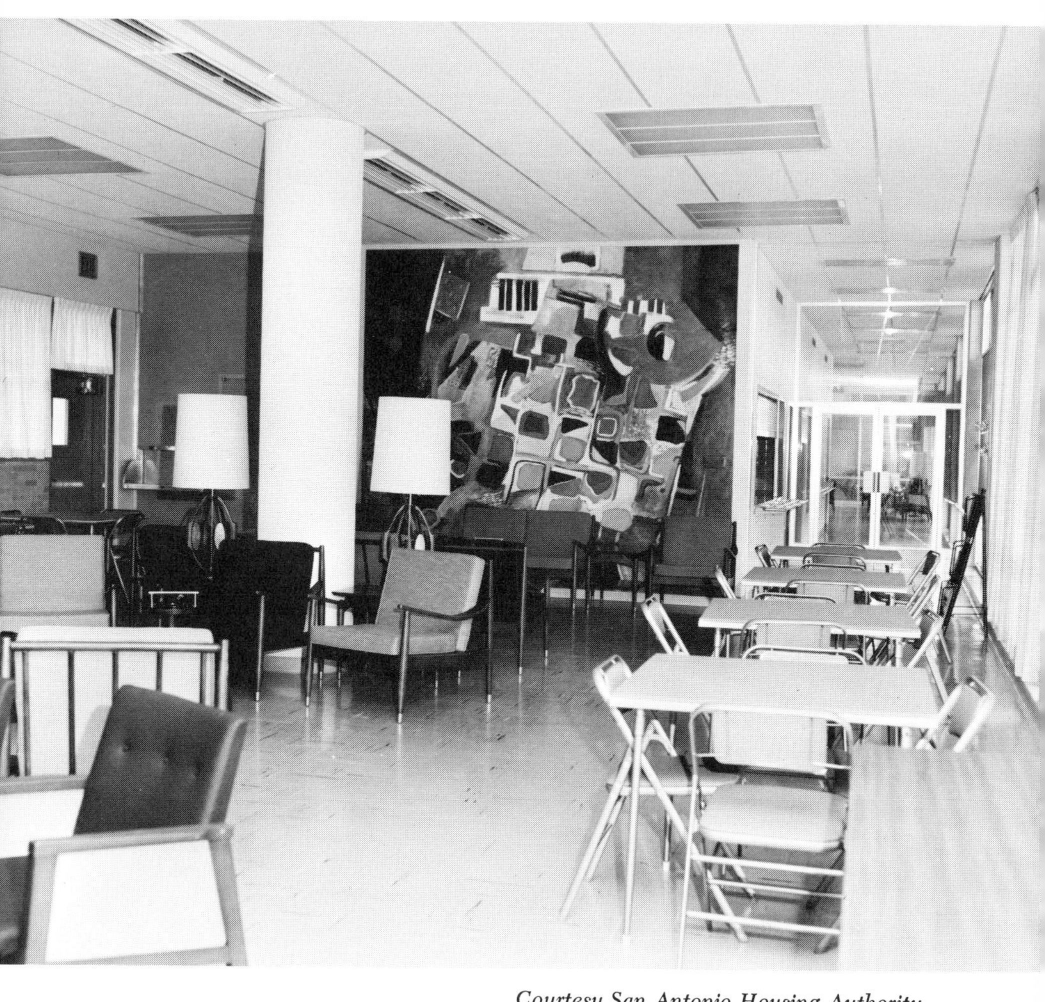

Courtesy San Antonio Housing Authority
Staff Photo

3. The Recreation Area in Readiness

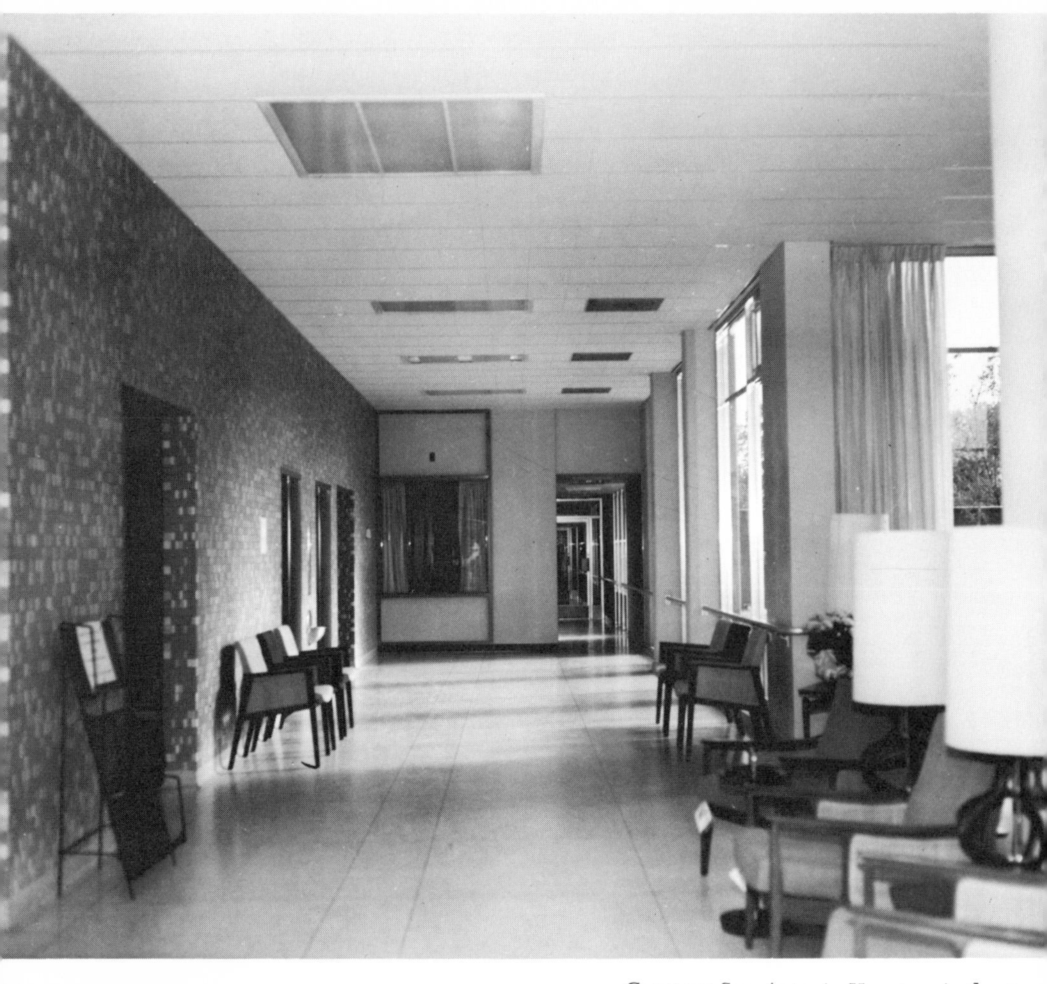

Courtesy San Antonio Housing Authority
Staff Photo

4. The Entrance Hall

Courtesy San Antonio Housing Authority
Photo R. J. Leydon and Associates

5. A Two-Bedroom Apartment

Courtesy San Antonio Housing Authority
Staff Photo

6. An Efficiency Apartment

Courtesy San Antonio Housing Authority
Staff Photo

7. A One-Bedroom Apartment

Courtesy San Antonio Housing Authority
Staff Photo

8. The Recreation Area in Use

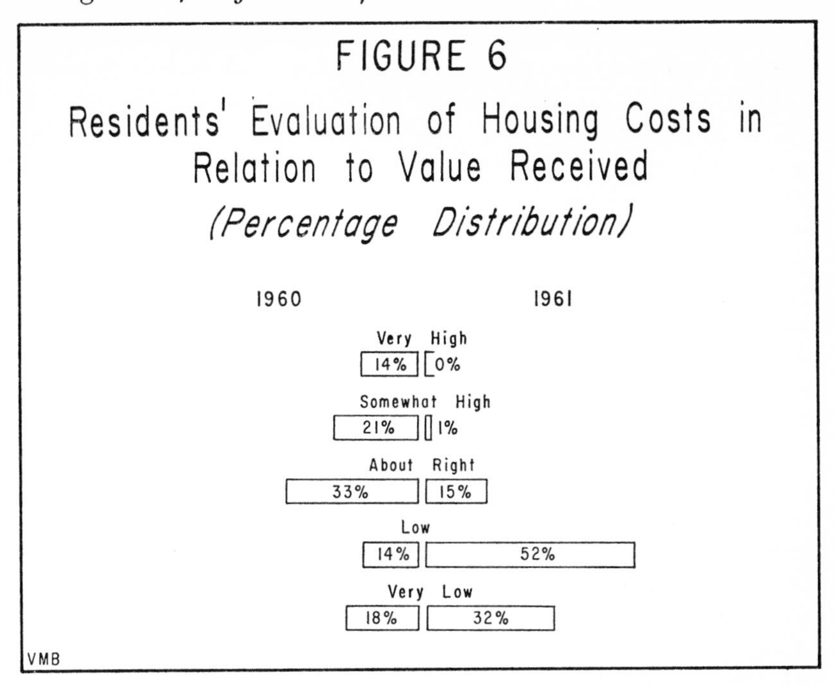

comparison was made only for people who had to pay for their food and did not include either residents or nonresidents whose meals were supplied by family or friends with whom they lived.)

This greater resistance by Plaza dwellers to the situation of rising costs was probably related to the pressure of other demands on fixed incomes. Food budgets were surely more limited for the one out of two who had to pay more rent to live in Victoria Plaza.

Probably related, too, was the contagion within the Plaza of the need to start "keeping up with the Joneses." Where these people had lived previously it was obviously impossible, in most cases, to make the home attractive. Worn, colorless, incompatible collections of furniture were suitable to their drab environments. Usually the situation seemed so hopeless that there was no point in trying to make it pleasant. Ego-involvement with place of residence and competitiveness in comparing it to others' were minimal.

Upon moving into Victoria Plaza, people identified closely with it and almost every one became "house proud." Not only did occupants take delight in the beautiful new building; each found it imperative to make his apartment worthy of the whole and a justification of his own admission. Too, it became important not to be outdone by a neighbor. Most residents were eager to visit back and forth. Some commented that, anyway, it would do no good to deny oneself visitors in an effort to hide inadequacies of furnishings, since they felt that people walking along the corridor could see into the apartment as they passed.

Looking ahead to the first occupancy, Housing personnel had been concerned at the possible reluctance or even inability of people this old to part with belongings they had had for years. Consequences might be serious if admission to the Plaza forced separation when old-fashioned furniture was too large for a modern apartment, or over-stuffed pieces were permeated with insect life. This proved to be less of a hazard than the temptation to buy new things "on time." Objections to disposing of inappropriate belongings were few and usually unimpassioned. Most residents welcomed the opportunity to acquire new, clean, comfortable pieces. At the time of the final contact, many Plaza dwellers were still paying on furniture they bought when they moved in or shortly thereafter, and counted payments remaining until they could add something else. Food money was one of the few ways to speed the process.

The same sort of thing happened in regard to clothing. Previously, worn and out-of-fashion clothes were suitable to the surroundings and were not intolerable because the person was with other people so seldom. In Victoria Plaza other residents and their friends could see how one dressed, even to do housework within one's own apartment, and it was necessary to appear "in public," before "outsiders" as well, when one went to the incinerator to dump trash, to the laundry room, or the mailbox. Accomplishment of these tasks is not usually possible to any householder without exposure to the view of other people. For most residents of the Plaza these jobs were much easier and more pleasant than previously, and they thoroughly enjoyed the convenience. However, whereas it had not mattered much how one looked in the old situation, now, in the beautiful new building, it did.

Basically, the interest in clothes stemmed from the fact that most residents continued to soak up companionship in an almost insatiable way. Though they complained a little at the inconvenience of such high visibility and lack of privacy, most spent as much time as possible in the company of others. Left-over and hand-me-down clothing was no longer necessarily acceptable, and residents tended to want more money for garments.

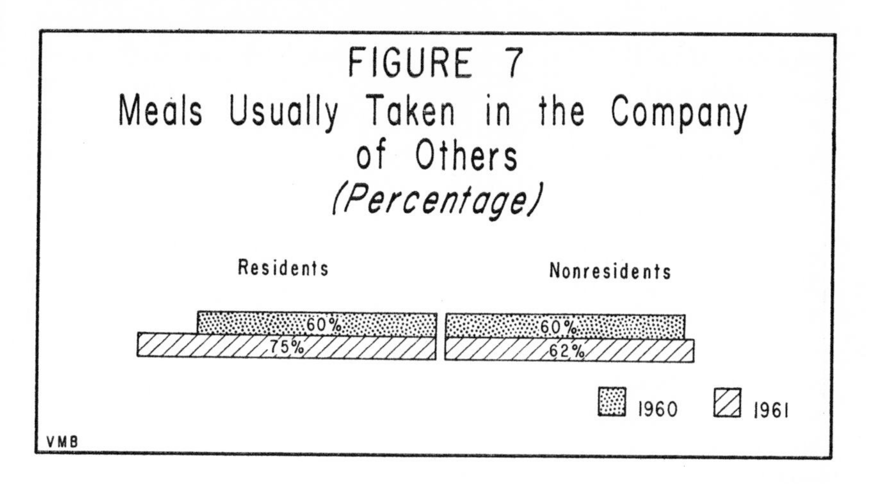

What was spent for furniture, clothing, and increased rent was not available for groceries. No regret was expressed over this. The choice was made consciously and voluntarily, and most would do exactly the same thing again. Life in Victoria Plaza was well worth any sacrifice. Also, residents' eating habits had changed in the direction of more frequent eating with one another (Figure 7). Probably there was some economy in this pooling of resources and, even more important to those involved, companionable meals were more enjoyable, no matter what the dish.

In describing their financial position residents tended to move from "can't make ends meet" toward "enough to get by" and "comfortable" while nonresidents showed no significant change (Figure 8). More residents expressed a feeling of security in their present source of income than they did in the baseline interview (Figure 9). Attitude Survey scores tended to move toward the positive end of the scale, indicating greater satisfaction with the funds available. However, residents were more likely to name money as their major problem in the 1961 interview (Figure 10).

Apparently the new ways of distributing their funds brought residents much more satisfactory lives than they had experienced previously. However, the new standard of living put pressure on their limited monthly income and in some instances led to dipping into capital. This jeopardizing of future income or reduction in emergency funds was a source of worry.

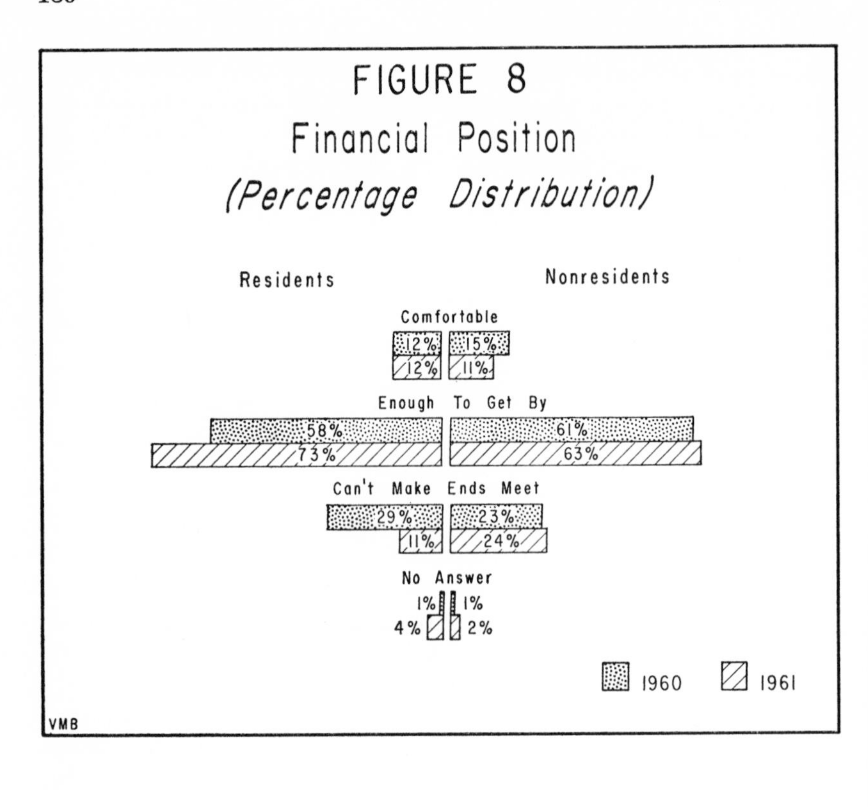
FIGURE 8
Financial Position
(Percentage Distribution)
Residents
Nonresidents
Comfortable
12%
15%
12%
11%
Enough To Get By
58%
61%
73%
63%
Can't Make Ends Meet
29%
23%
11%
24%
No Answer
1%
1%
4%
2%
1960
1961
VMB

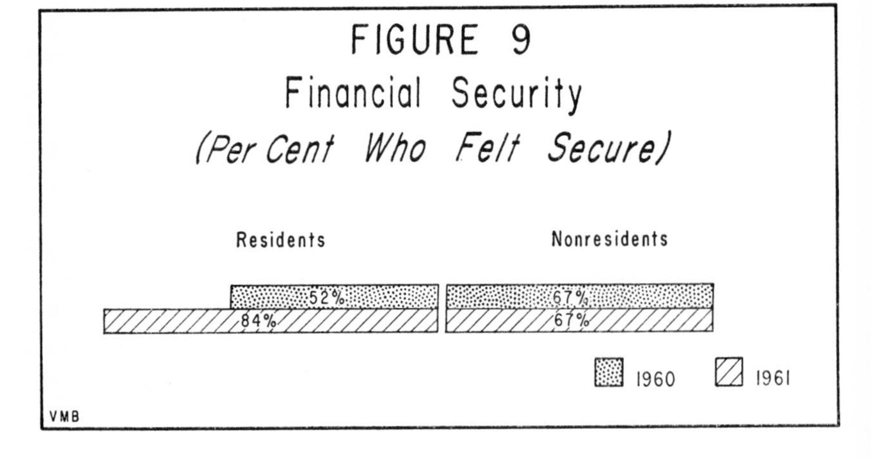
FIGURE 9
Financial Security
(Per Cent Who Felt Secure)
Residents
Nonresidents
52%
67%
84%
67%
1960
1961
VMB

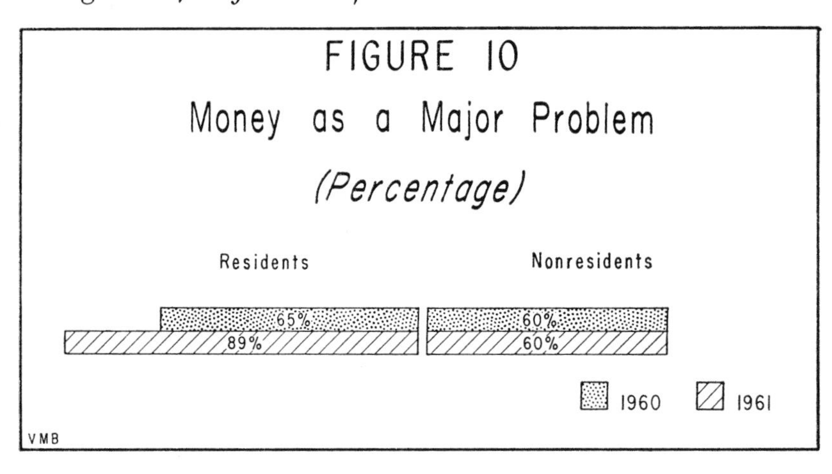

Activities and Relationships with Others

Residents showed many changes in the patterns of their lives, generally toward increased activity and social interaction, not toward disengagement. Memberships in clubs and participation in less formal group activities multiplied (Figure 11), and seven-day diaries showed a significant rise in time spent at meetings. More residents had assumed leadership roles in groups. They were not surfeited: the number of groups they wanted to join increased.

"Plaza-ites" tended to divide much more evenly regarding their present role of taking part in activities compared to what it had been

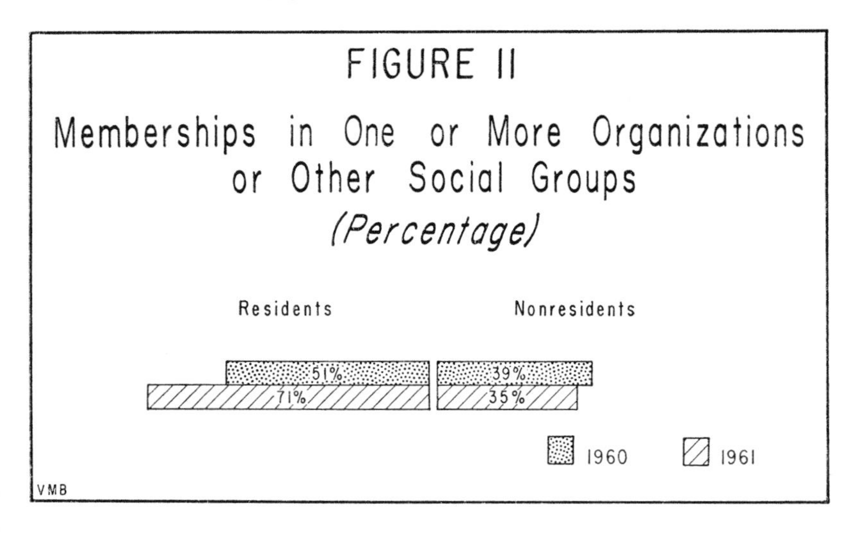

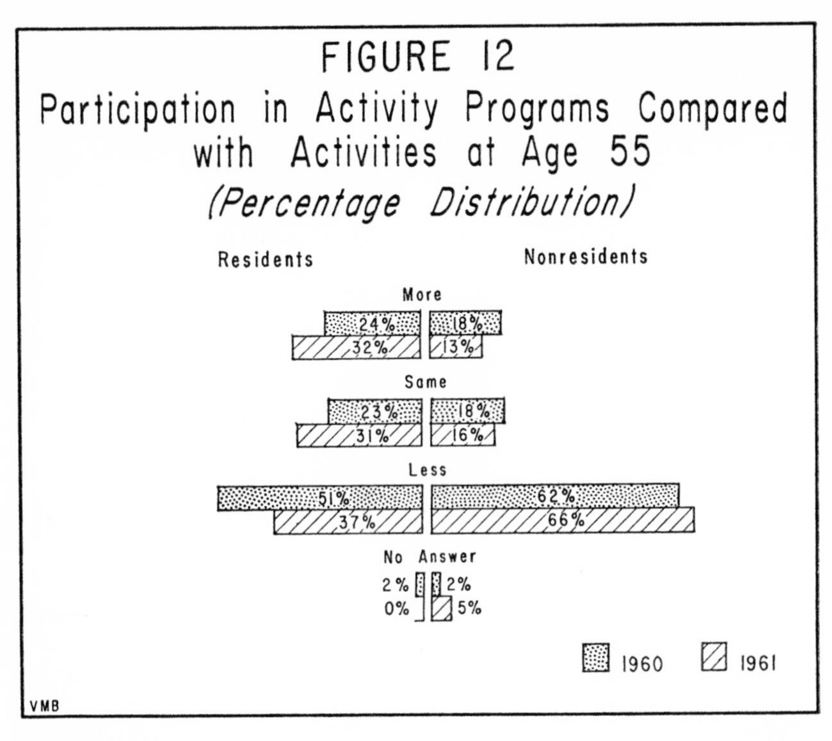

at age 55. A year earlier half of them had felt, as a majority of nonresidents continued to feel, that it was less (Figure 12). The number of leisure activities named by residents had increased, as had the proportion of active to passive pastimes and the proportion of social to solitary recreations. Diaries showed an increment in time spent on hobbies and a decrement in amount spent resting and sleeping, and in "lost time" which was not accounted for in any way.

While there was a tendency for nonresidents to have fewer close friends than a year previously, residents tended to have more. The typical (modal) number of "close friends" was seven for both groups in the initial interview. A year later, it was three for nonresidents and twelve for residents. Arithmetic averages (means) reflect less dramatic change. For residents, the mean number of close friends in 1960 was 10.8 and in 1961, 13.9; for nonresidents, the change was from a mean of 9.5 to that of 8.9.[2] Also, at the time of the second interview, residents professed a greater frequency of interaction with

[2] The large discrepancies between means and modes result from skewness

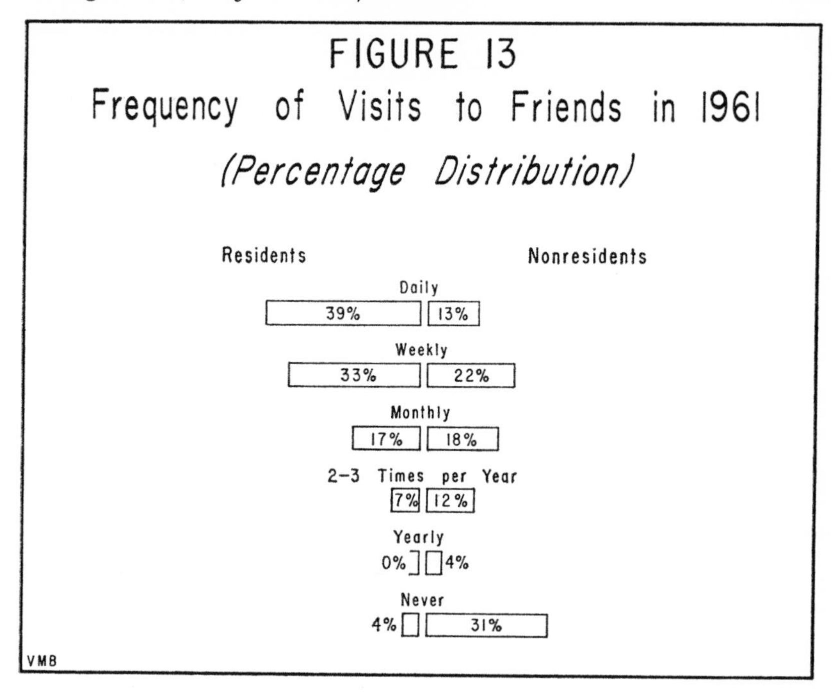

friends than nonresidents, both in visiting them (Figure 13) and in receiving visits from them (Figure 14). Tendencies were particularly divergent between the two groups for the response extremes "Never" and "Daily."

Compared to a year earlier, more of residents' close friends, and more of the people who came to visit them, were neighbors (Figures 15 and 16). "Old friends" and family members had become relatively less important in this regard. These figures do not indicate absolute decrease in these relationships with relatives and friends from former times, since they are expressed as percentages. Generally, the number of close friends, and the number of visitors, increased markedly for residents.

More resident women, and more nonresidents of both sexes, spoke daily by phone with members of their families in 1961 than in 1960. This seems to support the view of Cumming and Henry (1961) that kinship ties become increasingly important as the individual advances

---

of the distributions of responses. A few respondents insisted they had over ninety close friends.

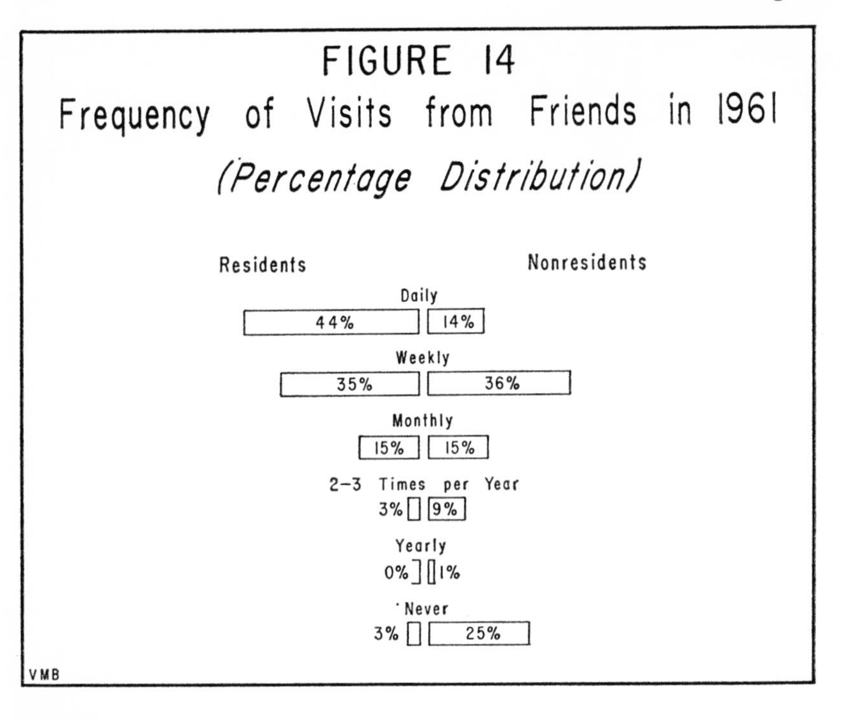

into old age, and their observation that women tend to maintain contacts with siblings and children to a greater extent han men do. However, his increase was not accompanied by decrement in other interpersonal contacts for resident women. Rather, it was a less impressive

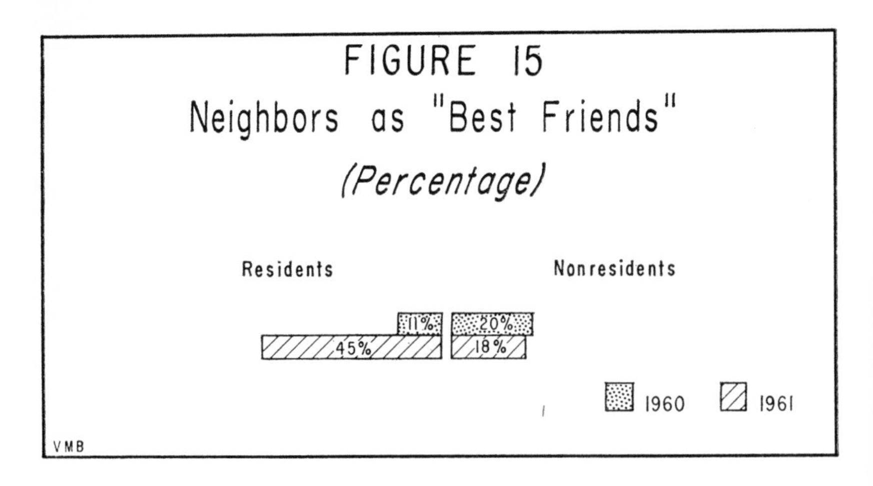

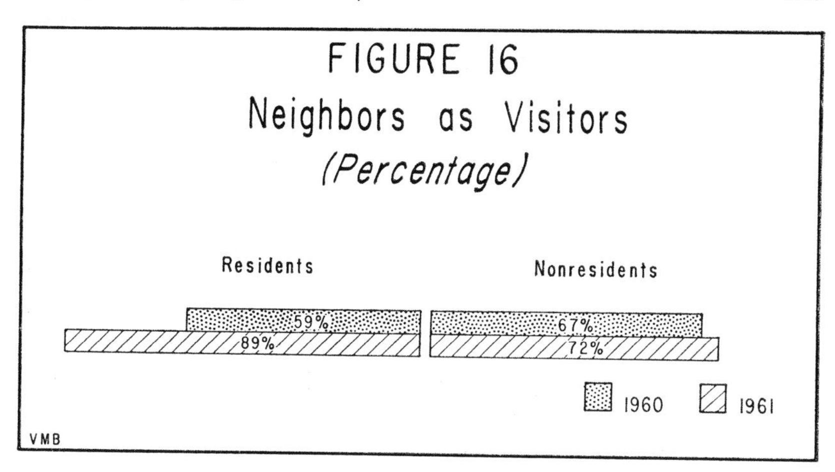

increase than that in other interpersonal relationships. Men who moved into the Plaza did not have more phone contact with their families, yet they showed, like the women, increments in the various indexes of peer social contact.

Surprisingly, there was no change in either group in the proportion who said they "never" talked with members of their families because they had no phones (15 per cent of residents, 25 per cent of nonresidents). House phones on the lobby floor of Victoria Plaza were available to everyone. Some people did not want to speak with their relatives strongly enough to use what they considered a "public phone." Incoming calls, of course, were not practical. Often this was not a serious problem, because the older person was with members of his family as often as he wished to be.

Attitude Survey scores indicated greater satisfaction with family and with friends for residents though not for nonresidents (Figures 17 and 18). These score changes probably reflect the generally higher morale of residents, but they also indicate improved relationships with kinship group members as well as with friends and acquaintances. Plaza residents enjoyed short visits to their children's homes where they were treated as guests and did not feel like imposers. They revelled in entertaining relatives, as well as old and new friends, in their beautiful apartments.

Companionship was mentioned with about equal frequency by both groups when asked in the first interview what were their major problems. By the time of the second, it was mentioned seldom by

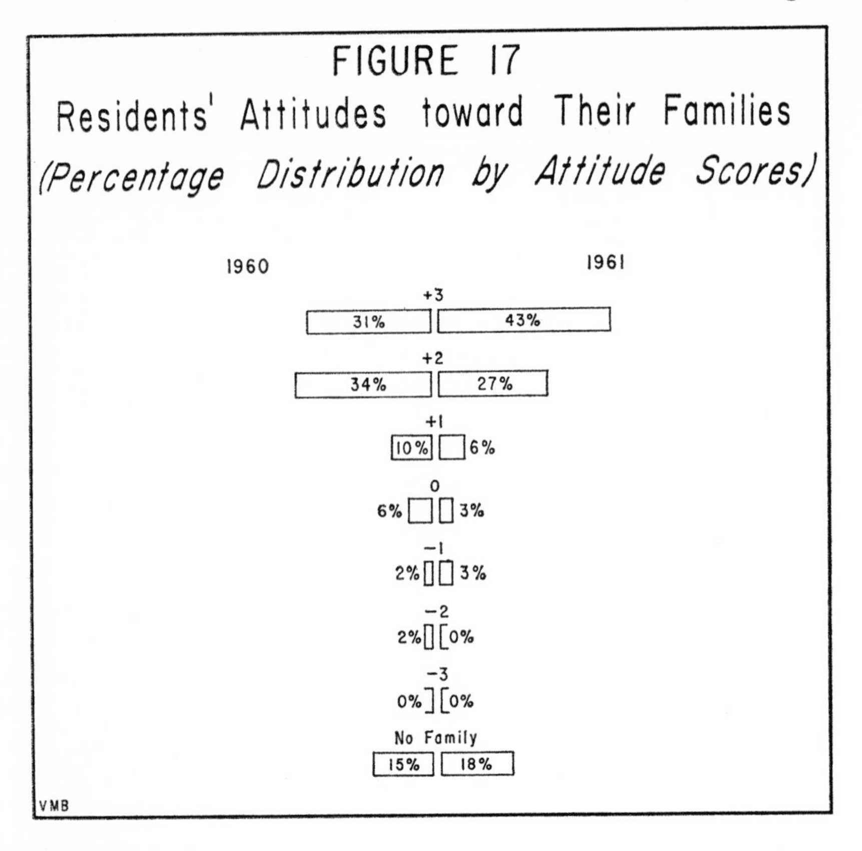

residents, but its incidence sharply increased among nonresidents (Figure 19).

Religion

Living in the Plaza had no significant effect on church attendance, which remained as it had been when all the people were applicants, as discussed in Chapter 3. For those who listened to church services on radio or television once a week or more, moving to Victoria Plaza seemed to reduce frequency, while for those who originally listened "once in a while" or "never" residence in Victoria Plaza was associated with an increment.

The same pattern was apparent in regard to attending church "socials." Those who habitually attended "once or twice a year" did not change, regardless of whether they moved to Victoria Plaza.

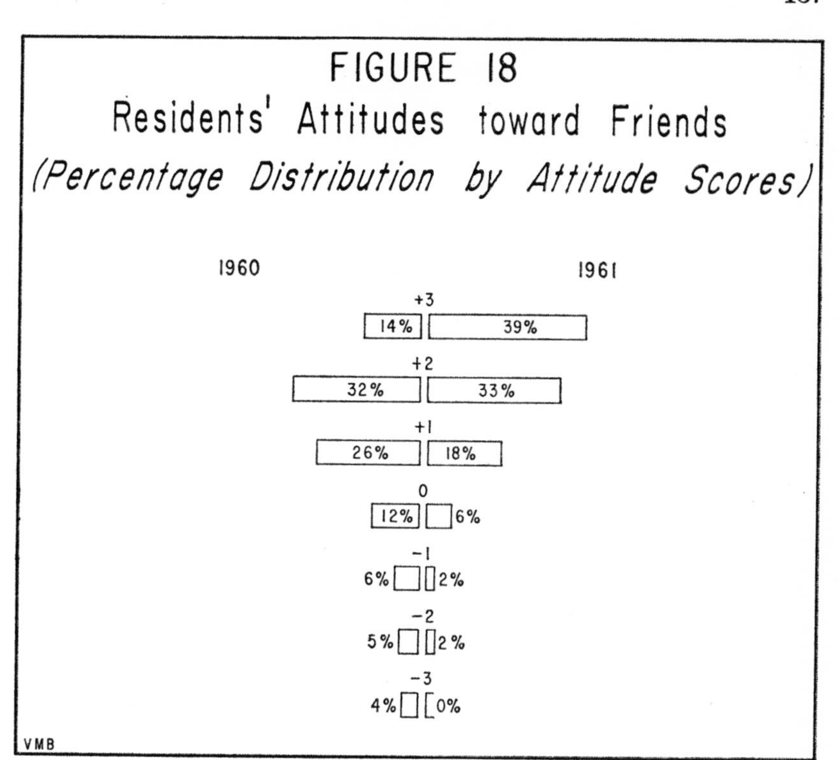
FIGURE 18
Residents' Attitudes toward Friends
(Percentage Distribution by Attitude Scores)
1960
1961
+3
14%
39%
+2
32%
33%
+1
26%
18%
0
12%
6%
-1
6%
2%
-2
5%
2%
-3
4%
0%
VMB

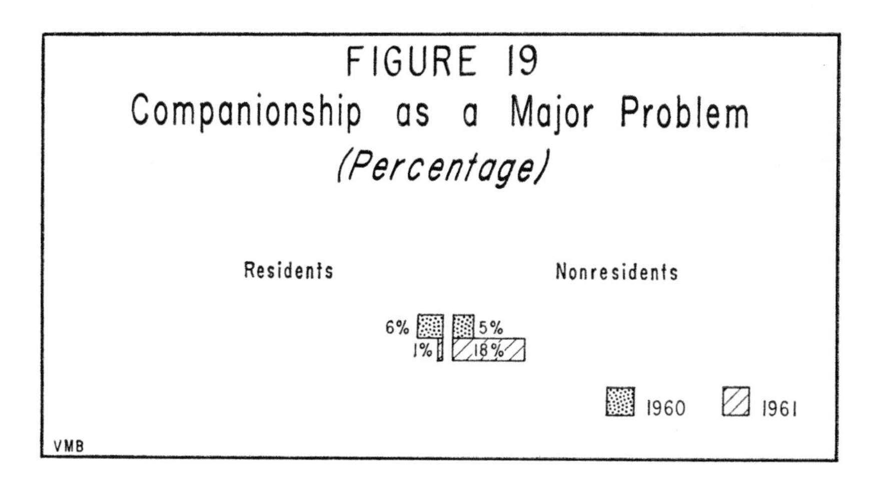
FIGURE 19
Companionship as a Major Problem
(Percentage)
Residents
Nonresidents
6%
5%
1%
18%
1960
1961
VMB

However, those who "never" went prior to residence in Victoria Plaza started to attend, while moving to the Plaza was associated with a drop in attendance for those who previously had gone to social events at church more frequently than once a year.

The pattern of change in regard to church social gatherings is easily explained on the basis of accessibility. Those who went to many church socials lived close by or had convenient transportation. Many of them, by moving to Victoria Plaza, increased the distance and/or made transportation more difficult. Also, many competing activities became available to them in the Plaza. On the other hand, most who "never" attended social gatherings at church did so through inability, not desire. When church groups offered social events in the Senior Center, these people were delighted to take part.

An explanation of the changed pattern of radio and television behavior is less obvious. However, Victoria Plaza afforded the opportunity for sociable radio and television listening and watching. This seemed particularly true for television. Many who had their own sets preferred to watch programs with other people, either in an apartment or in the lobby. Disagreements about which channel to watch on the lobby television set were not infrequent, but only the most heated led to anyone's leaving the viewing group. Sociability may have had a "leveling" effect on individual patterns of television viewing.

In spite of consistent and considerable change in participation in church social events and in attendance at radio and television religious programs, the stability of church-attendance habits suggests that such attendance may be, for these people, a relatively valid index of "religiousness," while participation in church social events and in group attendance at broadcast religious programs is more influenced by social factors. Apparently, the people for whom church services held deep meaning had managed, somehow, to attend them, in their earlier living situations, and they continued to do so, regardless of whether it was more difficult or easier after the move to Victoria Plaza. Participation in church socials and listening to or viewing religious programs, on the other hand, seemed to follow the pattern of change characteristic of most social activities consequent upon the move to the Plaza.

People who lived in the apartments reported an increase in visits from clergy and lay people from their churches. Fifty-five per cent received such calls between the interviews, while only 20 per cent had had such visitors in the year preceding the initial interview. This attention seemed to be a source of considerable satisfaction to them, as the absence or infrequency of such visits was cause for embarrassment and hurt earlier, and as it continued to be for those living elsewhere.

When these people were scattered in the community, workers did not seem to know that they existed, or how to find them if their names were available on church rolls. Another factor was the greater ease of visiting, since several people in the Plaza could be contacted in one trip, and if one was not at home, little time was lost in getting to another's door. As the research interviewers clearly demonstrated, much time and travel must be expended for each hour spent with older persons dispersed throughout the city. Clergymen, and members of guilds and circles, do not have time in unlimited quantities, and hours spent in fruitless search are discouraging.

During the period between interviews attitudes toward religion diverged between residents and nonresidents: religion became more important and more meaningful to residents, less to nonresidents. On the religion section of the Attitude Survey nonresidents' scores shifted consistently from the positive toward the negative, and residents' scores turned markedly in the other direction. Though there was no real difference between the groups in this respect at the time they were applicants, 75 per cent of the residents of Victoria Plaza, compared to only 50 per cent of the nonresidents, received the most favorable score on the basis of their responses during the final interview. For many the new living situation was literally the answer to fervent prayer. Not uncommon was a comment like this one: "I never really prayed before, but now I do, every day, in thanksgiving for getting in here."

Morale

Living in Victoria Plaza had a definite impact on people's views of themselves. Though the calendar showed them all a year or more older, fewer residents designated themselves as "old," "elderly," or "aged," so that the resident group was increasingly "middle-aged" (Figure 20).

Generally Plaza-ites were more favorable than previously in evaluating their overall accomplishments in life. Estimates of their present ability to work were better than they had been a year or more before. They currently considered their lives as of more use than

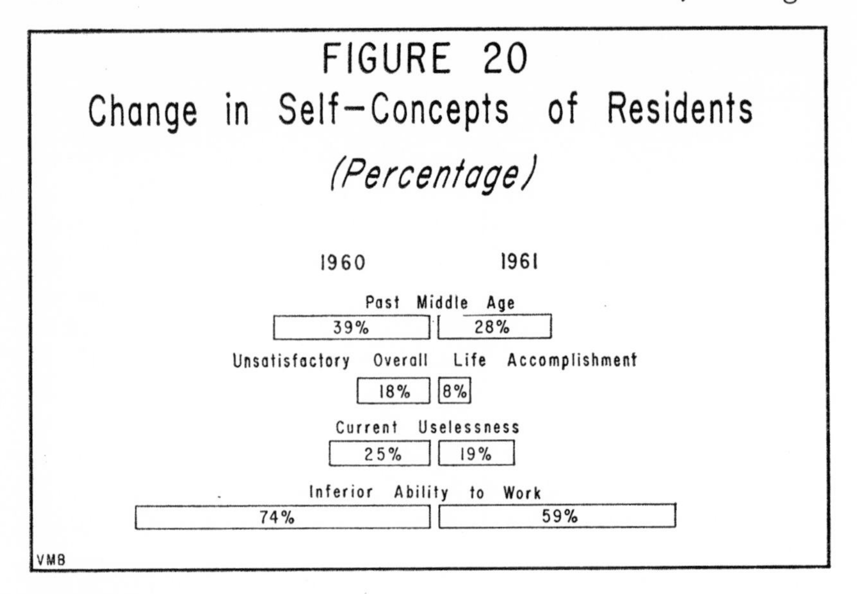

they had in the first interview, while nonresidents' scores on the Usefulness section of the Attitude Survey showed a tendency in the opposite direction.

Scores on the Happiness section of the Attitude Survey also showed change toward the positive end of the scale for residents, and in the opposite direction for nonresidents. The overall Attitude Survey score, which has been used as an index of general morale, showed the same pattern of change and counterchange. For example, scores above +15 were earned by 18 per cent of residents in the initial interview and by 36 per cent in the second, while comparable figures for nonresidents were 10 per cent and 9 per cent. Considering scores below zero, the percentage of residents in that category fell from 10 per cent to 5 per cent, and nonresidents increased from 11 per cent to 19 per cent.

Less than half as many of the residents, but twice as many nonresidents, worried about their own personal adjustment, compared to their 1960 responses (Figure 21). In 1961 fewer of the residents than in 1960 considered the present as the unhappiest period in their lives (Figure 22) and more termed it the happiest. Both changes were reversed for nonresidents. In describing themselves residents chose, from the list provided, a larger percentage of adjectives with favorable or positive connotations in 1961 than in 1960.

FIGURE 21

Personal Adjustment as a Major Problem

(Percentage)

Residents Nonresidents

9% 4% 9% 18%

1960 1961

VMB

Perhaps indication of improved overall feeling of competence to cope with life's demands is furnished by the reduction in the number of residents who felt that they had any problem of serious magnitude (Figure 23). Many more of them tended, when asked this question, to respond on the final interview, "I don't have any problem that I would call major."

Health

Residence in Victoria Plaza affected health, or at least individuals' evaluations of their health. In direct assessment of health on a five-point scale, residents' responses showed little change, while non-

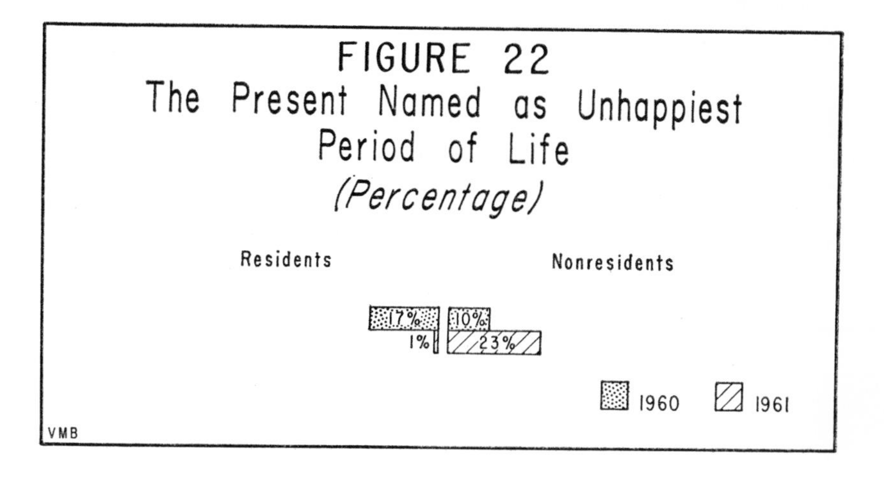

FIGURE 23
People with No "Major Problems"
(Percentage)

Residents Nonresidents

25% 27%
74% 29%

1960 1961

VMB

residents' shifted away from "good" and "excellent" (from 55% to 41%) and toward "poor" and "very poor" (from 14% to 22%). Attitude Survey scores of nonresidents tended to shift toward the negative, residents toward the positive end of the score scale. When asked about major problems, more nonresidents, fewer residents, mentioned health (Figure 24). They mentioned no fewer health problems when asked about them, but a smaller proportion of their complaints were among those previously classified as neurotic. Weekly time diaries showed an increase in amount of time spent in health care for the nonresidents, a decrement for residents.

It is questionable whether changes in the time reported as spent on

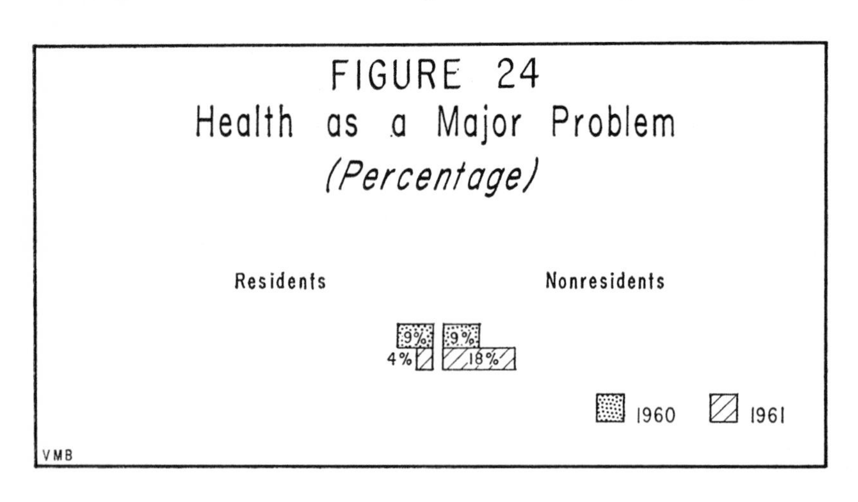

health care reflect alterations in habits, and whether changes in the other responses are accurate indexes of health status. It must be remembered that at the time of original interview all of these people were applicants for housing, and each one must have tried to present himself as healthy. At the time of the second interview all were in some measure relieved from this pressure, those in Victoria Plaza because they were secure, and those outside because their chances were poor. The differences may suggest better health or better feeling about health status, among those who were in the building.

Nonresidents consistently showed a tendency to change for the worse on items specifically aimed at attitudes toward their health, while residents' attitudes improved. The same thing was true for direct ratings of one's health compared to that of others of the same age: residents moved toward optimism; nonresidents toward pessimism. Residents decreased requests for medical services though nonresidents increased such requests during the same time period (Figure 5).

Disengagement

While the nonresident group showed a tendency toward disengagement during the period between first and second contacts, the resident group showed a contrary tendency in Disengagement Index scores. In a way, this may summarize many of the tendencies observed in attitudes and patterns of behavior: differential effect of residence in Victoria Plaza seemed to be in the direction of increased activity, more frequent contact with a wider circle of people, less "lost time" and less time spent in sleeping, in passive activities, and in solitude.

This reversal of disengagement was associated with more favorable self-concepts, improved interpersonal relationships, and increased happiness and satisfaction with past and present life, factors which suggest that this group of older people had been disengaging not from developmental readiness but from press of life circumstances. Given a comfortable and attractive physical environment and one rich in social possibilities as well, they seemed to re-engage and to enjoy it.

Summary

Changes consequent upon moving to Victoria Plaza were obvious in all measurements of life style, attitude, and adjustment which were used. They were consistently in the direction of "good adjustment" insofar as such a thing is defined for adults in general. They were away from passivity, seclusiveness, or disengagement. These changes, along with the continuing enthusiasm of residents for it, suggest strongly that Victoria Plaza was a full success in meeting the needs of this group of "middle-aged" people.

CHAPTER 8

Social Processes in Victoria Plaza

THE OPENING of Victoria Plaza afforded an unusual opportunity to observe the emergence of leaders and the formation of other interpersonal relationships within a group of people uprooted from a variety of backgrounds and simultaneously thrust into close proximity with one another.

Some Relevant Questions to be Considered

It is of both practical and theoretical interest to see how readily older people form new relationships. There is the danger that they experience such difficulty in making new associations that it is preferable to leave them in undesirable living situations rather than to move them and thereby demand social adjustment. Or it may be that though they cannot form new relationships this fact does not trouble them, since they are disengaging from the world of activities and people. At any rate, decisions regarding the housing of older citizens should take into account their ability to relate to strangers and a new way of life, as well as their affective reaction to this necessity.

One of the most urgently expressed frustrations of applicants was social isolation. Would a convenient supply of people solve the problem, or was the perceived need a "cover" for regret at the loss of old acquaintances joined with personal inadequacy to form new relationships? After a period of living so closely with many other people, were there longing backward glances at the "good old days" of privacy and some resentment at the demands of group living?

In any group-living situation early identification of potential leaders is desirable. "Natural" leaders from within the resident group should be able to ease the adjustment of others and to be of considerable assistance in interpreting management's roles and requirements. Furthermore, the strategic distribution of potential leaders with respect to each other in such residential facilities may be advantageous.

In addition, the question of the relative strength of personality characteristics vs. those of the building in determining such outcomes as leadership and popularity should be considered. Are friendships formed on the basis of similarity of background, commonality of present interest, or proximity within the building? Can leaders be identified prior to admission or created by assignment to highly visible apartment locations? Do social isolates exist because of previous development, and perhaps choice, or is this status forced upon them by assignment to apartments off the beaten path?

Background: The Building

Preparatory to any attempt to describe social processes within the group of residents, some additional background regarding the building and the people seems necessary. Victoria Plaza's eight residential floors are identical (Figure 25) in design, differing from one another only in elevation above ground level and in distance from the Senior Center (Figure 26). Obviously, on each floor apartments vary in con-

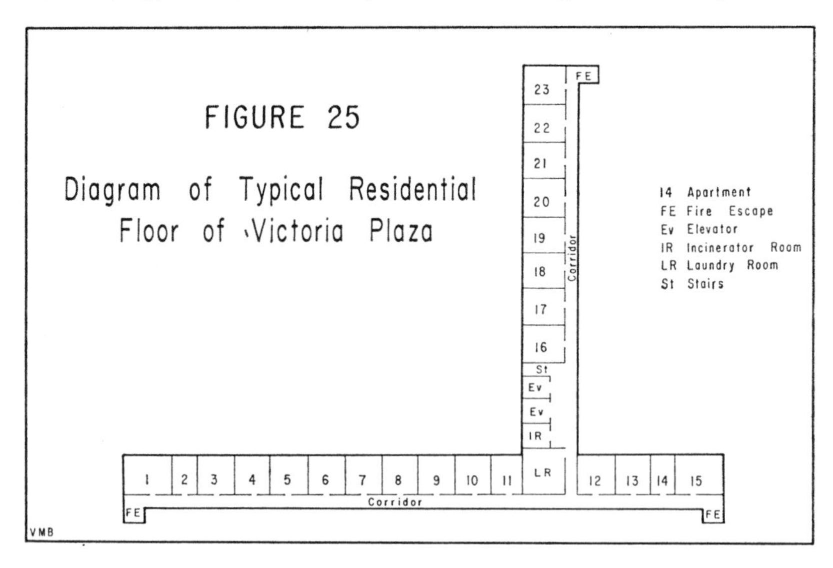

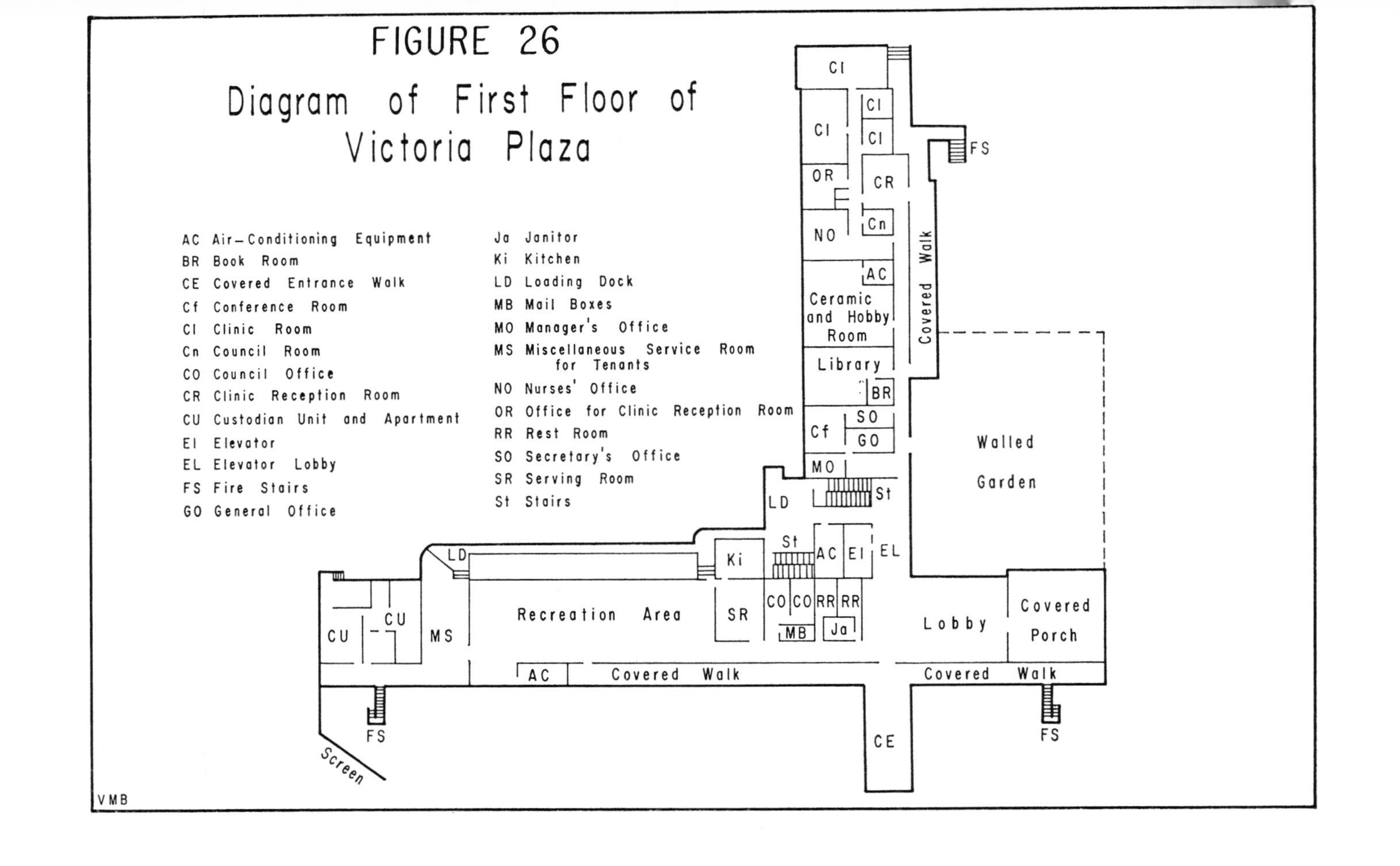
FIGURE 26
Diagram of First Floor of Victoria Plaza
AC Air-Conditioning Equipment
BR Book Room
CE Covered Entrance Walk
Cf Conference Room
Cl Clinic Room
Cn Council Room
CO Council Office
CR Clinic Reception Room
CU Custodian Unit and Apartment
El Elevator
EL Elevator Lobby
FS Fire Stairs
GO General Office
Ja Janitor
Ki Kitchen
LD Loading Dock
MB Mail Boxes
MO Manager's Office
MS Miscellaneous Service Room for Tenants
NO Nurses' Office
OR Office for Clinic Reception Room
RR Rest Room
SO Secretary's Office
SR Serving Room
St Stairs
Cl
Cl
Cl
Cl
OR
CR
Cn
NO
AC
Ceramic and Hobby Room
Covered Walk
FS
Library
BR
Cf
SO
GO
MO
St
LD
Walled
Garden
LD
Ki
St
AC
El
EL
CU
CU
MS
Recreation Area
SR
CO
CO
RR
RR
MB
Ja
Lobby
Covered Porch
AC
Covered Walk
Covered Walk
FS
CE
FS
Screen
VMB

venience to elevator, washroom, and incinerator chute, as well as in number of other people likely to go by in the course of normal activities.

From a research point of view it would be most desirable to assign residents to apartments completely at random. In this way individual characteristics which might influence social behavior would tend to be distributed throughout the population on a chance basis and would therefore tend to cancel themselves out in their effects on social processes. The research, of course, had no effect on placement of residents, but must take into account any determinants of apartment allocation which might influence interpersonal reactions.

The number of individuals in the family group and economic ability to pay for a larger apartment naturally had some influence upon the location to which the individual was assigned. The two two-bedroom apartments on each floor are at opposite ends of the longer hall. Only married couples or other family pairs or groups qualify for these. Some couples occupy one-bedroom apartments. Next to the two-bedroom apartments are two "efficiencies," and the remainder are one-bedroom apartments.

Furthermore, it was the aim of Housing Authority personnel to assign each person, insofar as possible, to the apartment of his choice within, of course, the size for which he qualified. This was true for floor number and for location of apartment on the floor. Prospective residents were much impressed with the efforts of the Housing Authority staff to locate them where they wanted to be. ("If I had to locate over two hundred people in three days I'd just take the list of names and start writing apartment numbers"; "They are so nice to go to all this trouble for us.") These efforts included interviews in which they were shown a layout of an apartment, to obtain some idea of possible furniture placement and of the location within the building. Subsequently they were taken on tours of the building, in small groups, to visit two apartments, in order to provide them a basis for expressing like or dislike of the location.

In most instances there probably was some expression of preference in regard to height. ("I asked them to put me any place except up high—so here I am on 9!" or "I'm glad I got what I asked for—up high where no one else's dirt comes down on me.") or centrality on the floor ("I wanted to be by the elevator—I'm the type's afraid I'll miss something!" or "It's wonderful! Everyone *has* to come by my door!" or, on the other hand, "Thank goodness my apartment is at the end of the corridor and on the wing away from the street. It is so nice not to have to be bothered with people!") or color scheme ("I don't care what story, and I don't even know what they mean by 'wing'—just let me have a blue one, any place.")

However, most acceptees were so overjoyed at the prospect of becoming residents that discrimination among locations had relatively little meaning. (See Chapter 6.) While Housing Authority personnel tried to assign each person the apartment he most wanted, it is by no means safe to say that locus of residence represents first preference in every instance. Assignments were also influenced by indecisiveness of applicants and by the pressure of time and volume of the simultaneous influx of residents. In view of the common lack of definite preference, and because of the pressure of processing such a large number of people in three days, it is probably fair to say that, in general, assignment of people to apartments was not essentially different than had it been done at random. That is to say, there is no evidence that people were assigned to apartments with any consistency in regard to age, health, intelligence, tendency to be involved in activities, or other characteristics which might be determinative of their development of relationships wtih other residents.[1]

Background: The People

Relevant also to understanding interpersonal behavior in Victoria Plaza is some knowledge of the social backgrounds of the people who became residents.

PARENTS, CHILDHOOD, AND YOUTH

Four applicants had parents still living, two fathers and two mothers. One was in the eighties, two were in the nineties, and one was over a hundred years old. Sixty per cent of mothers and two-thirds of fathers were reported to have lived past age sixty-five. Comparison with census data suggests either that the recollections were incorrect of that their parents lived to unusually old age. In 1900, 4.0 per cent of males and 4.1 per cent of females were over sixty-five; in 1950, 7.8 per cent of males and 8.5 per cent of females exceeded that age (Hauser and Vargas, 1960). Since there is evidence of a strong hereditary influence on longevity, it is not surprising that this group had long-lived parents.

[1] The top floors were filled first, so they probably included more people capable of making decisions and free in speaking their minds.

Eight subjects grew up with stepfathers and twelve with stepmothers. Five per cent disliked their father or stepfather, and 5 per cent their mother or stepmother. Overwhelmingly, however, recollections of relationships with parents were of "considerable" or "strong" attachment (75% for fathers and 80% for mothers).

Kinds of work at which fathers were employed during most of their lives fell in the middle occupational levels (Table 10). About a third were farmers. Many had small businesses of their own. A small number were day laborers and equally few were in the professions.

In regard to the financial situation of the family while the subject was growing up, most considered it "comfortable" while very few said that their parents either "couldn't make ends meet" or were wealthy. Many who reported that the family was financially "comfortable" when they were youngsters lived on farms owned by their parents. They remembered always having plenty to eat and everything they needed, but these satisfied requirements did not necessarily indicate affluence.

Nine out of ten remembered good health as children. The number of siblings who lived past five years of age ranged from none to a dozen. A mere 5 per cent of the subjects were "only" children, while 15 per cent had nine or more brothers and sisters. The typical number of siblings was five.

Recollecting the number of friends they had had in their teens, half reported "an average number" both of the same and of the opposite sex. However, nearly all the rest had "many" same-sex friends, while only a quarter of them remembered "many" friends of the opposite sex. Those with few friends usually commented that they lived on outlying farms, at some distance from other families.

As children, 85 per cent attended church once a week or more, according to their reminiscence. Most of those who reported church attendance less frequently lived in rural areas where church services were made available only occasionally by a circuit rider. Only three people (fewer than one per cent of the group) "never" went to church in childhood.

MARRIAGE

At the time of the first interview, 22 per cent were living with spouse, 52 per cent were widowed, 18 per cent were separated or divorced, and 7 per cent had never married. Compared to national figures for their age group the number of those divorced or separated from spouses was large.

Some interesting response discrepancies emerged. Thirty-one said they were "single," but when asked whether they had ever been married, only twenty-six said they never had. All five "single though married" people were women. Two were widows and one had been separated from her husband for over twenty-five years. One was divorced, but not proud of it, and the other refused to divulge current marital status. Each of these women had been living alone for many years and thought of herself as single.

A check on another discrepancy in the marital data, a difference between the number "married" and the number "living with spouse," disclosed that, to avoid the temptation of legal marriage to which he had succumbed many times, one man was living with a common-law wife, and tagged himself "unmarried" but "living with wife."

Though they were not outstandingly successful at it, people in this group seemed to like marriage. The typical pattern was once married (60%), but 30 per cent of the group had been married twice or more, one person eight times. He was reluctant about giving the interview at all and particularly hesitant during this section.

A third had been married in their teens, 80 per cent of them before they were thirty. As expected, women married younger. Most of the second marriages were during people's thirties and forties. The latest first marriage (of pre-Victoria Plaza days) was in the fifties. Six per cent of the applicants married again after they were sixty. Most (60%) considered their marriage(s) happier than the average. The happiest marriages were the first (and most of them only marriages). The one man who reported eight marriages considered them all happy, "up to a point." When that point was passed, he moved on to the next marriage!

Retrospecting about the first marriage, two-thirds would marry the same person if they had their lives to live over. The remainder—whose memories of married life were only of trouble, discord, and economic pinch—were evenly divided between being unsure, wanting to marry a different person, and not marrying at all.

CHILDREN

Members of this group had the average number of children for their generation—three (Whelpton and Friedmon, 1956). However, over a third of the group had no children living at the time of the first interview. In Shanas' (1960) aged group only 22 per cent had no living children. A third of those who had living children saw them every day, two-thirds saw them at least once a month. Fifteen per cent saw their children very infrequently because they lived at a distance.

Eighteen of the subjects had legally adopted children or had simply taken some into the house to raise. One person had gained six children in this way, and two others had acquired five each. Interviewers found it difficult to obtain a distinction between these and "own" children, since subjects considered it unimportant, and feelings about them tended to be much the same.

One woman said her two foster daughters were the most satisfactory of her several children. A bachelor had one of the warmest, closest, and most rewarding relationships with "children" of anyone in the group, though no blood or legal tie existed. He had developed a paternal relationship with his newsboy many years before, had put the young man through school, and at the time of the interview was taking the young man's children to school every day and picking them up every afternoon.

Only one in five felt that he was a help to a child or other relative, in any way, at the time of the first interview. It is surprising, in view of their very limited finances, that 5 per cent regularly gave money to relatives while only 10 per cent received money from them. Some applicants aided relatives with baby-sitting, sewing, nursing, cooking, and housework. Relatives assisted some of them by providing, in addition to money, a home, food and clothing, transportation, and entertainment. Apparently applicants were of the same opinion as Britton, Mather, and Lansing's (1961) subjects, most of whom felt that an older person should be responsible for himself but not for others, while he should be willing to receive help from others when necessary.

The question, "Do you feel your family is a real help to you now?" was usually not interpreted by the respondent as referring to financial assistance, but to social and emotional support. Fewer than two-thirds said "Yes." Most of them went on to comment in this vein: "It is wonderful just to know that I have them." When money was mentioned in answering this question, is was usually to the effect that there was no one in the family who could help them financially, but that this really did not matter. The meaning of family to these elderly people was the availability of others in the kinship group, should they be needed, for comfort and moral support.

Most of those who had families agreed that "My family likes to have me around," "I am perfectly satisfied with the way my family treats me," and "I think my family is the finest in the world." Half said they were getting more love and affection than ever before. However, one out of five wished his family would pay more attention to him, and one in ten said, "My family is always trying to boss me" or "My family does not really care for me."

OTHER CLOSE RELATIVES

Over half had close relatives living in the city, and two-thirds had some within the state. In addition to children, half of the applicants named more than eight living "close relatives."

It proved impossible to categorize "relatives" on any basis other than number. In many cases kinship was remote, if it existed at all, and any effort at clarification led to lengthy genealogical discussion. On the other hand, some people mentioned only brothers, sisters, and children, and did not include grandchildren. This lack of gratification in the grandparent role seemed the exception in this group, rather than the rule, as in that of Cumming and Henry (1961).

Interpretations of "close relationships" were so divergent as to defy categorization according to type or degree. Generally those who had many relatives, particularly if they lived in the immediate geographic area, named a few of them. Those having a small kingroup, or one with few members in this vicinity, mentioned people with whom they had some regular contact, even if the relationship was remote or nonexistent. Their equation of present contact with kinship is demonstrated by the fact that only one per cent said they had close relatives with whom they never had contact. Seventeen per cent had no close relatives, even accepting their own broad definition of the term.

Though the typical (modal) frequency of face-to-face encounter with relatives other than children was monthly, there were nearly as many who had contact only two or three times a year or every two or three years. The few who saw other close relatives daily were living with them. Communication by phone and mail was much more frequent than were personal visits. The typical pattern for both telephone and mail contacts was once a week. Women communicated with relatives more frequently than men did, through every medium.

FRIENDS

Attitudes toward friends as measured by Burgess *et al's* Attitude Survey (1948) were strongly positive. Typically the applicants agreed, "My many friends make my life happy and cheerful" (80%), though most would be happier "If I could see my friends more often." Nearly a third had "no one to talk to about personal things," and half that many seemed to suffer badly from lack of friends, having "so few friends that I am lonely much of the time," and at the same time realizing that "I never dreamed that I could be as lonely as I am now."

However, only 5 per cent had no "close friend" (one who would go out of his way to do a favor). These few tended to be such "independent" individuals that they did not need or want to ask a favor of anyone, or they had outlived friends and lacked energy or opportunity to form new relationships. On the other hand, twice the number reporting no close friends insisted they had twenty or more. Several reported over a hundred. When the interviewer commented on the very large number of intimates, they were insistent. One furnished names and addresses to document her close friendships. The mean was eleven friends and the mode seven.

When possible, friendships were categorized as to background or source. It was not always clear whether the relationship was brought about by the common activity or whether the person joined the church or club because of the friendship. In most instances it seemed likely that the friendship was a result of the shared interest. More women than men had church and neighborhood friendships, while those related to club and business contacts showed no sex difference. Many whose friendships seemed to stem from neighborhood association were living in Victoria Courts, a bungalow-type public-housing facility.

A third of the group neither paid visits to friends nor received visits from them. Some who had no visitors had no friends. Many more did not want friends to see them in impoverished and unpleasant surroundings. Physical limitations and unavailability of transportation hindered their calling upon others.

A sharp drop in frequency of contact with friends since age 55 was felt. Over half of the applicant group thought they saw their friends less often. Poorer health, inconvenient geographic location, and unavailability of transportation were important reasons for reduction in interaction with friends.

Death had taken the friends of some. On the other hand, a few saw friends more frequently because of deaths which freed them for visiting. Work acted both for and against seeing friends also. Nearly as many said retiring from work allowed them to see friends more frequently as said they no longer saw friends whom they formerly met on the job. The most frequent reasons, by far, for greater contact with friends was more free time than at age fifty-five.

Women use the phone much more frequently to contact others than did men. Half of the women and 20 per cent of the men used it daily. The one woman who had not used a phone for over twenty years was stone deaf. From comments in this and other sections of the interview, it was apparent that interviewees depended heavily on the phone for social contact, since they were so limited by finances, transportation, and physical condition. Many used it for daily contacts with children. Plans for phones in Victoria Plaza were a matter of concern and occasioned frequent questions addressed to interviewers. It was obvious that applicants would prefer to continue living in unpleasant surroundings if moving to the new building meant giving up the availability of a phone.

Highly significant sex differences existed also in regard to correspondence. Women wrote and received more letters. This sex difference occurred in the number of people to whom letters were written, but not in the number of people from whom letters were received. Men wrote fewer letters and to a smaller number of people. They also received fewer letters, but they received mail from as many different people as did women. Though number of correspondents ranged from none to dozens, the commonest was two.

Sources of Information on Social Behavior in Victoria Plaza

As already discussed in Chapters 6 and 7, interview and test responses indicated that moving to Victoria Plaza was associated with widespread changes in interpersonal relationships and other probably related alterations in life style. For example, those who moved tended to reduce the amount of sleep and rest they normally took, as well as that spent in passive ways, and their time diaries recorded less "lost" time which was simply not accounted for in any way. At the same time, they spent more time in active leisure pursuits and in those which involved participation of other people.

In addition to comparison of interview and test responses, from applicant status to established resident status, for the same individuals, over a period of a year to fifteen months, sociometric data were collected at intervals during that time, to provide further information regarding formation of interpersonal relationships within the group of residents. Every three months the residents were asked to name the people they would select to fill certain roles (Appendix A). Nominees were not limited to the residents of the Plaza.

No questions with negative implications were included in the sociometric questionnaire. Every nomination could be taken as a compliment. Two considerations determined this limitation to the positive. The less serious was residents' reluctance to make negative judgments about each other by name for fear that such expressions of opinion would accentuate interpersonal problems ("I'd just as soon not say. I have to *live* with these people, you know!") In this resistance they resembled servicemen who are members of groups isolated from other social contact or under some unusual stress. (Sells, 1961). Residents were freely and even spontaneously critical about "those gossipy old hens" or "the lobby boys" or "porch sitters" but shied away from attaching unfavorable statements to individuals except in repeating gossip to their interviewer—usually to demonstrate how gossipy everyone else was.

More important, the Housing Authority and Senior Community Center managers felt that peer ratings on items with negative connotations might focus grievances, particularly through subsequent discussion of such questions and speculation as to others' responses which anyone familiar with the Plaza must anticipate.

Collection of these data was itself a revelation of that intense interest in what others were saying about one which contraindicated inclusion of negative items. The first round of sociometric data was collected just as the interview and test data were. With only two interviewers, this took a period of several days. They had not been started more than an hour or two when the entire building was literally buzzing with speculations about people's answers to the various questions. As each resident finished, he or she was set upon by neighbors and other friends and exhorted to "tell all"—not about the task, but about his choice of "best friend," and so on, and to exchange opinions about what others had said or would say.

Other testing was spread over several weeks, yet apparently residents were able to keep their own counsel about it after the examiner had explained the need for withholding discussion until everyone had finished, so that each person's own reaction could be obtained, uninfluenced by those of others. Apparently this was all very well and good as long as questions were about past history and present knowledge and opinions—but not when they were about the other residents, and possibly oneself. Some residents seemed almost obsessed with finding out what others had said on the sociometric questionnaire—about themselves first of all, and then about the people they especially liked or resented. Worse, they tried every means, fair and foul, to extract promises of "votes" from those not yet officially questioned.

There is no way of knowing how much this exchange of information, advice, and even pressure affected the results of the first sociometric responses. However, some effect must be assumed, and the emotional uproar aroused was clearly not desirable. For those unfortunate persons who happened to be last, the stress became almost unbearable. Not only was it prolonged, but as each wave of respondents finished the task, they eagerly turned to pressuring those remaining.

For the second and third collections of sociometric data no warning was given and a much larger crew of data collectors descended suddenly upon the building. The same elevator took interviewers to each wing of each floor. They started at the apartments farthest from the elevator, and made it clear that exchange of information was not wanted. The only access to other residents not yet polled was past the window of an apartment in which an interviewer was working and which he faced, and residents were painfully aware of how visible they would be. This effectively eliminated "politicking" which might influence nominations, and there seemed to be little more interest, after the fact, than there was about any other data.

In addition to the problem of pressure and influence, another limitation on this measure should be noted. Some residents, most of them men, did not know the names of people they wanted to nominate. Though interviewers did the best they could with such statements as, "Oh, you know, that old guy I play pool with every day, what's hisname," they were by no means always able to supply the name. This type of omission was greatly increased by the necessity to use many interviewers in the collection of the sociometric data. Only the two who did the majority of the data collection were sufficiently well acquainted with what the residents did, and whom they did it with, that they could suggest possible names. Interestingly, men who had spent many hours together, perhaps every day for a period of months, sometimes did not even recognize each other's names when they were supplied.

This failure may indicate lack of alertness or ability to learn on the part of these individuals or it may suggest that names were not of importance to them. The latter seems likely in many cases. The men did not use, or seem to need, names in their social intercourse. They did not phone each other or call for one another at their apartments, as the women were wont to do, but usually met, by offhand mutual agreement, in the lobby. Their social contact seemed largely determined by participation in activities. Another person was one's "bridge partner" or "billiard opponent."

For scoring purposes the questions comprising the sociometric questionnaire were divided into two categories. To the first were assigned those which seemed to relate to friendship behavior, and to the second those which referred to leadership qualifications. Each resident's nominations were tabulated separately for each pool of items into a companionship score and a leadership score (Appendix A).

For analysis of group processes, the two were maintained as separate scores since, while they have something in common, they are far from identical. (Data from the final collection of sociometric material indicated a correlation between the companionship score and the leadership score of .17, significant at the .05 level.)

Getting Acquainted

The plan had been to collect sociometric data at approximately three-month intervals until the patterns of social interaction became stable. With few exceptions, social roles were well defined at the end of the first three months the building was open, and there was little change to the sixth, or to the ninth month, despite procedure differences.

The number of individuals named as "best friends" increased, and as time went by a greater per cent of Plaza residents' visitors and "best friends" were other residents. A comparison of initial Attitude Survey scores with final scores indicates that satisfaction with friendships increased, suggesting that the earlier common complaint at social isolation was based in realistic frustration. Moreover, it seemed to be a frustration which was readily relieved, for most people, but putting them into physical proximity with other individuals about their own age and with similar economic resources.

Though satisfaction with family improved for most residents, the frequency of contacts with family members tended to be less for residents than it was for applicants; and with each sociometric, the proportion of family members named became smaller.

Friends outside the building also became less crucially important. They too were nominated less frequently as the sociometrics progressed. It surely would be incorrect to conclude that people "threw over" their old friends. Rather, they were less totally dependent upon them and perhaps even enjoyed them more because of the reduction of their tension. The typical description of change in friendships during the follow-up interview was that old friendships had been maintained and new friendships formed with Plaza residents.

For the most part, applicants complained of their social isolation, acceptees launched into campaigns for becoming acquainted, and residents continued such efforts vigorously. After a year and a half in the building the need for other people still seemed insatiable.

Generally those residents who wanted to widen their circle of acquaintances needed no special assistance to do this. Techniques varied, though favorite gambits among women were comparison of forebears and progeny, and search for common religious interests and leisure-time pursuits. Billiards and dominoes were social lifelines for men, who tended to be somewhat less outgoing, perhaps only because they were a minority. Even after months in the building men tended to stay together at a table game, before the television set, or in a discussion of their previous occupations or the political or economic scene. However, visitors who remarked on the obvious segregation by sex usually agreed it was no different from what they often observed on social occasions among their own friends.

Generally, then, this group of people seemed eager for, and capable of, formation of new social relationships. Though the study included no comparison data, it is difficult to imagine a group of any other age which would have been more effective in becoming acquainted.

Within this general readiness for social interaction were there identifiable determinants of the particular relationships formed? One possibility was that characteristics of the high-rise building influenced the interpersonal behavior of people living in it.

Impact of Characteristics of the Building

ELEVATOR

The elevator is the core of the building, affording access from one residential floor to another, as well as to the Senior Community Center and the outside world. Moreover, the closer an apartment is to the elevator, the greater the proportion of other residents who must pass the occupant's door as they go about their own activities. Therefore it seemed likely that, whether as cause or result, there would be a relationship between distance from the elevator and both popularity and leadership.

Neither sociometric score was related to centrality or nearness of apartment to the communication core of the building, the elevator. Apparently, ease of access and visibility to others bore no relationship to how well one was acquainted in the building, and leadership qualities were neither dimmed by residence off the beaten path nor improved by living in a commanding position. The results of the three collections of sociometric data were essentially the same in this regard. This consistency supports the assumption that residents were assigned to apartments pretty much at random (in regard to determinants of social behavior), and emphasizes the lack of impact, over an extended period of time, of location of apartment within any residential floor.

PROXIMITY OF APARTMENTS

With a group of people this age, generally not acquainted with each other, how important a role does propinquity play in determining which individuals will become acquainted with each other and enter into social activities together? One might suspect that the process of one person's becoming acquainted with other residents would spread out from his apartment, and that the probability of his ever getting to know another resident would be inversely proportional to the distance between the two apartments.

But the expected did not occur. Though there was more social interaction with the person next door than with one at the other end of the hall, the majority of social contacts were with people on different floors of the building. This was true not only for selection of best friends, but also for visiting and eating together.

HEIGHT OF FLOOR

It was considered possible that the floor on which a person lived might influence his popularity. Residential floors differ only in elevation. Impact of floor number might come about through the resultant difference in distance from the ground-floor Senior Community Center. Modes and means on the popularity score from the third collection of sociometric data are shown in Table 16. No consistent relationships between floors and scores is indicated.

TABLE 16

The 204 Residents' Popularity within the Resident Group According to Height of Apartment

Floor Number	*Score on Third Sociometric*	
	Mean	*Mode*
2	5.38	7
3	7.81	8
4	12.35	8
5	8.30	5
6	13.85	8
7	9.62	5
8	7.08	6
9	7.04	8

The rather high means for people on the fourth and sixth floors may reflect at least in part the residence there of some interesting individuals with general visibility. A widely known and admired resident was a man who married during that first year of the Plaza's occupancy for the first time, at the age of ninety-two. His bride, in her eighties, lived on the same floor. The progress of this romance was followed eagerly by people throughout the building and, consequently, the hero and heroine became well known.

On the same floor was the handsomest man in the building, one who would be outstandingly good-looking in any group. In addition he was intelligent, well educated, had beautiful manners, and was generally charming. Since the occupants of apartments were predominantly women, it is perhaps not surprising that his popularity score soared.

Also on that floor was a tiny, brisk, gray-haired ex-school teacher who became known to everyone in the building because, sooner or later, she told each one what he should do about something. She bossed everyone in the Plaza as if he were a pupil in her third-grade class. Most people found the experience rather delightful, and few were offended, because her intentions were obviously good, and her appearance and manner charming.

On the sixth floor lived a woman active with various art forms, who entered every hobby show in the building and many in the community outside it. She became well known in this way, as well as by the voice with which she hailed people as they came up to the front of the building—from her apartment window six stories higher.

Another apartment on that floor was occupied by "the Greek," a former restaurant owner, who was almost instantly transformed from near invisibility to the focus of general attention when he bought a brand-new (not second-hand) car, and a fire-engine red station wagon, at that.

Impact of Characteristics of the Residents

Location of his apartment within the Plaza had little effect upon an individual's assumption of a leadership role among the residents, upon the number of people who chose him as a companion, or upon the particular people with whom he formed acquaintanceships. As pointed out in the previous section, some people became easily and widely known because of some dramatic characteristic. Generally the patterns of social behavior seemed to develop as they did because of traits of the individuals involved.

RECIPROCATED FRIENDSHIPS

One approach to understanding interactions was to analyze the reciprocal choices on the companionship items. In other words, people who named each other were identified, and an attempt was made to discern the reason for this mutual regard. The role played by acquaintance prior to living in the Plaza was one thing to consider. Some indication of its importance is given by the fact that six pairs of people named each other as "best friends" in the first interview, while seventy-six pairs did so in the third collection of sociometric data, taken after about nine months in the Plaza.

Some basis for the formation of friendships was furnished by common interest in an activity or hobby, or membership in the same church. In regard to personality similarity or complementarity, both patterns were observed. Some close friends seemed to be very much alike in major traits. In other cases one member was quite unlike the other in important ways. For example, one friend might be excessively dominant and the other compensatingly dependent. Some warm relationships obviously satisfied the need of one person for assistance of some kind, and the capacity of the other for "mothering."

In many cases no observer saw any rationale for what was obviously a close and meaningful friendship. One of the most baffling was the persistent, warm, but Platonic relationship between a charming but "fast" gentleman, who flaunted several heterosexual interests outside the Plaza, and an equally delightful but Puritanical "single lady."

The only adequate summary of this analysis seems to be that people became friends because they liked each other and enjoyed being together, and that reasons for this mutual attraction were as varied as the individuals involved.

POPULAR INDIVIDUALS

There were some characteristics which related to "companionship votes" from the group as a whole (Table 17). Those people who re-

TABLE 17

Traits Correlating with Frequency of the 204 Residents' Nominations on Companionship Items

Trait	*Correlation Coefficient*	*N*
Use of Senior Center	.48**	204
Participation in planned activities	.18**	204
Unaccounted+passive use of time	–.18*	119
Number of raters who knew him	.29**	204
Happiness	.30**	204
Nervousness	–.25**	204
Talkativeness	.35**	204
Artistic, sensitive nature	.27**	204
Tidiness	.16*	204
Chronological age	–.24**	204
Wechsler I.Q. (Verbal)	.20*	103
Gift-acceptance: poised	.17*	166
Adjectives: % agreement with interviewer	.18**	204

* Significant at the .05 level of confidence.
** Significant at the .01 level of confidence.

ceived many votes tended to spend much time in the Senior Community Center, using it in an informal way as a recreation area. To a lesser extent they participated more than the average resident in the planned activities that went on in the Center, such as formal meetings and organized programs. Diaries showed less time spent passively or sleeping or not accounted for in any way.

People with more "friendship" votes were better known to the nine staff members who were asked to make the trait ratings. Moreover, these staff members (plus the two interviewers) tended to rate them as happy, talkative, artistically sensitive, tidy, and not easily upset or made nervous. Generally they were younger and brighter. According to the ratings made when they were presented with tokens of thanks for their participation in this study, they were more poised in that situation than was the average resident. Their self-concepts seemed to be more realistic, as indicated by the per cent agreement of their self-description with that of the interviewer, both using the adjective check list.

LEADERS

Activity and sociability scores were related to leadership scores in approximately the same way as to companionship scores, with a few exceptions (Table 18). Leadership was not correlated with taking part in planned activities in the Senior Community Center. Leaders tended to use the ground floor area for informal recreation, as did the people with many "friendship" nominations. Both spent much time there playing dominoes or cards or pool, watching television, or simply visiting with others. However, those people most often perceived as leaders did not participate more than the average resident in the planned programs and more formal activities of the Center.

Like people with many "companionship" nominations, leaders were known by more of the raters, and their ratings on the behavior traits were similar. Leaders, like populars, showed closer than average agreement of self-description with interviewer description on the adjective check list.

Similar, too, was their tendency to show less time unaccounted for in their diaries, or recorded as something like "just sat." However, leaders were more likely either to have a job or other regular commitment of time, or to be desirous of having one. Another possible index of greater forcefulness and drive among leaders is the TAT score obtained by taking the ratio of verbs to nouns used by the

TABLE 18

Traits Correlating with Frequency of the 204 Residents' Nominations on Leadership Items

Trait	*Correlation Coefficient*	*N*
Use of Senior Center informally	.39**	204
Number of Raters Who Knew Him	.25**	204
Happiness	.23**	204
Nervousness	−.20**	204
Talkativeness	.29**	204
Artistic, Sensitive Nature	.23**	204
Tidiness	.15*	204
Unaccounted+passive use of time	−.18*	119
Regular Responsibility Score	.19**	204
TAT: Ratio of Verbs to Nouns	.24*	111
Adjectives: % Agreement with Interviewer	.14*	204
Wechsler I.Q. (verbal)	.21*	103
Education	.18*	204

* Significant at the .05 level of confidence.
** Significant at the .01 level of confidence.

person in telling his three stories. This score was significantly related to leadership nominations, and not to friendship nominations.

An interesting difference relates to brightness and education. Leaders tended to be both brighter and better educated than average, while popularity on a companionship basis was related to I.Q. but not to amount of education. Intelligence seemed to be an advantage, both to being liked as a person and to being perceived as a leader. However, while residents would rather be led by a person with more education, this did not affect their selection of friends.

Leadership, like friendship, had a variety of styles. One approach to its understanding is to view the relationship between elective office in the organization of residents and nominations on the sociometrics.

RESIDENT ORGANIZATION OFFICERS[2]

The president of the residents' organization received the highest sociometric score on leadership. However, he received no nomi-

[2] The material in this section has been changed to protect the identity of individuals.

nations on "companionship" items. Apparently residents did not seek his company, though nearly everyone would put his name forward if leadership were needed. The number of times his name appeared on leadership items increased from sociometric to sociometric. His election as president occurred prior to sociometric data collection. No doubt visibility as president of their organization, and presiding officer at the meetings, contributed to his almost unanimous selection as leader after people had been in the building nine months, but there was probably more to it than that.

He had been a typical successful "salesman," and quickly brought himself to the notice of other residents by his outgoing, back-slapping approach to them. Perhaps also as in his salesman days, and unlike many of the men, he impressed his name upon those he met. However, he was somewhat overbearing in his relationships with others, tending to monopolize conversations and to determine group activities. People did not immediately think of him as a comfortable companion, but he was highly valued by other residents as a "smart" person who could "get things done," even should this involve manipulation of Plaza management when there was misunderstanding or conflict of interest. ("He can even 'jolly up' ——— ——— [a staff member]".)

The secretary of the resident organization had a similar pattern of sociometric choices: a top score on leadership and no votes as a friend or companion. This woman, an ex-school teacher who had been married but who insisted upon being called "Miss," prided herself on her "direct approach." As one of the interviewers commented: "When she says 'Hop!' everybody does. No one dares question her." But interviewers noticed that people tended to disappear at the approach of her purposeful stride unless they needed her to represent them to another resident or a member of the Housing Authority staff.

The treasurer presented quite a different picture of interpersonal relationships. This man, always dressed in shades of brown and tan, was hardly ever seen outside his apartment by the interviewers. His neighbors also commented on his love of isolation. It is not clear how enough other residents became aware of his accountancy experience to elect him treasurer. On the final sociometric he received no companionship nominations and only two on leadership items (as compared to over one hundred each for the president and for the secretary), and perhaps the main reason for these was the familiarity of his name on account of his treasurership. He did an excellent job with the organization funds, having been a bookkeeper all his life. Generally, residents were grateful for his efficiency in their behalf, but they perceived his role in the organization as one of routine competency rather than of leadership. His name did not occur to them in connection with sociable activities.

In addition to these general officers were two representatives from each floor who, with the officers, sometimes met with members of the building management about matters of concern to the resident group. Leadership and friendship scores for these sixteen people showed no consistency. Neither the basis for their election, nor the effect of their performance of duties as floor representatives fell into a pattern discernible in sociometric nominations.

One floor representative had almost as many leadership votes as the president and secretary, and in addition was one of the people most frequently nominated on the friendship items. She was a well-liked and much respected member of the Plaza community. Her life was not, and had not been, a bed of roses, but she managed always to see a bright side. For example, her husband was hopelessly and lingeringly ill, and she spent several hours each day visiting him in the hospital, yet she always returned to the Plaza with a smiling face and a joke to tell. She looked fifty rather than seventy, with a good figure and an attractive face. People liked her because she was fun to be around and admired her because they knew she had more right than most of them to be gloomy.

Another floor representative, who received no leadership and only three companionship nominations, was in a somewhat similar situation except that her husband was becoming confused in his thinking rather than being physically ill. A meek, quiet, sweet little person, she would do anything for a friend, and was dearly treasured by the few she had. However, she was so retiring that it was difficult for people to get to know her.

A big, robust, talkative hail-fellow-well-met, much like the president except not so capable, received only one leadership nomination; a female floor representative who was involved in all sorts of leadership activities outside the Plaza, but who was in the Plaza so seldom that few knew her, also received only one vote.

Generally, floor representatives who received many friendship nominations on sociometrics were physically attractive, had a good sense of humor, were endowed with friendly dispositions, were considerate of other people, and went out of their way to be cooperative and helpful. Those who were nominated for leadership roles, whether or not they held office in the organization, were forceful and intelligent people who could get things done. Some leaders were popular as companions. Others were not. No consistent relationship was discerned between election as floor representative and nomination on the sociometric questionnaire. Elections were held early in residency, because the organization was intended to facilitate adjustment and acquaintance. The sociometric responses used in this section of the report were obtained after the group had been living in the Plaza for about nine months, and so they are based on more general acquaintance among residents. Subsequent elections might more closely resemble sociometric choices.

Summary

In summary, according to the sociometric indexes, the residents of Victoria Plaza showed no reluctance and experienced no difficulty in forming new relationships. The ways in which they went about achievement of this end, and the bases for choice of the particular people they selected, were highly individualistic. Characteristics of the building itself, and of the location of the individual's apartment within it, seemed to have no appreciable effect on social activity. Apparently determinative were personality and behavioral characteristics of the people involved, which would allow prediction regarding the likelihood of an applicant's becoming a popular resident or playing a leadership role, but which would not foretell the particular intimates any person might later select.

CHAPTER 9

Measures of Tenant Morale or Adjustment

GENERALLY HIGH MORALE and good adjustment among residents of the Plaza were suggested in the preceding chapters which report their evaluations of Victoria Plaza and its Senior Center, the patterns of change in attitude and behavior that were different for residents and for unsuccessful applicants, and the proliferation of stable social bonds among tenants.

This chapter and the two following it deal with differences in "morale" or "adjustment" among residents of Victoria Plaza and with efforts to identify characteristics of applicants which predict these individual variations. Such information may supplement legal requirements when the number of applicants for public housing exceeds the number of available units and suggest admission criteria for privately financed facilities.

Problems in Selection of Residents

During long months of construction on Victoria Plaza, Housing personnel continued to work over their files, reviewing old applications and processing new ones. After qualifications were checked, there remained the task of informing the ineligible. When completion of the building became imminent and Housing personnel were confronted with the necessity for notifying those who could get ready to move, they had nearly as many qualified and eager applicants as would fill two such residences.

Evidence presented in previous chapters leaves little doubt that the Housing Authority succeeded admirably in choosing initial occupants. However, selection was an excruciating task for those involved. It is one thing to turn a person away because he does not meet requirements; quite another to choose between two equally well qualified.

Group differences between applicants who moved to the Plaza and those who did not were few, and those which existed were about as likely to reverse formal selection policy as to follow it (see Chapter 5). These facts suggest that, after the initial eligibility screening, Housing Authority standards were of little additional use to admissions people charged with the task of eliminating nearly half the qualified applicant group. Perhaps, beyond the first screening, selection might as well have been at random. If so, this should be ascertained so that selectors might be relieved of the burden of trying to improve on chance. On the other hand, if there are additional characteristics of individuals which make some of them even slightly better risks as tenants, effort should turn to putting this information into the hands of selection personnel.

It is probably true in most urban centers, as in San Antonio, that this type of dwelling is not available at present for all interested people in the older age group. To maximize the usefulness of existing facilities it would seem wise to admit those most likely to be happy in them and to fit into the kind of social environment provided.

From the individual's point of view it is no kindness, in the long run, to move him into a situation which makes demands he cannot or does not want to meet. By moving he may have "burned his bridges," leaving himself with no recourse but to stay. Generally, people seeking apartments in Victoria Plaza did not have many alternatives. Some applicants in substandard houses were even more worried about the possibility of losing these residences than they were about their inadequacy. Similar fear of being evicted by a landlady determined the secretiveness necessary for some data collection sessions. Few people in this group could afford to "try out" Victoria Plaza, retaining an option on another residential possibility.

Because of the constant proximity of residents and, to some extent, the group living which is a consequence of the structure and administration of such a building, it is requisite that "misfits" not be included, and that residents be compatible. An unhappy or antisocial person may have little impact on his neighbors in a cottage-style community, or even in the anonymity of the typical commercial apartment house. Victoria Plaza, with a Senior Community Center on the ground floor, and a Resident Organization with officers and floor representatives, provided quite a different social context.

It is possible to get some idea of characteristics conducive to positive adjustment in Victoria Plaza by considering its first group of residents. Generally delighted at the outset, they continued, after living in the Plaza for a year or more, to be almost euphorically happy. Some criticized features of the building, but they usually did so with a view toward improving plans for future construction. Overwhelmingly they valued the clean, beautiful surroundings and modern conveniences. Irritations between tenants were relatively minor and were far outweighed by the enjoyment of social contact. While staff members had serious difficulty with one person, and occasionally observed or received complaints about annoying behavior or personal antagonisms, the adjustment of residents seemed much less a problem than did community liaison. This is clearly documented in the day book[1] kept by the social group worker in charge of the Senior Community Center.

Nevertheless, though "maladjustment" was so rare as to be almost nonexistent, there were discernable differences in the degree and quality of "adjustment." While nearly all individuals would score on the "positive side," there was a range.

Mention has already been made of the man whose violations of sexual and modesty mores were so flagrant that other residents insisted he be asked to leave, and of the other who was credited with introducing roaches to the Plaza. They were the extremes among a minority of residents whose ways of life offended their neighbors.

Dissatisfied tenants were similarly infrequent. After living in the Plaza for several months, one woman unexpectedly moved out. This one spontaneous removal was consistent with her history of frequent changes in place of residence. In a few months she returned, pleading to be readmitted. Many other tenants were free with criticisms of the building, its other occupants, and its staff. But criticism is not equivalent to unhappiness. Freedom to voice minor dissatisfactions may be

[1] Made available through the courtesy of Dorothy O'Neill.

requisite for good morale. However, satisfaction ranged all the way from praising Victoria Plaza as "Heaven on earth" to acceptance of it as the best available place to live.

Life in the Plaza seemed to provide total solution for the problems of some residents, but it was not a panacea for all. Extreme examples are the dramatic change for the better in the woman described in the first chapter, and the deterioration of another woman over the same period.

At the time of the first interview, no one would have known that she was in her seventies. A large woman, but beautifully proportioned and with splendid carriage, she was perfectly groomed, with silver-gray hair done in a becoming and up-to-date style, and peaches-and-cream skin which was artfully and tastefully made up. Delightful as her appearance was, her manner matched it. Alert, widely read, genuinely interested in people, this was a most charming woman.

She enjoyed her job, which involved direct selling, and knew, furthermore, that it helped her resist the temptation of too much alcohol. She had postponed retirement as long as possible, and was delighted at admission to the Plaza, particularly because it would be approximately coincident with forced retirement. It was her hope that the beautiful surroundings and the companionship of other people would provide the stimulus for sobriety and good grooming which even part-time work after age sixty-five had supplied.

Unfortunately, it did not. She began to anesthetize herself more frequently with highballs, later with cheaper wine. She had to be hospitalized, at one time, for a "heart attack" which was generally assumed among her neighbors to have been alcoholic. The last time her interviewer called on her she was wearing a mussed, misshapen, faded housedress from which buttons were missing. Her hair was stringy, her face puffed and without make-up. The shape of her body had changed—sagged and grown heavy.

As in any situation, some people "adjusted" better than others. There were individual differences in experienced satisfaction with the situation and in social-stimulus value to others within it. Identification of background and personality characteristics related to this variation will allow prediction of adjustment and, thereby, improved tenant selection for the Plaza and similar facilities.

What Is Adjustment?

Even with a consensus on the desirability of locating predictors of "adjustment" or "morale," there is considerable room for disagreement, or at least variation, in regard to the meaning of either term. Each denotes a concept that is, at best, complex and elusive. Both can be defined in terms of social-stimulus value or competence, or of inner satisfaction. Components of any such definition must depend upon the context, and each reflects the point of view of the definer.

All of these uncertainties are accentuated in research with aged people. If old folks converge to stereotyped similarity, reduction of individual differences makes such prediction both difficult and relatively meaningless. On the other hand, aging may not only make a person "more like he was" but also less concerned with what others think of his actions. Then behavior ratings and inner experience of "adjustment" may diverge with age.

Though this has not been determined it is suggested by the literature. Correlations over a twenty-year period are sufficiently high to indicate consistency through time, yet leave room for some change (Kelly, 1955). Though there is some evidence that personality constricts with very old age, there is also indication that, in the process of aging, the variety of activities, emotions, and needs increases up to a point (Hall, Lindzey, 1958). Generally it has been found that score variability among older people exceeds that of any other age group, and there is evidence that some persons show more pronouncedly in old age traits which they evidenced in earlier years.

Decreased monitoring of behavior because of "what others will think" has been pointed out (Aronson, 1960, 1962) and was clearly demonstrated by some people interviewed for this study. "Gentlemen" satisfied lifelong desires by going around in their undershirts despite sour looks and sharp comments. "Sweet old ladies" shocked experienced interviewers, not only by the content of what they said, but also by the language in which it was expressed. Not uncommon were comments like, "Now that I am——years old, I can do and say what I please!" One delightful little woman regretted that she had never been in jail—and it would not be surprising if she yet managed to fill this gap in her experience.

In earlier phases of life their personal desires often were modified, delayed, or sacrificed because of responsibilities to others—particularly to parents, spouses, dependent children, and employers. They tended to feel that their reactions need no longer be limited by the role expectancies for "Mr. Jones' employee," "Mr. Smith's wife," or "Johnny's parent." At last, each could be himself.

Such individuality and desire for richness of experience should not be confused with the much rarer deteriorated and bizarre behavior such as that of the one man expelled from the Plaza. In addition to being grossly filthy in person, dwelling, and speech, he brought prostitutes into his apartment in such a way that other residents could scarcely remain unaware of them. The much larger number simply hungered to live life to its fullest and did not want, merely for conformity's sake, to miss anything. Such potential diversity, however, does argue against any simple definition of adjustment. The equation of inner satisfaction with social-stimulus value is particularly questionable.

Another characteristic of "adjustment" as used here is its specificity to the environmental setting. Though adjustment seems to generalize from one situation to another, and best-adjusted applicants probably became best-adjusted residents, Victoria Plaza was a distinctive environment. One research goal was to discover characteristics of people most likely to adjust to this high-rise apartment building, which was especially designed for a homogeneous age group and which included a "public" Senior Community Center. This may, or may not, be synonymous with prediction of adjustment in general. Morale may, instead, be predicated upon degree of improvement of physical or social surroundings. Or the new environment may even impose novel stresses on a previously well-functioning personality.

Perhaps the most difficult problem of criteria is that of defining adjustment for people past middle-age. Is disengagement superior to involvement, or vice versa? Is resignation or lack of zest necessarily unhealthy in a poor, lonely old person? What is the adjustive physical self-concept for a lame and half-blind octogenarian?

In setting up criterion measures for this study, the planners made every effort to avoid prior judgment regarding components of adjustment as a general concept. This was an investigation of adjustment of older people in a particular type of environment. Relationships of adjustment to such variables as disengagement, activities, sociability, and self-concept were explored, not assumed.

Indexes of Adjustment or Morale

One important decision remained: how was an individual to receive his score on "adjustment to Victoria Plaza?" Establishment of a criterion measure or measures is, of course, prerequisite to any effort to predict the criterion variable. Prior to attempts at using applicants' background information or test scores to forecast residents' morale, it was necessary to state explicitly the procedure for determining the level of each tenant's morale.

Unfortunately, morale or adjustment is not subject to direct measurement. For assessment of such covert variables, recourse is often taken to ratings by people familiar with those being studied (Flyer, 1964).

Interviewers had many contacts with residents during a period of fifteen to eighteen months, collected voluminous information about each one of them, and seemed in excellent position to assess their reactions to the new residence situation. Members of the staffs of both the Housing Authority and the Community Welfare Council had been assigned to the project even earlier and, particularly in the case of Housing Authority personnel, contacts with some people dated back many years. Both staff members and research interviewers could provide well-informed evaluations of the person in his new environment.

Peer judgments are useful as criteria also. They assumed particular importance in this situation involving proximity of residential units and sharing of certain facilities. From one point of view, the opinion of other residents might be accepted as *the* index of adjustment. However, peer judgments may not coincide with those of management or research workers. As one man said in response to a staff member's derogatory comment about another's chewing tobacco: "None of *us* minds it—and she doesn't live here."

Objectivity is, of course, one favorable characteristic in any criterion measure. Subjectivity tends to introduce bias and decrease dependability. Plaza and Center staff members, research interviewers, and peers had more or less objective views of residents. However, each of the three groups probably tended to obtain them from rather different viewpoints. Administrators must perceive behavior in light of institutional goals and plans; janitorial staff in terms of overall maintenance problems; both in terms of a forty-hour work week.

A resident may exhibit quite different behavior to staff members in different roles. The building manager was overheard to remark, when she in turn happened to overhear a conversation between a tenant and the assistant janitor, "Why I just can't believe that's that sweet little Mrs. ———!"

Occupants generally tended to talk of the adjustment of others in terms of its impact on themselves. People they did not like, they avoided; those whose company they enjoyed and sought were "well adjusted to Victoria Plaza." Also, residents' reactions to each other were in terms of all-day, every-day living together, with little likelihood, or desire, for change. ("That's all right for her to say— she only works here. These people are my neighbors, and I expect they always will be.")

Research staff members had probably the most disinterested view of residents. Though relationships were cordial and even warm, they were limited. Occupants' behavior was instrumental only to the need of the interviewer for information, not for companionship nor for success of a community project which commanded national as well as local attention.

In addition to these viewpoints with varying degrees of objectivity, there was another perspective which is usually considered to have little or no objectivity—that of the person himself. A purely subjective feeling of satisfaction must be accepted as one definition of morale, and persistent unhappiness indicates less than perfect adjustment to one's situation, no matter what other people say.

Each of these different viewpoints seemed a valid one for assessing adjustment: (1) the person's, despite its subjectivity, to provide the inward aspect of morale; (2) his peers', since adjustment involved relationships with other residents; (3) staff members', because morale and adjustment were part of their job; and (4) research workers', because of their relative lack of personal involvement and their fund of information about each person.

Since there seemed adequate reason to expect the four to be different, separate scores were developed for every resident, to represent each approach to his morale or adjustment. This procedure provided opportunity to see whether the differences in viewpoint seriously affected evaluation, or whether ratings of a resident's adjustment were similar, whether made by himself, his neighbors, the staff, or the interviewers.

THE FEELING OF HAPPINESS AS AN INDEX OF MORALE OR ADJUSTMENT

Fortunately for the residents, although disconcerting from a research point of view, most items which were included to obtain self-evaluations of adjustment to Victoria Plaza were useless. Nine months after the Plaza was opened, and again in the final interview, subjects were asked to rate their satisfaction with Victoria Plaza on a seven-point scale. In the first case nearly 90 per cent indicated satisfaction while only one person expressed extreme dissatisfaction. In the second, only one (the same) woman's reaction was unfavorable, and every one of the other residents said he was satisfied, most of them extremely pleased.

On the assumption that "feet speak more clearly than voices," moving out of the Plaza and the number of moves within the building were set up as indexes of maladjustment or dissatisfaction. However, practically all transfers from one apartment to another were made because the person no longer qualified for so large an apartment after the death of a spouse or sibling. Too few people moved out of the Plaza to make this a useful criterion: five died and one required hospital care; only one person was so obnoxious that he was asked to leave, and another left in a huff.

Self-description as "contented" or "dissatisfied" in the final interview was another prospective criterion. Here again, response distributions made the item useless. Ninety per cent were "contented" and only 5 per cent "dissatisfied." Obviously there were differences in satisfaction among residents. However, they were within a narrow range of pleasure in their improved situation, within which the simple rating scales were not adequate to make useful distinctions. Some of the "dissatisfied" felt so with themselves, rather than the Plaza. For example, the attractive woman who had deteriorated into a "wino" blamed only herself for being unable to accept retirement from her job. In regard to the Plaza she experienced gratitude and guilt.

No doubt these responses reflected consistent, genuine satisfaction. Contributing to the extremity of the ratings was the inevitable tendency of residents to compare their situation in Victoria Plaza with that at the time they were applicants, or with what it would be if they were evicted. Efforts to have them use as a reference point either "compared to others" or "compared to what you would like to be" were not successful. In their view, anyone not satisfied in Victoria Plaza had only himself to blame, and no one wanted to identify himself with such ingrates. ("Sure it's not perfect, but it's near to Heaven as I'll get on this earth—and anybody who don't say so ought to get the H—— out!" "I'll never complain about a thing; the only ones who do are the people who don't keep their places nice. You ought to see some of those apartments, dirty and not fixed up at all.") Comparison with the ideal seemed foolish and childish, since realistically they could look forward to nothing better. Comparison with other residents was evaded. Contrast with pre-Victoria Plaza living was extreme and favorable.

Another index of resident satisfaction, and one which had special merit, did not materialize. The highly skilled social group worker who was director of the Senior Community Center planned to keep a day-by-day account of complaints, suggestions, and comments which residents brought to her. In addition to its other obvious values, it was to provide for this study an objective, even numerical, index of resident dissatisfaction. However, pressure on this staff member's time was so great that it was not possible for her to keep such a record. During that first year, liaison with other community agencies was a full-time job, as her day-book attests.[2]

The only self-report indicator of adjustment to Victoria Plaza which had a statistically useful distribution of scores was the happiness section of the Attitude Survey (Burgess *et al,* 1948). Therefore this measure of satisfaction was used as the criterion of adjustment to Victoria Plaza from the resident's viewpoint.

Its limitations as an index of adjustment to Victoria Plaza should be kept in mind. The items in the scale are listed in Table 19. Obviously they do not elicit direct evaluation of happiness in the new residential situation, though it seems reasonable to suppose that responses reflect it.

Limiting, too, is the range of answers, even here. The responses of residents also, in percentages for each item, are given in Table 19. Obviously, this was a generally happy group of people, or at least they gave responses congruent with happiness. Further indication of the narrow range and the bias toward happiness is given by the distribution of overall scores, derived according to the standard instructions of the scale's authors, which is given in Table 20.

The criterion of happiness finally used is not one of the measures designed for this purpose. Others were discarded because they did not differentiate among people. Though the one used shows a more adequate range of scores, it suffers somewhat from the same fault. Fortunately or unfortunately, depending upon point of view, this situation probably reflected homogeneity of mood of residents as much as inadequacy of measuring instruments.

[2] *Ibid.*

TABLE 19

The 204 Residents' Responses to Attitude Survey Items on Happiness (Percentage Distributions)

	Agree	*Disagree*	*Don't Know*
1. This is the dreariest time of my life.	10	90	0
2. I am just as happy as when I was younger.	59	35	6
3. My life could be happier than it is now.	30	59	11
4. I seem to have less and less reason to live.	6	91	3
5. These are the best years of my life.	26	66	8
6. My life is full of worry.	9	91	0
7. My life is so enjoyable that I almost wish it would go on forever.	52	41	7

POPULARITY WITH OTHER RESIDENTS AS A MEASURE OF ADJUSTMENT

One of the Housing Authority's stated aims was to select individuals with capacity for the type of community living maximized by characteristics of the building. The person employed by the Com-

TABLE 20

The 204 Residents' Scores on the Happiness Section of the Attitude Survey (Percentage Distribution)

Standard Scale Score	*% of Incidence*
+3	16
+2	33
+1	19
0	19
–1	7
–2	4
–3	2
Total	100

munity Welfare Council for the Senior Center in the Plaza was a social worker trained in group work. One of her responsibilities was to facilitate group activities and development of healthy social relationships. Lack of interpersonal contact had been a major complaint among applicants.

Although not equated with any other factor—personal happiness for example—acceptance into the peer group of other residents may, for some purposes, be the most suitable "definition" of adjustment. It might not differ widely from residents' ratings of each other on "adjustment to Victoria Plaza." Acquaintance with a person tended to be equated with his adjustment: one's friends were obviously well adjusted, acquaintances were doing all right, but there was some question about strangers.

The score used as an index of group acceptance, or popularity, was the total number of times an individual was nominated by other residents on all questions in the third sociometric questionnaire (Appendix A). The range of scores was adequate, running from zero to well over one hundred.

Scores on the third sociometric were used, rather than those on the first or second for two reasons. The time of data collection was closest to that for the other adjustment criteria, and it allowed maximum opportunity for people in the Plaza to become acquainted. The third sociometric was administered about nine months after the first people moved into the building. Though this is not a direct estimation of "adjustment to Victoria Plaza," it may actually be a more direct indicator of one important aspect of overall "adjustment": broad and favorable interpersonal relationships within the resident group.

The strength of this criterion was somewhat curtailed by the absence of predictor information for several extremely popular people. It was mentioned earlier that names of fifteen applicants were added after the initial period of interviewing had ended and while data collectors were trying to obtain as many test responses as possible before completion of the building and announcement of its first occupants. Twelve of the fifteen moved into apartments immediately, and five of these were among the residents with the highest number of sociometric nominations. This, of course, dilutes what can be said about the most popular residents. Since these people were not interviewed or tested as applicants, no predictions regarding their popularity could be made. This elimination of people at one extreme of the score distribution would reduce the apparent relationship between predictors and this criterion measure.

ADJUSTMENT OF RESIDENTS AS PERCEIVED BY STAFF MEMBERS

Evaluations of the morale and adjustment of residents of such a facility as Victoria Plaza by those professional people responsible for it are of particular importance. These individuals are concerned with such basic characteristics in the resident group, and are in position to observe behavior related to them. In addition, these administrative personnel are the ones who make decisions about residents or prospective residents, decisions based on their evaluations regarding morale and adjustment.

The manager of Victoria Plaza and the director of the Senior Community Center located on its ground floor were asked to rate each resident on a seven-point scale of adjustment to the Plaza (Appendix A) after all other data had been collected. The manager rated almost every resident. Though the Center director's ratings were disappointingly incomplete, it seemed desirable to include her judgments in the criterion, not only because of her position, but also because she was a skilled social worker. Unfortunately, community contacts and tours of the Center required so much of her time during the first year that she was not sufficiently well acquainted with many of the residents to rate them. Each resident's criterion score was the average of the two staff members' ratings of him, or the one rating which was available.

ADJUSTMENT OF RESIDENTS AS RATED BY RESEARCH WORKERS

Because of the limitation of their involvement compared to that of residents and of staff members, interviewers were assumed to have a more objective view of behavior and relationships in Victoria Plaza. Having collected voluminous information about residents, and having had contact with them at intervals over the period of more than a year, they were well informed about these people.

Both of the interviewers completed ratings on practically all of the residents. Their judgments were combined into an average score for each ratee.

The Four Views on Adjustment

There were, then, four separate definitions of adjustment of residents, starting from the assumption that this is not necessarily a unitary concept, but that an individual's "adjustment" depends in part upon the index selected for its measurement. The first task, after deriving the four scores for each individual, was to assess their similarity. In case of near identity, it would be expedient to eliminate three and use the one measure easiest to obtain in future situations of a similar nature, or to provide a more reliable criterion measure by combining them.

It is obvious from Table 21 that, while the various indexes of adjustment to Victoria Plaza have something in common, they are by no means interchangeable. All intercorrelations are positive and significant beyond the 5-per-cent level of confidence,[3] but the per cent of variance[4] in one criterion attributable to that in another ranges from three to fifty-eight, justifying the decision to use several indexes of adjustment, and requiring continuation of their treatment as separate.

For example, popularity among peers bears little relationship to happiness. Knowing a resident's sociometric score would give almost

TABLE 21

Relationships among Adjustment Criterion Measures on the 204 Residents

	Happiness (Self)	*Popularity (Peers)*	*Adj. to Vic. Pl. (Interviewers)*
Popularity (Peers)	.16*		
Adj. to Vic. Pl. (Interviewers)	.52**	.31**	
Adj. to Vic. Pl. (Administrators)	.27**	.49**	.43**

* Significant at the .05 level.
** Significant at the .01 level.

[3] Such a correlation coefficient would occur by chance alone only five times out of a hundred, so it indicates that the relationship is probably a genuine one likely to be found again in a similar situation.

[4] Another way to look at the relationship between two variables is to see how much information one gives about the other. If the correlation coefficient is zero, prediction of one, based on knowledge of the other, is no better than chance. As the correlation coefficient increases, prediction of one, based on information about the other, improves. The per cent of variability in one score which can be predicated, or accounted for, by knowledge of the other, is the square of the correlation coefficient.

no information about how happy he was. Conversely, knowledge of his happiness score would not appreciably improve a guess as to his popularity. This is not surprising, since popularity was not the goal of every resident. On the contrary, a few persons sought admission to Victoria Plaza primarily to escape constant "togetherness" and to gain freedom to carry out the rest of their lives according to their own desires. One put it: "For the first time in my life I don't have to please other people," and another: "Thank goodness, they put me at the end of the corridor so it is easy to be alone."

Social isolation and unpleasant interpersonal relationships were important motivators for making application to Victoria Plaza. Generally, residents immediately set about making friends within the building, and they continued to be sociable over the period of observation. Still, it was clear that "popularity" was not a universal requisite for happiness. In addition to the minority who preferred to be alone, a much larger number basked in the friendships of a few others and neither sought nor would have been gratified by "popularity" among the many.

As anticipated, residents' popularity among their peers was more closely related to administrators' estimates of their adjustment to Victoria Plaza than to residents' evaluations of their own happiness. This is understandable, since those responsible for the program felt that its goal was not only individual gratification but also support of the group. Interviewers' ratings of adjustment seem to have been influenced more by popularity than were residents' feelings of happiness, though less than administrators' judgments of adjustment. Interviewers' estimates of adjustment had more in common with residents' feelings about their own happiness than did administrators' ratings.

The directors of the Plaza and the Center, quite understandably, did not consider as optimally adjusted those people who were delighted to have, at last, a little corner of their own in which to stay and do as they wished. Research interviewers were more likely to judge such a person well adjusted, since his own needs were being well met. On the other hand, administrators probably tended to give a higher "adjustment" rating to the person who forced himself, perhaps at some private cost, to participate in group activities, because they felt he had been successful in meeting the demands of his situation.

Another indication of the difference between "adjustment" ratings by administrators and by interviewers is provided by the fact that, on various subsamples of residents, the correlation of interviewer's with interviewer's, and those of administrator's to administrator's, tended to be about .50, while those between administrator-interviewer pairs were near .20.

As an additional comment on the importance of viewpoint, it should be pointed out that two items expected to measure about the same phenomenon and asked of the same observers were ratings of adjustment to Victoria Plaza and ratings of residents' happiness (Appendix A). These turned out to be obviously not synonymous (Table 22). They were more nearly equated, evidently, in the view of interviewers than in that of administrators. Apparently, again, the difference in viewpoint of the rater was important. This community was planned, not only for the happiness of individual old persons, though that was highly desired, but also for a particular sort of semigroup living which would give mutual satisfaction to all residents of the Plaza.

Surely happiness as judged from the outside was not identical with that experienced from within (see Table 22). The intercorrelation matrix for the happiness rating, as expected, showed no consistent differences between subtypes of raters, so the score used was the average of them all.

It would seem that while adjustment to Victoria Plaza held a different connotation for administrators than for data collectors, "happiness" had a common meaning to them. Though interrater agreements were satisfactory on this item, pooled ratings did not mirror

TABLE 22

Relationship of the Adjustment Indexes to Ratings of Happiness for the 204 Residents

	*Happiness Rating**
Adjustment to Vic. Pl. (Interviewers)	.76**
Adjustment to Vic. Pl. (Administrators)	.43**
Popularity (Peers)	.30**
Happiness (Self)	.25**

* This score is the average of ratings by administrative, service, and research personnel. Differences between raters in the various roles, in their perceptions of residents' happiness, were neither predicted nor apparent in inter-rater correlations.

** Significant at the .01 level.

the self-evaluations of residents. Observers who made the ratings, though they had different relationships with residents and different views of their adjustment in the Plaza (as indicated by rating intercorrelations on that item), agreed fairly well with each other in judgments of residents' happiness. Their views did not coincide with those of the residents.

For both administrators and interviewers, but particularly in the case of research personnel, evaluation of the happiness of a resident was closely related to perception of his adjustment to the Plaza. Apparently they felt that being happy was a normal consequence, or an important aspect, of good adjustment. However, the relationship holds up only when their ratings of residents' happiness are used in conjunction with their observations of adjustment. Correlations between adjustment ratings and residents' expressions of their own happiness are considerably lower (see Table 22).

Summary

Comparison of various indexes showed that even "adjustment to Victoria Plaza" was not the same thing for research and administrative personnel, to say nothing of the disparities of each of these from happiness and popularity. For this reason the search for predictors of "adjustment" was really not one search, but four. The next two chapters describe that process. Chapter 10 explains the selection of items that were tried as predictors; Chapter 11 reports how successful they were, singly and in combinations, in predicting the four different indexes of morale or adjustment.

CHAPTER 10

Methodology of Prediction of Morale or Adjustment

ADVANTAGES of being able to predict an applicant's success in such a situation as that of Victoria Plaza have been discussed. Prior to analysis of the 1960 data, four criteria of adjustment were defined, as discussed in Chapter 9. At the same time a set of prospective predictors was listed. Their selection is discussed in this chapter. A year after the predictions were made, criterion data (happiness, popularity, administrator rating, and interviewer rating) were collected, and the predictive efficiency of the system was tested.

Selection of Prediction Items

As a first step in the attempt to predict adjustment a year or more later, three people familiar with the situation at Victoria Plaza were asked to indicate characteristics of prospective residents which they considered most important in attempting to forecast adjustment there. For this purpose no distinction was made among the four measures of adjustment. Each judge was given a list of items on which data would be available for the entire group and was asked to check the twenty-four variables he considered most relevant to adjustment in Victoria Plaza. This meant, unfortunately, elimination of such possible predictors as the Wechsler-Bellevue, MMPI, Sentence Completion, TAT, and time-diary scores, since time had not allowed administration of these instruments to everyone.

To maintain statistical respectability, it was predetermined that about two dozen predictor variables would be appropriate, considering the number of people on whom measures would be available.[1] After the three judges had made their selections, working independently, the three sets of variables were compared. Those checked by at least two judges comprised a list of twenty-two predictors.

These twenty-two measures fell into categories based upon the effort and cost involved in obtaining data: (1) those typically on application blanks, (2) additional items collected in this study during an interview, but which probably could be converted to pencil-and-paper form, (3) those which inevitably involve the judgment of an interviewer.

Five personality or behavior-trait ratings were added as a fourth category. In a strict temporal sense this was not prediction, since information would become available only concurrently with the adjustment measures. Also, these data were collected on residents, not applicants, though the traits probably are fairly stable and enduring. However, it seemed of interest to investigate relationships between adjustment and these variables.

Another limitation on these measures of personality traits is that they were obtained through ratings by people who had had at least a year to observe the residents. However, Tupes and Christal (1958), using the personality-trait-rating instrument which was adapted for purposes of this study, present evidence that length of acquaintanceship did not affect the factor structure, from group to group, where length of acquaintanceship varied from three days to nearly a year. This suggests that such ratings could be made validly on short acquaintance. The trait ratings were included to see whether knowledge of them added significantly to prediction of adjustment in the Plaza. If so, an effort could be made to select or develop instruments—rating scores or any other type—suitable to an admission situation.

The efficiency of each category of predictor item was assessed separately, as well as in combination with others. In any practical selection situation, the contribution of a predictor must be weighed against its price in time and money. Little extra effort on the part of the staff would be required to use routine application-blank information, should it promise to improve selection of tenants. If a significant

[1] Limitation of the number of predictors in relation to the number of people guards the dependability of conclusions drawn from the results.

contribution is made by interview items, an attempt could be made to convert them to "cheaper" paper-and-pencil form. Should interviewers' evaluations make a unique contribution, the feasibility of adding such observers to the staff might be considered. If personality-trait ratings significantly improve prediction of adjustment, development of measuring instruments which could be used with applicants would be warranted.

Also, it was important to avoid recommendation of items which essentially overlap or which make the same contribution to predictive efficiency. For example, it is possible that objective interview items and subjective interviewer judgments both improve tenant selection, but that when you have applied one, addition of the second has no further effect. If such turned out to be the case, a selection staff might choose either to use only the objective items, or to throw away that information and use only subjective judgments made during the interview.

Below are the predictor items, grouped according to the "expense" probably involved in obtaining information. The statistical plan included viewing the relationship to each index of adjustment of (1) each item singly, (2) each category or "cost level" of items, and (3) the various combinations achieved by successively adding, to the "cheapest" group of items, each "higher-priced" group, one at a time, until all items were included.

Application-blank Type Predictors

The first category of predictor items was composed of inexpensive or even "free" information which appears routinely on application blanks:

1. Chronological age
2. Education (as indicated by the highest school grade attended)
3. Marital status (comparing those married and living with their spouses to all others, whether single, widowed, divorced, or separated)
4. Monthly income
5. Job level of the work done by the man (or by the husband of the woman) during most of his working years

All of these items are objective and involve the kind of information people are accustomed to furnishing when filling out any kind of form. These data could be available to Housing Authority personnel, or to management in any similar situation, at little or no extra effort.

Scoring is straightforward, and utilization in a selection system could be handled by a clerk.

Questionnaire Predictors

Items making up the second category probably could, for economy, be converted to pencil-and-paper form for the interviewee to fill out. Results presented here were obtained by excellent interviewers, and the feasibility of duplicating them without the interpersonal contact would have to be tested. However, the items selected were not among those which interviewers believed would be difficult for applicants, with the exception of some Attitude Survey questions. In regard to those, difficulty arose from the ambiguous form of the statement, rather than from inherent item difficulty or reluctance on the part of applicants. Except for the few with poor vision, motor disturbances, or handicapping nervousness, most of this group of applicants could have answered the questions on paper.

These items were potential predictors of adjustment in the new housing situation, not as necessarily realistic reports of applicants' histories or attitudes, but simply as their verbal behavior at the time of applicancy. For example, in regard to the second item below, the attempt was not to predict future adjustment on the basis of the actual number of friends during childhood. The task was to determine whether the type of person who reports having had many friends as a teenager will adjust to a new living situation more adequately than a person who says he had few. Even on items dealing with current behavior and attitudes, there is no assumption that response reflects reality. There is only the prediction that the verbal behavior itself is related to adjustment capacity.

1. NUMBER OF "CLOSE FRIENDS"

Responses to this question ran from zero to over one hundred. On the hunch that either extreme may be indicative of difficulty in interpersonal relationships, this score was squared.[2] The prediction was that applicants who reported about the average number of "close friends" would be more successful as residents of the Plaza than would applicants naming very few or extremely many.

[2] This manipulation allows for a curvilinear relationship between number of "close friends" and the criterion measure, with one change of direction in the curve expressing the relationship.

2. NUMBER OF FRIENDS DURING THE EARLY TEENS

The interview included questions on the number of friends of the same sex and of the opposite sex. Answers were tabulated in terms of applicants' recollecting that they had more than most people, about the average number, or fewer than usual among their contemporaries. The score used here was the average of responses to the items about boy friends and girl friends.

There is, of course, no way to know how closely the reminiscences of these people, so many years later, reflected the reality of their youthful years. However, the item was included on the basis of two beliefs. First, outgoing, friendly people probably will be happiest in the close, almost community-type living imposed by the physical form of Victoria Plaza, and second, this trait very likely remains fairly constant through life.

Perhaps a question about long-ago could be answered more truthfully, since there would be less need for defensiveness. The number of friends at present was arbitrarily determined, to a considerable extent, by physical and social conditions in which applicants were living. Responses to questions about previous years might give clearer indication of capacity, willingness, or desire for friendships than would factual account of interpersonal contacts at present. Readiness might be more important in predicting social success when moved into a situation affording different opportunity for it.

There is no assumption that people's responses tally with realities of the time they were growing up, but only that they may reflect interest in sociability and confidence in their own competence in this area, perhaps better than similar questions about current times.

3. CHURCH ATTENDANCE

Religion may be an escape for people unable to adjust successfully to the demands of life, or a source of strength which enables individuals to meet life's problems more adequately. The latter point of view was accepted here, and a positive relationship was predicted between strength of religious belief and future adjustment in the Plaza.

Though it has obvious inadequacies as an index of religiousness, church attendance has the advantages of objectivity and directness. Among this group of people considerable effort was usually required to get to church. Applicants received disappointingly little personal attention from people connected with churches, so their motives in attendance would not be primarily social. Few could use church as a place to make an impressive appearance. As a matter of fact, a number said they did not go to church as often as they would like, because they did not have appropriate clothes or because they could not make an adequate contribution of money and had no skill which was valued by other members of the congregation. It seemed likely that those people who attended church regularly did so out of some essentially religious need or conviction, and that this might well be related to their capacity for adjustment.

4. PREFERENCE FOR ACTIVE, SOCIAL PASTIMES

During the initial interview each applicant was asked what he liked to do in his leisure time. Regarding each pastime he mentioned he was asked whether he usually did it alone or with other poeple.

All activities named by applicants were listed in alphabetical order, and two judges rated them as "active" or "passive," and as "solitary" or "social," with nearly 100-per-cent agreement. However, these judges' assignments of activities to the categories "social" and "solitary" were by no means always the same as an applicant's perception of them as activities he pursued "alone" or " with others." Some activities, such as contract bridge, would seem to require other participants. However, one respondent's treasured possession was a gadget which allowed her to play four hands of bridge by herself. On the other hand, several applicants said that napping was one of their favorite pastimes, and that they usually napped with others rather than napping alone.

The score used as an adjustment predictor was compiled by giving each applicant one point for every pastime he named which the judges considered "active" and another point for every one which he said he usually did in the company of other people. This decision was based on the assumption that the person involved knew better than anyone else which things he did sociably and which in solitude. The prediction was that, the more sociable and the more active pastimes an applicant named, the likelier he was to achieve successful adjustment in Victoria Plaza.

5. NEUROTIC-TYPE HEALTH PROBLEMS

In the section of the interview on health, applicants were asked about physical conditions which "bothered" them. Again, two judges working independently agreed completely on those which were likely to indicate neurotic tendencies rather than primarily physiologic ones: sleeplessness, bad dreams, tiring too easily, food not tasting good, feeling blue, nervousness, disliking noise, worrying, and forgetfulness. The total score was simply the number of such conditions a person mentioned. The larger an applicant's score, the worse the chances predicted for his adjustment as a resident.

6. ATTITUDE TOWARD PARENTS DURING THE EARLY TEENS

Relationships with parents are generally accepted as important determinants of character and personality. Teen years were selected for scrutiny because, during this period, intergeneration conflict is most likely. People who recall strong and healthy relationships with their parents at that time probably grew up incorporating few conflictive tendencies and enjoying generally pleasant interpersonal associations. Insofar as self-concept is based on perception of forebears, it too should be more favorable, and further conducive to good adjustment. For the attempt to predict adjustment to Victoria Plaza, an average was taken of the scores (on five-point scales) representing recollection of relationship with father and with mother.

7. ATTITUDE TOWARD ONESELF

The original intent was to use a "self-attitude" score designed for Peck's Sentence Completion Test.[3] However, time ran out before it was possible to obtain data on more than about half of the applicants who were assigned apartments. As a substitute index of self-estimation, an average was taken of scores on three of the Attitude Survey scales: health, present ability to work, and usefulness. Favorable self-concept of applicant was considered conducive to good adjustment; unfavorable self-concept, to poor adjustment.

8. ATTITUDE TOWARD OTHERS

Again because of the absence of sentence-completion responses from so many applicants, the score planned for this purpose was replaced by the average of two Attitude Survey scores: friends and family. Better adjustment was predicted for applicants with positive attitudes toward their families and friends, worse adjustment for those with negative scores.

[3] Article in preparation.

9. DESIRE FOR GROUP MEMBERSHIP

Applicants were asked what groups or organizations they would like to join, supposing such affiliation were possible. Considering the close group-living structured by the Plaza, desire for such membership seemed a favorable indicator for adjustment. For the purpose of prediction, no attention was paid to the type of club, but simply to whether or not the applicant wanted to join one or more.

10. DESIRE FOR ACTIVITIES

In addition to increased availability of other people, moving into the Plaza would open up to residents a variety of lesiure-time activities, which might, but did not necessarily, involve club membership. If one were to get the most out of the new situation, and also if he were to give to it what was considered desirable in the eyes of planners, the resident should be favorably inclined to taking part in various activities. In order to see whether applicants' expressed interest in activties was predictive of later adjustment in the Plaza, an "activities wanted" score was derived for each person. This score was simply the number of activities he mentioned, when asked what things he would like to do if he had the opportunity.

11. AGE IDENTIFICATION

Each person was asked his age group. So many were "middle-aged" that the only statistically sound procedure was to compare them with the relatively few "old," "elderly," and "aged," all taken together. The prediction was that Victoria Plaza would be more suitable to a "middle-aged" person than to another, regardless of calendar years.

12. FEELING ABOUT THE FUTURE

Applicants were asked how they felt about the future. Then they were asked whether they ever thought about the end of life and, if so, what. Responses were easily categorized into those which indicated secure acceptance or eager anticipation, as against those which showed fearful avoidance or apprehension. This predictor was a combination of scores on these two items, with the expectation that people apprehensive about the future and anxious at the thought of dying would not adjust as well to Victoria Plaza as those who felt prepared for the future and unafraid of the thought of death.

Interviewer Evaluations

It seems likely that, with people as alert and capable as these applicants, information regarding items in the previous section could be obtained in a written questionnaire, in most cases. However, on the basis of the applicant's responses and of observations of him during interview and test sessions, the interviewer recorded several judgments of him. It may be that an interview is useful for selection purposes, not only to collect factual information, but to provide opportunity for observation of applicants which will allow trained interviewers to make subjective judgments.

1. CONFUSION

Interviewers were alerted to watch for signs of confusion shown by applicants during the interview and testing contacts. The most common types were confusion in regard to dates, places, and names. Separate ratings of these, each on a five-point scale, were averaged to provide an overall "confusion" rating, which was expected to correlate negatively with later adjustment.

2. DISABILITY

Also to be noted by the interviewer were any signs of disability, such as defective vision, deafness, or crippling, which tended to interfere with interview and testing procedures. The assumption was made that these might also interfere with normal activities of self-care and interpersonal relationship in Victoria Plaza.

3. SENILITY INDEX

At the close of the initial series of contacts with each applicant his interviewer filled out the Senility Index for him, and it was scored in the standard way (Cavan *et al*, 1949). Though the Plaza was designed for older citizens, it was not planned for the senile. Signs of senility, therefore, should contraindicate successful and happy adjustment there.

4. DISENGAGEMENT INDEX

Similarly, the interviewer rated each of his interviewees on the Disengagement Index (Appendix A). Disengagement was predicted to be a deterrent to adjustment in Victoria Plaza. Despite the special safety features and the limitation to older tenants, the design of the building, inclusion of a Senior Community Center, and attitudes surrounding plans for the Plaza, all pointed to an active, interested, sociable clientele.

5. DESIRABILITY AS A TENANT

The interviewer was asked to give, as part of his summary for each applicant, his general evaluation of the person as a potential resident of Victoria Plaza. His statement was translated into a score on a five-point scale and used as one of the predictors.

Trait Ratings

Not available among initial data was some information about applicants which might be predictive of their adjustment in the Plaza. It seemed worthwhile to use estimates collected later, in order to obtain some idea of whether or not effort should be made, in future studies, to include these variables. Personality or behavior-trait ratings were averaged across all of the eleven raters who knew the resident sufficiently well to make a judgment regarding the characteristic (items are given in Appendix A).

Raters were the manager of the Plaza, the director of the Senior Community Center, the latter's secretary, the Public Health nurse, the city recreation worker, and the public librarian assigned to the Plaza, the man in charge of the building's maintenance, his assistant, the night watchman, and the two data collectors. Unlike the judgments of adjustment to the Plaza, there were no consistent differences between raters on these personality or behavior traits.

1. LIKABILITY AS A PERSON

The first item provided at the two extremes of a seven-point scale these reactions: "From a purely personal point of view, I like this person" and "From a purely personal point of view, I dislike this person." This scale was designed to evoke a unitary response to a multiplicity of information and impression about the ratee. It calls for an integrated summary of the total social-stimulus value of the applicant for the rater.

This item was included in the trait-rating schedule for several reasons. For one, it provided opportunity to study rating bias. Interviewers and others might, quite inadvertently, present a more favorable picture of a person to whom they took an immediate liking, and a less favorable view of one who happened to rub them the wrong way. Of course this is a chicken-and-egg problem: they might very well like the person because he had the favorable characteristic. However, these data provide opportunity to test for interrater differences in likable characteristics of ratees, and to see whether these seemed to influence their perceptions of residents.[4] It was placed first among rating items to alert raters to the possibility of bias, in hopes that this would minimize the effect of personal liking on other trait ratings.

The item was included as a predictor for the rather simple reason that people who were well liked by this number and variety of raters would probably be well liked by other people generally. An important predictor of adjustment to Victoria Plaza should be how likable the person seems to others, regardless of the specific traits comprising this social-stimulus value.

In addition, four less general characteriestics expected to bear upon adjustment in the Plaza were used.

2. CONGENIALITY

Residents were rated on a seven-point scale running from "superior" and "above others" (in the sense of snobbishness) to "congenial" with other people.

3. NOSINESS

It was anticipated that undue interest in the affairs of others, and zeal in disseminating such "news," would be handicaps to acceptance among residents, and therefore to adjustment in the Plaza. However, the extent of gossip that developed in the Plaza, and the concern with it, were far beyond expectation.

4. NERVOUSNESS

Another personality characteristic probably relevant to adjustment to community living, and one which should be measurable prior to admission, is the tendency to worry, to be easily upset, to become overwrought, and to be overly sensitive, vs. the ability to maintain one's equilibrium despite distractions and interruptions, and to remain calm.

5. FASTIDIOUSNESS

As concerned as applicants generally were with the ugliness and

[4] Paper in preparation.

unavoidable dirtiness of their living situations, it seemed obvious that they would tend to reject and dislike anyone who was assigned an apartment in Victoria Plaza and who did not keep it and himself clean and attractive.

Two rating items were combined to obtain scores for this last trait. One runs from, "Tidy, overprecise, especially over details. Drives other people to be the same. Strict, fussy, pedantic. Insists on everything being orderly. (In these respects rather 'uncomfortable to live with')" to, "Rather careless of detail, lazy." The other has as one extreme, "Artistically sensitive to surroundings, art. Fastidious, not too easily pleased," and as the other, "Not showing artistic tastes. Not interested in artistic subjects. Insensitive to esthetic effects." In the Personality Trait Rating Instrument (Tupes and Christal, 1958) from which the one for this study was adapted these two ideas were contained in only one item. However, the raters for this study insisted that more than one personality characteristic was involved, and that they could not make sensible ratings on the item, so it was divided into two, to obtain their judgments. Ratings on the two were then combined to produce the predictor score.

In setting up the prediction equation it was assumed that the difficulty was due to inexperience on the part of the raters, since these traits had proved quite stable, through several samples of young adult males (Tupes and Christal, 1959), and the relationship between the two parts of the split item was not yet known for this group.[5] As a further consideration, it was undesirable to use sections of the split item separately, unless necessary, to protect the ratio of predictors to people on whom data were to be available.

First, all twenty-seven characteristics listed above were used jointly to predict adjustment to Victoria Plaza. Accuracy of the prediction was checked against residents' adjustment scores. This process was carried out separately for each criterion of adjustment. In other words, all twenty-seven predictors were used simultaneously to estimate residents' scores on the happiness section of the Attitude Survey. Then the same twenty-seven were used to predict the popularity score on the third sociometric questionnaire. In similar manner, the complete set of predictor variables was used to estimate adjustment ratings made by administrators and those made by research interviewers.

[5] Paper in preparation, presenting interrater agreements and comparing factor analysis with those of Tupes and Christal.

Furthermore, this was carried out in such a way that items were identified in order of the importance of their contributions to the prediction of adjustment. First, the one predictor which would do the best job of estimating adjustment was selected. Then was chosen the one among the remaining twenty-six which, added to the first, would improve prediction most. The third was identified as the item which, taken together with these two, would most benefit predictive efficiency. This process was continued until addition of items did not significantly improve estimation of the adjustment criterion.

The statistical representation of the first step, prediction of an adjustment measure by the one "best" predictor item, was in terms of a zero-order correlation coefficient.[6] The next step involved computation of the multiple-correlation[7] between the two predictor items (the first selected and the one which, added to it, increased the prediction most) and the measure of adjustment.[8] Then a test was made of the statistical significance of the difference between the zero-order correlation and the multiple-correlation coefficient. If addition of the second item improved prediction significantly, that item was recorded, and the search continued for another piece of information among the group of twenty-five items which would further increase the multiple-correlation coefficient. Increase in size of the multiple-correlation coefficient is, of course, indication of improvement in

[6] The zero-order correlation coefficient expresses the degree of relationship between two variables. If there is no relationship the coefficient is zero; perfect relationship would be represented by a coefficient of 1.00.

[7] A multiple-correlation coefficient, similarly to a zero-order correlation coefficient, represents closeness of relationship. It has the same range of size—from zero, which indicates absence of relationship, to 1.00, in case of total agreement. Multiple-correlation differs from zero-order by determining the relationship of one variable to two or more others, simultaneously.

[8] Either zero-order or multiple-correlation coefficients may be interpreted in terms of prediction. In case of no relationship, represented by a coefficient of zero, information regarding scores on one variable helps not a bit in predicting scores on the other. If possession of voter registration shows no relationship to adjustment, then there would be no use in trying to improve selection of residents by inquiring whether applicants were prepared to vote. On the other hand, if income had a correlation of 1.00 with adjustment (which it does not), perfect prediction of residents' adjustment could be made on the basis of applicants' income. Real data do not produce coefficients of 1.00, but the closer a zero-order or a multiple-correlation coefficient approaches the size of 1.00, the more accurate the predictions which can be made on the basis of the variables involved.

accuracy of the selected predictor items in their task of estimating adjustment.

This multiple correlation analysis was used, in addition to the more traditional approach of viewing separately the ability of each item to predict the criterion, because it provides more useful information.[9] Zero-order correlations were computed between each measure of adjustment and every prospective predictor (Appendix D). These indicate strength of relationship between the two, and therefore likelihood or accuracy of predicting one from the other. However, it is not advantageous to consider only one piece of information at a time, when selecting applicants. For example, if both marital status and Senility Index score are known to bear an important relationship to adjustment, selection personnel would prefer to take into consideration both of these characteristics, concurrently, when considering an applicant. Human behavior is multiply determined, in most instances, and multivariate analysis, such as this multiple-correlation technique, assists in viewing it more realistically. The chances of any applicant to succeed in Victoria Plaza were determined by many factors, none operating alone and independently. Multivariate analysis allowed assessment of the simultaneous impact of many.

When only zero-order correlations are available it is not clear how much overlap there is among predictors or, in other words, how many of them are needed. For example, interviewer rating on alertness and I.Q. scores on the Wechsler-Bellevue might each show a sizeable zero-order correlation coefficient with adjustment. However, multiple correlation of the two with adjustment might be no higher, or so little higher that the improvement in prediction would not justify collection of both kinds of information. Then the more "expensive" could be eliminated, with little or no loss of efficiency.

The practical problem is not identification of the one characteristic which shows closest relationship to adjustment, but determination of that combination of variables which predict it best. The several characteristics showing highest correlations with an adjustment criterion may all be measuring the same underlying variable, so that, after the first, others add little to improvement of prediction. On the other hand, a piece of information with much less impressive

[9] Availability of electronic data-processing equipment made multivariate analysis possible.

zero-order correlation to adjustment may add appreciably to predictive efficiency, if it does not overlap with others, so that its contribution is unique.

In this evaluation of subsets of predictors, effort was made to determine how much of a contribution each made to the prediction of adjustment and, therefore, how valuable each would be in future selection of tenants.[10] Since all twenty-seven predictors working together would do the most efficient job, this level of accuracy was accepted as the standard against which to compare subgroups of items. This was done separately, of course, for happiness, popularity, administrators' ratings of adjustment, and interviewers' ratings.

One at a time, each subgroup of items was eliminated, to see whether or not its absence impaired prediction of adjustment. If the more "expensive" trait ratings or interviewer judgments could be omitted without seriously lowering estimation of adjustment, much effort and cost could be avoided with no reduction in efficiency of future selection procedures. If elimination of one of these types of information resulted in serious incapacitation of prediction, use of trained interviewers and development of new instruments should be considered. Omission of even the relatively "cheap" admission-blank information was tested. If it adds nothing, admissions staffs can more wisely invest the time spent, beyond what may be required legally, in processing it.

After testing the effect of eliminating application-blank, interview-item, interviewer-rating, and trait-rating items, one group at a time, the same procedure was followed for pairs of groups. It was conceivable that two types of information could be dropped from consideration without seriously reducing prediction of adjustment. At least this possibility was well worth testing, before any recommendations were offered to admissions personnel. Any addition to their work loads should be of demonstrable value.

[10] The multiple correlation between the full set and one of the criteria was computed and compared with the various multiple correlations obtained by eliminating, one at a time, each of the subsets. If the loss of a piece of information does not affect the multiple correlation significantly, it is probably not making an independent contribution to the prediction of adjustment and might well be omitted in the future. On the other hand, if the multiple correlation drops radically at the elimination of certain information, that predictor is making a unique contribution and should be retained. Data processing systematically tested each possible combination of subsets of predictors, in comparison to the full set, for each criterion measure.

Finally, three groups of items were simultaneously eliminated or, to put it another way, each subgroup's ability to predict each adjustment criterion was compared with the ability of all four groups working together. Application-blank information alone, interview-item responses alone, interviewer ratings alone, and trait ratings alone, were used to predict adjustment, and the performance of each was evaluated in view of what all of them were able to do when used together.

Similarly, within each of the four subsets of predictors, the independent contribution of each item was observed.[11] Just as interviewer ratings, for example, may simply duplicate the contribution of more objective information from interviewers, one application-blank item may bear the same relationship to later adjustment as another, or one behavior trait may be related to another in such a way that the second adds nothing to the prediction based on the first. From the theorist's viewpoint of attempting to understand adjustment, clarification of such relationships seems wise; surely from the practical point of view of the person in a selection situation, the economy in both time and money is important. If several pieces of information duplicate each other in prediction, some can be eliminated. This is particularly important when relatively "expensive" information adds little to that which can be collected easily and cheaply, but it is still helpful even within a pool of items of equal "cheapness" or "expensiveness."

The results can be, of course, only as effective as the original selection of predictor variables was wise. Other items of each type were available, and quite possibly those selected were not the best ones. However, the procedure prevented inadvertent capitalization on chance, which improves the prospects for successful application of the resultant system to selection of tenants for similar situations.

Other Relationships

For development of such a system for prediction, however, only a

[11] In order to obtain information about the contribution to prediction of adjustment made by individual items within each pool, the computational procedure was to start with the largest zero-order correlation between any one predictor and the criterion measure. After this was recorded, a second predictor was selected, always the one which, together with the first, would bring about the greatest improvement in correlation with the criterion measure. In this way, one at a time, predictors were added to the multiple correlation either until all were in, or until those which were left would make no significant contribution.

limited number of variables can be used, for statistical reasons. In addition to the twenty-seven variables in the prediction equation, data were collected on others of interest in relationship to adjustment in the Plaza. Some were omitted from the prediction system simply so that it would not contain an excessive number of variables. Others could not be included there because time had not allowed collection of data from enough people. For these, zero-order correlations were computed with the four adjustment measures.

Chapter 11 deals successively with each of the criteria of adjustment, first discussing results of the attempt to predict it by means of the set of predictors, and then presenting additional information afforded by the zero-order correlations.

CHAPTER 11

Predicting Adjustment

CHAPTER 9 DISCUSSED adjustment in Victoria Plaza. Four ways of looking at morale or adjustment led to the determination of four related but separate indexes. Chapter 10 presented the selection of applicant characteristics possibly predictive of adjustment and explained the technique for identifying those characteristics, and those combinations of characteristics, to do the best job of accounting for individual differences in adjustment to the Plaza.

In this chapter the results of these attempts at prediction are presented and discussed. Each criterion of adjustment was treated separately throughout the statistical procedures, and each is discussed separately here. Patterns of relationship with the predictors clarify differences between the four types or definitions of adjustment. Application of these results to another situation would involve, first of all, decision regarding which "adjustment" is the goal. Different selection bases would be used, depending upon the standard of "adjustment": happiness of the residents, their popularity among the peer group, adjustment evaluations by staff members, or adjustment ratings by research people.

Predicting Happiness

All four types of predictor together correlated .56 with the Attitude Scale for happiness; so they accounted for about 30 per cent of the variance in happiness scores. This represents an improvement in prediction which would be useful in a selection situation. However, prediction of happiness was less accurate than that of any of the other three criteria of adjustment, and some attention should be paid to its improvement. It is not possible to say how much the relatively poor prediction was due to inappropriate choice of predictor and criterion variables, how much to the unreliability of predictor and criterion instruments, or how much to the difficulty inherent in making predictions for members of any relatively homogeneous group.

The Attitude Survey score was a make-shift criterion measure. Those which were planned for the study, and which dealt directly with satisfaction with living conditions, were abandoned because they did not differentiate among residents (see Chapter Nine). Even the index used, the happiness score from the Attitude Survey, showed a skewed distribution: only 13 per cent of respondents scored below the middle of a seven-point scale, while 68 per cent scored above it (Table 20).

It is probably safe to say that every person was happier with his living conditions in Victoria Plaza than with those he had had previously. Applicants were dissatisfied with their surroundings; residents were generally delighted. The improvement in environment had been great, and residents enjoyed the Plaza and were grateful to be in it. Any judgment for which living conditions a year before were used as standard of comparison would probably give rise to responses such as were obtained—for the most part useless in attempting to discriminate the least from the most delighted, among an almost euphoric group of people.

A statistically more adequate indicator might have been the number of criticisms people made about the Plaza and the Center, and the number of suggestions they offered for future facilities. Interviewers' impressions were that these would not be valid criteria. Some residents failed to make recommendations out of apathy rather than satisfaction. Only a person who spent time in the Senior Community Center, and was involved in its activities, would be in position to make negative comments about it. Some residents demonstrated clearly that it is possible to be, concurrently, extremely appreciative of good housing and bitterly self-reproachful because of personal inadequacies.

Criticisms and suggestions probably did not reflect unhappiness in the new situation, with the possible exception of concern for gossip. Freedom to suggest improvements may actually indicate high morale.

Negative comments were realistic reactions to the situation, generally given in an effort to avert similar conditions in similar facilities. It is relevant here that desire to give information which might benefit future generations of old folks was probably the strongest motivation among these people to give so much time and effort to the research. This was most clearly indicated in the final collection of data, by the excellent cooperation of residents secure in their apartments and of unsuccessful applicants who remained in substandard or stressful situations.

Conversely, absence of critical comments may have resulted, in some cases, from reluctance to voice them rather than from failure to perceive faults. Obvious impediments to expression of dissatisfactions were the pervasive gratefulness of residents and their intolerance of people who did not show appreciation. Characteristics which residents disliked in each other were largely determined in this way, again with the possible exception of gossip. Criticisms of others were mostly elicited by their failure to "live up to" the Plaza, either by not keeping themselves or their part of the building neat and attractive, or by failing to lead the independent, self-sufficient style of life which they valued and for which the Plaza and the Center obviously were designed.

In such a situation there may be advantage in a criterion measure based on the observations of others. The eleven raters agreed fairly well in their evaluations of the happiness of the residents. These ratings, like the Attitude Survey questions, were not oriented toward reactions to the Plaza. This lack of specificity may be an advantage, despite the fact that the indexes planned for this study were directed at satisfaction with housing. The real problem, after all, is whether improved housing increases the enjoyment of life in general.

Dispersion of these happiness-rating averages was much broader and less skewed than that of the Attitude Survey scores (Figure 27). However, the composite rating showed relatively little relationship to the score on happiness derived from the residents' responses (Table 22). The decision here was to retain the resident's own expression, despite its limitations.

Selection of tenants to maximize their happiness as residents is a legitimate goal, and probably residents' assessment of their own satisfaction is more valid than any other index. It would seem profitable to attempt the devising of a more sensitive indicator of happiness, though not one more closely related to satisfaction with living in the new residence. These people gave every impression of being a great deal happier than they had been, but there remained marked individual differences in satisfaction which should be measurable, and which would improve the efficiency of predictions regarding applicants.

In regard to efficient and economical prediction of the happiness index in this study, the analysis indicated that elimination of either trait ratings or application-blank information did not cause an appreciable loss (Appendix D, Tables 18 and 19). Retention of application-blank material in preference to behavior-trait data is clearly indicated. In the first place, it is really "free," requiring no data collection in addition to routine Housing application, and only simple additional processing for selection purposes. In the second place, traits were estimated through ratings of the people when they were residents. The traits could be used in selection only after the rating approach had been validated for applicants or other measuring techniques suitable to the time of application had been developed. When

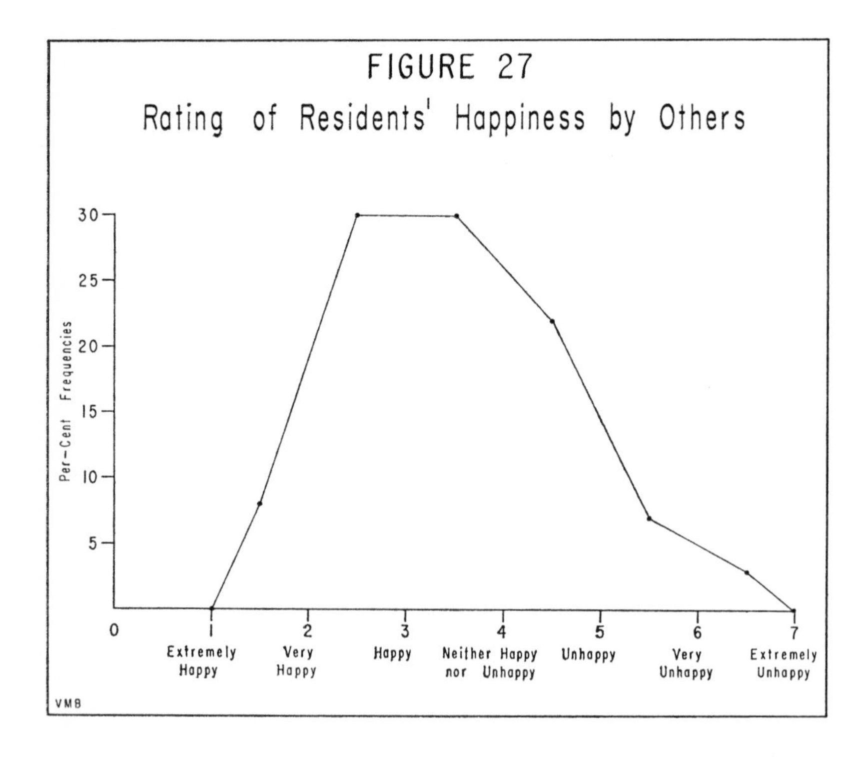

difference in "price" of two overlapping predictors is so great, the decision of which to keep is easily made.

Elimination of interviewer judgments reduced efficiency of the prediction system significantly but not drastically. However, when interview items were omitted, the relationship between predictors and happiness score dropped sharply.

Furthermore, when pairs of types of predictor were considered, the interview items seemed most important. The lowest correlation coefficient in which they were involved is .49, while the highest in which they were not included is .36. The usefulness of the interview items is further substantiated by the correlation of .47 with the happiness score, when no other information was used. All by themselves, the objective items from the initial interview, which probably could be converted to paper-and-pencil format, accounted for nearly a quarter of the variance in residents' scores on happiness.

Among interview items, it is interesting to note that the most important single pieces of information were identification with the "middle-aged" rather than with the "old," "elderly," or "aged"; optimistic or secure attitude toward the future and toward the end of life, rather than pessimism or fearful avoidance; expression of confidence in one's own usefulness and ability to work; recollection of a strong and warm relationship with one's parents during the teen years; present satisfaction with family and friends; number of activities in which interest was expressed, should the situation permit participation; and expression of a desire to join some particular organization, or more than one.

Table 23 shows results of the first seven steps in the statistical analysis. Attitude-toward-the-self was the item most closely related to happiness score, so it appears first. Then, one at a time, other items were added to self-attitude, according to the rule that whatever item made the largest increase in the multiple correlation should be selected.

In summary, these results indicate reasonably accurate prediction of self-report of happiness. If happiness of the individual, as expressed by him, is accepted as a goal, then use of these predictors would definitely improve selection of tenants. The most useful type of information was that obtained in the interview but probably reducible to paper-and-pencil form for most applicants similar to these. Collection of this information could easily be added to application procedures. Scoring is simple and could be handled by an office clerk

TABLE 23

Interview Items Most Important in Predicting Happiness for the 204 Residents

Predictors	*Correlation**
Self-Attitude	.300
+ Feeling about the Future	.383
+ Age-group Identification	.424
+ Attitude toward Parents during Teens	.435
+ Attitude toward Family and Friends	.440
+ Number of Activities Wanted	.445
+ Interest in Joining Some Group	.452

* All, with the exception of the first, are multiple-correlation coefficients. Zero-order correlations between these characteristics of applicants and their happiness as residents are presented in Appendix D, Table 26.

after very little special instruction. The cost of adding these procedures would be well justified by the improvement in tenant selection.

Those residents who were happiest after a year in Victoria Plaza had been applicants with excellent capacity for adjustment anywhere: secure in their own ability, in their relationship to life and death, and in their relationships to other people both in the past and currently. Less important, though relevant, they were interested in activities and in group participation. These latter were needs which Victoria Plaza and the Senior Community Center were specifically designed to meet.

Predicting Popularity with Other Residents

All four types of predictor, working together, accounted for about one-third of the variance in popularity scores. The correlation coefficient of .56 between the predictors and the number of peer nominations promises useful improvement in tenant selection if popularity is accepted as an index of adjustment. Again, as with prediction of happiness, an improved criterion measure might allow demonstration of a larger correlation coefficient. Some difficulties with peer judgments among members of such a group are probably inherent and unavoidable. Among these are the reasonable reluctance of administrators to allow titillation of such eager tongues, the unwillingness of residents themselves to make negative assessments about each other, and the not uncommon lack of relationship between familiarity with a person and with his name. On the other hand, acceptance of an individual within such a resident group is important, and selectors may be particularly interested in its prediction. With another group, instead of the overall number of nominations on all items of the sociometric instrument, those questions indicative of leadership might be eliminated for this purpose leaving for use in deriving the criterion measure only questions indicating friendly relationships. Such separate scores were made, in this study, for investigation of social processes (see Chapter 8). It is clear that "friendship" or enjoyment of the companionship of a person, is not the same thing as perceiving him as a person who can or does show leadership qualities. This confluence of two different variables in the criterion measure for "popularity" may have reduced correlations with predictors.

Eliminating any one of three types of information—application-blank, interview-item, or interviewer judgment—reduced insignificantly the efficiency of predicting the overall popularity score which was used (Appendix D, Tables 20 and 21). As long as the behavior-trait ratings were included in the system of predictors, any one other kind of predictor variable could be dropped. However, if the trait ratings were not included, there was significant and sizeable drop in the predictive efficiency of the system, regardless of what remained in it. As a matter of fact, if the entire interview was eliminated—both objectively scored questions and interviewer ratings—and only application-blank data and trait ratings were used, popularity could be predicted about as well as with all of the information.

It should also be noted, however, that the prediction of popularity was significantly improved by the use of any one of the types of information, and that, even when trait ratings were eliminated, the correlation of remaining predictors with popularity was .45. The two "cheapest" sources of prediction—application-blank and interview items—correlated .40 with the criterion.

Table 24 lists the order of the items of application-blank and behavior-trait information, as they entered into the growing multiple-correlation coefficient. Again, the process started with selection of the variable showing closest relationship to the popularity score. This was the trait rating of congeniality with people rather than "superiority" or superciliousness.

The characteristic which, added to the congeniality score, would most improve prediction of popularity was that of being tidy, even

TABLE 24

Application-Blank and Behavior-Trait Items Most Closely Correlated with Popularity of the 204 Residents

Predictors	*Correlation with Popularity**
Congeniality	.364
+ Tidiness	.430
+Tendency To Gossip (reversed)	.482
+ Marital Status	.501
+ Nervousness (reversed)	.506
+Age (reversed)	.527
+ Education	.531
+ Income	.534

* All, with the exception of the first, are multiple-correlation coefficients. Zero-order correlations between these characteristics of applicants and their popularity as residents are presented in Appendix D, Table 26.

overprecise, and of driving others to be the same; insisting that everything be orderly; being artistically sensitive to the surroundings and to art; being fastidious and not too easily pleased. The definition even included, "In these respects rather uncomfortable to live with." The other end of the scale, which tended to characterize people who were not popular, was that of being careless of detail, lazy, insensitive to, and uninterested in, the artistic and esthetic.

The trait selected third, to improve still further the prediction of popularity, was that rating which ran from "nosey and a gossiper" to "minds own business and refuses to gossip." Residents who remained aloof from gossip tended to be more popular than those who minded everyone's business.

Marital status appeared next in order to increase the relationship of predictor system to criterion measure. People who were living with their spouses at the time of application to Victoria Plaza tended to become more popular residents than did widowed or divorced applicants, or those who had never married.

Nervousness, sensitivity, tendency to become overwrought was the next characteristic, again from the trait-rating list. Those who were judged to have a high degree of nervousness were less popular.

The following three items all were of the application-blank type: chronological age, highest grade completed in school, and amount of present income.

Feasibility and desirability of using these biographical items in tenant selection are questionable. It would not make sense to give advantage, in admission to public housing for the aged, to youngest married couples with largest incomes. Anyway, these biographical characteristics add relatively little to the predictive efficiency of five trait ratings, used alone. The four personality traits mentioned above, superciliousness, carelessness, nosiness, and nervousness, with the addition of one other rating: "From a purely personal point of view I like this person" to "From a purely personal point of view I dislike this person," accounted for only a little less of the variance in popularity scores than did the two complete sets of behavior-trait ratings and application-blank items, used conjointly.

Absence of overlap between variables which predicted happiness and those related to popularity is striking. In regard to popularity the clear-cut advantage of behavior traits over all other kinds of information available about residents suggests the desirability of developing for them measures suitable to applicants for any situation in which peer relationships are considered important. Congeniality, tidiness, and nervousness probably could be judged by interviewers at the time of application. Those who collected data for this study thought this would not have been more difficult than other judgments they made about each applicant at the time of initial contact.

Interviewers did record their personal reaction of liking or disliking each applicant, after the first set of contacts. For the leaseline study, requirement of this judgment was put in as a warning against rater bias and a test for it. For purposes of the prediction study, this turned out to be a fortunate happenstance. For people who lived in the Plaza these ratings correlated .95 with those made a year or more later. Furthermore, the later ratings were similar to those made at the same time by administrative and service personnel of the Plaza and the Center. These findings suggest both that the social stimulus value for "likeableness" is stable and that ratings made on the basis of initial interview contacts were valid and would be useful in a selection situation.

However, interviewers were doubtful about their ability to make judgments regarding nosiness and tendency to gossip. Some applicants gave themselves away the first time they spoke. Many, though, were so preoccupied with their own problem of finding a more adequate or more secure place to live that the peccadillos of others did not catch their attention. Also, social isolation, common for applicants, provided meager material for gossip and little opportunity to exchange it.

Furthermore, Victoria Plaza provided, as many residents later claimed, a hot-house environment for rumor. Among over two hundred people under one roof, some were bound to be engaged in intriguing pursuits. If not, there was always someone ready to speculate about what was going on unseen. Orientation of the balconies, and location of the Senior Community Center with respect to the building entry and elevator, were "made to order" gossip-producers, as more than one resident pointed out. A few of these were gloating busybodies, but more were disgruntled subjects of the grapevine. The public areas provided residents with grounds, whether justified or not, for the further complaint that "the outsiders" had free access to their private lives, which seemed even worse than intrusion by fellow Plaza-dwellers.

The formula for popularity among Plaza-ites seems fairly straightforward. Disliked in the subcommunity were those people who acted as if they thought they were better than their neighbors, who were careless and untidy, and who gossipped. On the other hand, married couples were more popular, as were people who were relatively calm and not easily upset. Younger folks tended to be more popular, and results suggest that higher socio-economic level in earlier years of life, as well as at the present, may have had a favorable bearing. The degree of education of the applicant and "level" of the job of the man of the house during the middle years of life added slightly to prediction of the popularity score, as did income at the time of application.

Predicting Administrator Ratings of Adjustment to Victoria Plaza

When the study was being planned it seemed likely that administrative personnel would have a different interpretation of adjustment to the new situation than would research interviewers. This was borne out by interrater correlations on this item. The two administrators (director of the Senior Center and manager of the residence) tended to rate people similarly. The ratings of the two interviewers showed fairly consistent agreement. However, correlations between judgments of either of the administrators and either of the interviewers were lower.

Therefore, two separate criterion scores were maintained. One was the average of the ratings given the resident by the two interviewers. The other was the average of that given him by the two administrators. Or, when only one administrator knew him well enough to rate him, the rating of that one administrator was utilized. For ease of exposition, because predictors are similar and yet in important ways different, these two adjustment indexes are discussed together.

In predicting administrator or interviewer judgments of adjustment, once more the personality or behavior traits were overwhelmingly important (Appendix D, Tables 22, 23, 24 and 25). In each case, within the limits of chance, trait ratings alone did as good a job of prediction as all four types of information, used together. No other type of variable, or combination of types, came close to the predictive efficiency of this pool, with either the administrator or the interviewer evaluations of adjustment to the Plaza. In addition, relationships were close (represented by correlation coefficients of .76 and .82), accounting for about 60 per cent of the variance in administrators' ratings and nearly two-thirds of that in interviewers'.

It should also be pointed out that use of only the "cheaper" predictors would improve tenant selection to a useful degree. Simply the factual items from the interview which either were or probably could be on an application blank correlated .49 with administrators' ratings of tenants' adjustment and .43 with interviewers'.

As Tables 25 and 26 show, the personality or behavior traits carried different weights in prediction of adjustment assessments by administrators and interviewers. Likableness of the resident as a

TABLE 25

Behavior Traits Most Closely Correlated with Administrator Ratings of the 204 Residents' Adjustment in Victoria Plaza

Predictors	*Correlation Coefficient**
Nosiness	.531
+ Congeniality	.700
+ Tidiness	.726
+ Nervousness (reversed)	.738
+ Personal Liking	.744

* All, with the exception of the first, are multiple-correlation coefficients. Zero-order correlations between these characteristics of applicants and administrator ratings of their adjustment in Victoria Plaza are presented in Appendix D, Table 26.

TABLE 26

Variables Which Contribute Most to the Prediction of Administrator Evaluations of the 204 Residents' Adjustment to Victoria Plaza When all Four Types of Information are Used

Predictors	*Correlation Coefficient**
Nosiness	.527
+ Congeniality	.697
+ Participation in Activities	.728
+ Confusion in Initial Interview (reversed)	.742
+ Nervousness (reversed)	.750
+ Church Attendance	.760
+ Tidiness	.772
+ Feeling about the Future	.774
+ Marital Status	.777
+ Disengagement Index (reversed)	.779
+ Senility Index (reversed)	.781
+ Number of Friends during Teens	.782
+ Attitude to Parents during Teens	.783
+ Income	.784
+ Attitude toward Friends and Family	.785
+ Interviewer's Estimate of Success Made at First Interview	.787
+ Age Identification	.788
+ Interest in Activities	.789
+ Education	.790

* All, with the exception of the first, are multiple-correlation coefficients. Zero-order correlations between these characteristics of applicants and administrator evaluations of their adjustment to Victoria Plaza are presented in Appendix D, Table 26.

person accounted for about half the variance in interviewers' ratings, while it made the smallest contribution to prediction of administrators'. On the other hand, the tendency of the resident not to mind his own business was the single best predictor of administrators' ratings, while it did not make any contribution to prediction of interviewers'.

Though the "personally like-dislike" score had the disadvantage of being based on ratings, it was the average of the judgments of eleven raters, and included reactions of administrators as well as of interviewers. This was not a situation in which interviewers perceived as best adjusted those they liked and as poorly adjusted those they disliked. Rather, they tended to perceive as well adjusted those residents who were liked generally by all full-time and part-time staff members with whom they came into contact at Victoria Plaza and in the Senior Center, as well as by the data collectors. Administrators' perceptions of adjustment seemed to be much less influenced by this social-stimulus characteristic of residents, or at least less closely related to it.

An attempt should be made to devise a predictor of nosiness and to clarify its role. As measured here, this trait was strongly related to administrator perceptions of adjustment, but inversely related to popularity among peers. From other evidence it is apparent that gossip was the cause of perhaps the most serious unhappiness in Victoria Plaza. As indexes of the tendency to stick one's nose into the business of others and to spread embroidered accounts of it, ratings probably would not be satisfactory. This behavior tendency is not necessarily open to observation in an intake interview, and there may be behavior change with this type of alteration in environment. What is needed is an index of readiness to exhibit the behavior if placed in such a seductive situation as the Plaza.

The personality-behavior traits showed such a close relationship with adjustment ratings that applicant scores on them alone should predict resident adjustment satisfactorily. Nevertheless, it is interesting, in order to understand a little better what administrators and interviewers conceived as "adjustment," to look at the order in which pieces of information entered the prediction system when all four types of information about the resident were available.

Exactly as when only personality or behavior traits were being considered, the tendency to mind others' business showed the closest relationship with adjustment ratings of administrators, and so became the first member of the prediction system (See Table 26). Congeniality came second, as the variable which, together with nosiness, produced the greatest improvement in prediction. (These two traits are not synonymous. The correlation between them is .09.)

However, in the situation in which the pool of available predictors included all types, and not just trait-rating items, the third most important piece of information was the number of activities the applicant listed as those in which he participated prior to living in Victoria Plaza. Fourth in importance was the interviewer's rating of the applicant's confusion in regard to dates, times, and names, during 1960 contacts.

From there on, as items were added to improve prediction of administrator ratings, two of the remaining behavior traits—nervousness and tidiness—appeared, interspersed among application-blank, interview-item and interviewer judgment items. Likeableness as a person did not make a sufficiently important independent contribution to be selected as a member of this set of predictors. Generally those items which helped most to account for the administrator ratings pointed toward activity, desire for activity and involvement, competence, and an outgoing attitude toward others.

A glance at variables not included among the twenty-seven confirms this interpretation (see Table 27). Tendency to make use of facilities in the ground-floor Senior Community Center was practically synonymous with "adjustment to Victoria Plaza" in the eyes of

TABLE 27

Characteristics Not Included in the Prediction System Which Correlated Closely with Administrator Evaluations of the 204 Residents' Adjustment in Victoria Plaza

Characteristics of these People	*Zero-Order Correlation Coefficient*	
As Residents:		
Frequency of Using the Senior Center	.92**	
Talkativeness	.59**	
Number of Raters Who Knew Resident	.52**	
Welcome of Outsiders to the Senior Center	.45**	
Regular Responsibility	.41**	
Participation in Victoria Plaza Activities	.40**	
As Applicants:		
(Disengagement Index Score	–.45**)	
Number of Sociable Leisure Activities	.36**	
Number of Active Leisure Activities	.35**	
Attitude Toward Father during Teens	.34**	
Number of Leisure Activities	.30**	
Attitude Toward Mother during Teens	.29**	
Frequency of Correspondence	.25**	
Number of Activities Interested in	.24**	
Alertness in Initial Interview	.21**	
MMPI: F Scale	.21*	(N=101)
Number of Close Friends	.20*	
I.Q.	.19*	(N=104)
Time Diary: Time Spent in Meetings	.18*	(N=203)

* Significantly larger than zero at the .05 level of confidence.
** Significantly larger than zero at the .01 level of confidence.

administrators. In addition, those residents perceived by administrators as best adjusted to the Plaza generally "talked to everybody," welcomed "outsiders" into the Senior Center, and took part in activities of the organization of apartment holders sponsored by the Housing Authority. Most of the eleven raters knew them, a fact which is another indication that they were outgoing and interested in many activities.

Furthermore, the well-adjusted residents tended to have had higher "regular responsibility" scores as applicants. Toward this score they were given points for having a job or doing volunteer work on a regular basis, and points for saying they would like to have such a definite, routine commitment of their time, were it possible. Though expressing an interest costs nothing, and some who appeared eager might never become involved no matter how easy it became, credit was given for expression of interest because of the extremely limited opportunity of most of these people in their pre-Victoria Plaza situations.

The outstanding characteristic of those applicants later to be judged by administrators as well adjusted was their tendency to have low Disengagement Index scores. Actually the Disengagement Index score enters into the prediction system. However, it is included here again, since it was the measure taken on applicants which had the highest zero-order correlation with administrators' ratings on adjustment, made a year or more later. At the time of first interview they did not appear to be losing interest in people, belongings, activities, or mental stimulation.

Other traits are highly consistent with the Disengagement score. As applicants, people who would receive favorable ratings on adjustment to Victoria Plaza tended to report a larger number of leisure-time pursuits. More of their activities were done in the company of other people, and were active rather than passive. In addition, they could think of more activities in which to participate, given the opportunity. They had more close friends, or at least reported more; and they were more active correspondents. They spent more time in meetings. Their tendency to alertness was indicated both by higher ratings during the initial interview and by I.Q. scores for the sample to whom the Wechsler-Bellevue was administered. A tendency to assume a favorable façade is suggested by the F-Scale scores of the sample who took the MMPI.

Predicting Interviewer Judgments of Adjustment

Table 28 shows the steps in the analysis of data through which items were chosen to predict ratings by the interviewers, when all four types of information were available. Here, as with prediction of the administrator rating, the most influential items were personality or behavior traits. Four behavior traits plus likeableness accounted for nearly two-thirds of interviewer ratings (Table 29). The tendency to be nosey and to gossip, which was the single most important predictor of administrators' ratings, did not make an appreciable contribution to prediction of interviewers. On the other hand, personal liking of the raters in general, while relatively unimportant for administrators, kept first place with interviewers.

TABLE 28

Variables Which Correlate Most Closely with Interviewer Ratings of the 204 Residents' Adjustment to Victoria Plaza When All Four Types of Predictor Information Are Used

Predictors	*Correlation Coefficient**
Personal Liking	.684
+ Congeniality	.774
+ Nervousness (reversed)	.793
+ Job Level	.794
+ Tidiness	.800
+ Physical Disability (reversed)	.802
+ Church Attendance	.803
+ Attitude to Parents during Teens	.804
+ Interest in Joining Some Group	.806
+ Interviewer's Estimate of Adjustment Made at Initial Contact	.807
+ Senility Index Score	.808
+ Interest in Activities	.809
+ Disengagement Index (reversed)	.810
+ Self-Attitude	.811
+ Attitude toward Family and Friends	.812
+ Age (reversed)	.814
+ Education	.815
+ Number of Friends (squared)	.817
+ Marital Status	.818
+ Present Income	.821

* All, with the exception of the first, are multiple-correlation coefficients. Zero-order correlations between these characteristics of applicants and interviewer ratings of their adjustment to Victoria Plaza are presented in Appendix D, Table 26.

TABLE 29

Behavior Traits Most Closely Related to Interviewer Ratings of the 204 Residents' Adjustment to Victoria Plaza

Predictors	*Correlation Coefficient**
Personal Liking	.683
+ Congeniality with Others	.773
+ Nervousness (reversed)	.788
+ Tidiness	.793

* All, with the exception of the first, are multiple-correlation coefficients. Zero-order correlations between these characteristics of applicants and interviewer ratings of their adjustment to Victoria Plaza are presented in Appendix D, Table 26.

Many of the pieces of information in the system predicting interviewers' judgments of adjustment were the same as those in the system predicting administrators'. However, interviewers' ratings seemed to be less closely related to activity and sociability than were administrators'.

This idea is supported strongly by the zero-order correlations presented in Table 30. Interviewer ratings of adjustment to Victoria Plaza were closely related to the happiness of the resident and the

TABLE 30

Characteristics Not Included in the Prediction System Which Also Correlated with Interviewer Evaluations of the 204 Residents' Adjustment to Victoria Plaza

Characteristics of the People	*Zero-Order Correlation Coefficient*
As Residents of the Plaza:	
Rating of Happiness	.76**
Acceptance of Aging	.68**
As Applicants:	
(Senility Index	— .39**)
Attitude Survey Score on Happiness	.20**
I.Q.	.20** (N = 103)
Time Diary: Unaccounted Time	— .19** (N = 202)
Number of Neurotic Problems	— .14*

* Significantly different from zero at the .05 level.
** Significantly different from zero at the .01 level.

ease and grace with which he was accepting the process of aging, as these were perceived by others. Scores on happiness and on acceptance of aging were averages of ratings by administrative and service personnel as well as the interviewers.

Interviewers' ratings of adjustment also correlated significantly with applicants' scores on the happiness section of the Attitude Survey administered as part of the first set of contacts, though it is a much less close relationship than that with averaged ratings of the happiness of residents. A significant relationship occurs also with a time-diary score, but here it is with the amount of time for which the applicant was unable to account,[1] rather than, as in the case with administrators' ratings, the amount of time spent attending meetings. Each person's score was the per cent of time, over the period of a week, in which he did "nothing." This "lost time" score was devised as a possible index of wasted life and lowered morale. Applicants with little "lost time" became better adjusted residents.

Further indication of the greater concern of interviewers with inner experience of residents than with their social behavior was shown by the modest but significant correlation of their adjustment ratings with the number of health problems mentioned by the interviewee which had been predesignated as probably of neurotic origin.

Again, the piece of information available at the time of first contact which showed closest relationship to the adjustment rating was one which had been included in the prediction pool, the Senility Index score. Applicants showing fewer signs of senility were subsequently among those residents judged by interviewers as adjusting better to the situation. These ratings were made by the same people, but with a time interval of from a year to fifteen months.

Administrators' and interviewers' ratings of residents' adjustment to Victoria Plaza proved to be rather accurately predictable. A preselected set of variables accounted for about two-thirds of each. However, "adjustment" to administrators was not synonymous with "adjustment" to research interviewers, and the best predictor systems are not identical. In general, the administrative view of adjustment seemed more closely related to the social behavior of the person, while that of the interviewer was influenced relatively more by the ratee's inner satisfaction.

[1] Paper in preparation.

Summary

Prediction of differences in adjustment to the Plaza seems quite feasible, even when dealing with this prescreened and relatively homogeneous group of residents. Especially if a shortage of units continues, it will be worth while to supplement other admission standards in order to admit applicants most likely to adjust to this type of facility. Consideration of characteristics of relatively poor adjusters, in relation to the various indexes of adjustment, might suggest alternate plans for housing some old people.

The primary problem in such settings as Victoria Plaza will be to decide which "adjustment" is the goal. Selection will be carried out differently, depending upon the definition of adjustment in terms of tenant happiness, popularity within the resident group, administrators' evaluations, or those of research interviewers. Once that decision has been made, intake procedures can be selected or devised to provide relevant information about applicants.

These results suggest that the amount of improvement, using any of the four definitions of adjustment, would be well worth the effort, in a practical selection situation. Even the utilization of several items of information routinely collected on application blanks or amenable to such collection would improve tenant selection, thereby maximizing the usefulness of such facilities and minimizing damage to individuals for whom they are not suitable.

CHAPTER 12

Some Implications of the Studies

Impact of Environmental Setting

EVIDENCE OF THE DRAMATIC EFFECT of improved life setting on this group of older people was overwhelming. It appeared not only in increased satisfaction with the residential situation but also in more favorable attitudes concerning the self and toward others, in improved physical and mental health, and in more active and sociable patterns of life.

The environmental change was deeply and almost unanimously satisfying to the people who lived in Victoria Plaza. They had wanted to move, they were delighted to be selected as residents, and after living in the Plaza for a year or more they continued to revel in all it offered of physical comfort and convenience and of social opportunity.

In most ways the resident group moved toward usual norms for good adult adjustment. The nonresidents exhibited less change. That which did occur tended to be toward passivity, reduced social contact, and lowered morale.

Residents entered into more activities of all sorts, but particularly those pursued in the company of other people and those of an active rather than passive nature. Contacts with members of the kinship group and with old friends comprised a smaller proportion of total interpersonal contact for residents. This did not represent an absolute decrease in time spent with old friends or family members, but was an artifact of the impressive increase in new friendships and in social-group activities. Typically they made new friends while keeping old ones. Concurrently, residents expressed increased satisfaction with their friends and with their families.

Nonresidents' diaries showed an increase in time spent sleeping and napping, "just sitting," and that which could not be accounted for. Residents spent less time in each of these, but more time working on hobbies, at meetings, and informally with other people.

Though a calendar year had passed, more residents were "middle-aged," fewer "old," "elderly," and "aged." They showed generally improved self-concepts—not only in regard to present competence, health, and happiness, but also in evaluations of their lives as a whole. Even recollections of childhood were more favorable than they had been a year previously.

There seemed to be only one reversal. The number of residents for whom money was a "major problem" increased, though the number of such people among nonresidents did not. There had been no change in income for either group. Rent was not cheaper for residents: one out of every two residents was paying more rent than when he applied for public housing. Also the beauty of the building stimulated purchase of new furniture "on time," and increased sociability made old or hand-me-down clothes unacceptable. The very little bit of recreation money could not be sacrificed. What went was food. While nonresidents' expenditures for food increased slightly over the period, that of residents decreased. In terms of total food budget, the drop was rather sharp. Residents expressed greater satisfaction with what their money purchased, and they felt more secure in regard to financial matters. However, money tended to come to mind when residents were asked if they had any major problems.

The considerable change among Plaza residents indicates that rigidity is not an intrinsic component of the aging personality. The behavior of these people calls into question the difficulty, with increasing age—as distinct from decreasing opportunity—of forming new social relationships. The results suggest that old people's dissatisfactions with the circumstances of their lives are realistic reactions to difficult physical or social situations, and that the expressions of discontent will cease when the causes are alleviated. The relative consistency of nonresident records over a period of time supports attribution of resident change to housing. Also it lends confidence to the initial research material as realistic report of conditions and reactions. Had there been a successful attempt on the part of applicants to manipulate responses to maximize likelihood of acceptance, significant alterations should appear in the later material from nonresidents.

Changes exhibited among residents in their attitudes and ways of living were generally toward activity and informal social contacts, not at all toward disengagement. The findings suggest that more attention needs to be paid to the role of the setting in determining the experience and behavior of old people. It points also to the necessity for more careful scrutiny of traits considered to be age-related. Some environmental conditions may so regularly accompany chronological aging that their effects are mistaken for those of age itself.

The new facility was not all things to all people. It did not, for example, cure alcoholism, a tendency to exhibitionism, or antipathy to soap and water. Nor was it the ideal situation for all residents. Had such choices been open to them, some would have preferred to live in a different part of town, or in a small house with its own yard, or among people varying more widely in age, or in a situation which did not so much emphasize contact with any sort of people at all.

For them Victoria Plaza was the best situation they could obtain, and they were grateful for it because the alternatives open to them were much less attractive. Residents were only reacting like people who toured Victoria Plaza when they voiced extremely favorable comments about the beauty of its design, the imaginative and pleasing use of building materials, the comfort and convenience of the apartments, and the welcoming atmosphere of the recreation area. Certainly a major portion of the satisfaction with Victoria Plaza stemmed simply from the fact that it was a desirable residence. In comparison with the places from which they had moved or in comparison with any others they could obtain at present, it was extremely attractive.

The overwhelming nature of the Plaza's success probably resulted partly, also, from characteristics of the people who took up residence there. They had expressed interest in such housing and had taken active steps to secure it, they were generally capable of caring for themselves and their apartments, and they were strongly motivated by the need for autonomy. Perhaps it is important, too, that they had not lived all of their lives in substandard residences or in social isolation. Such adjustment would not be expected in old people who had never had good housing and did not go out of their way presently to obtain it, or who were physically or psychologically dependent.

However, the rather comprehensive background information collected on this group suggests strongly that most old people in this country today are much like them. The fact that the changes came about in a group of individuals who were simply getting along as well as they could, as normal members of a community, rather than achieving visibility either through acknowledgments of physical or economic helplessness or through identification with some privileged group, supports the prospect of more general improvement of the later years of life, through changes in the environmental setting in which they are living.

The striving for autonomy prevalent among members of this group was not a denial of, or distaste for, interdependence with other people. Quite the contrary, most of them recognized their need for others. Social isolation and interpersonal friction were major sources of applicants' (and nonresidents') dissatisfaction. However, most of these people wanted to maintain their own households as long as possible, and they wished to feel free to make decisions for themselves. Above all they dreaded becoming burdens, financially or emotionally, upon members of their families. They did not want to strain the highly valued bonds of kinship by constant contact under uncomfortable housing conditions. They did not want to make demands for separate housing which would curtail the budgets of younger households. The conclusion that they resisted accepting help from their families would be incorrect. Rather, they did not want only to take, but also to give. If they could make no positive contribution, at least they wanted to minimize the drain or stress on relatives.

Too, love for children and grandchildren did not preclude interest in other people. Actually, the older people who enjoyed the best relationships with their families were the ones who also had the most satisfactory friendships. Applicants perceived as particularly hazardous to sound family relationships their own lack of peer-age social life and consequent emotional dependence on the kinship group. As residents' friendships extended, their satisfaction with their families increased.

Two reservations may limit this evaluation of Victoria Plaza's apparent success. One stems from the fact that the people studied were the first occupants of the building and that they moved in almost simultaneously. The other arises from the fact that the expressions of satisfaction and the other indexes of change were based on only a year to fifteen months of experience in the situation. First occupants may be a special group. The resulting prestige and in-group feeling may even be detrimental to the adjustment of replacements. Also, though there is no evidence of this on the basis of informal observation, it is possible that satisfaction will moderate with time. However, as long as alternatives remain so limited, it seems unlikely that any significant swing toward dissatisfaction will occur. Possibly, too, the general reactions toward activity, sociableness, interest in personal appearance and pride in home are temporary. A basic process of disengagement may only have been interrupted or delayed. Informal contacts with residents suggest that, for the large majority, reengagement continues and is thoroughly enjoyed.

Future Tenant Selection

There are obvious advantages, to individuals and to institutions, in improving selection techniques for such residential facilities as Victoria Plaza. This improvement involves, first of all, detection of applicant characteristics predictive of success or failure after exposure to the new situation. The more similar the people, the more difficult it is to make differential predictions. This group of residents was fairly homogeneous in many ways, since all had preselected themselves by making application for housing and all had passed the Housing Authority's initial eligibility screening and its final selection procedures. However, this is the sort of group with which selection systems will have to deal in the future.

Development of selection devices is simpler, too, when there is a clear-cut indicator of success vs. failure. However, satisfaction with the Plaza was nearly universal, and other indexes of adjustment showed most of the residents to have been successful. Nevertheless, there were sufficient differences among the people, both in characteristics at time of application and in degree of adjustment to residency, to allow development of selection techniques which should be useful in screening future tenants for this or a similar facility.

A critical issue in any practical situation will be the definition of adjustment. Selection items will vary in importance, and even in kind, from one view of adjustment to another.

If adjustment is equated with residents' expressions of their own happiness, preference should be given to those applicants who consider themselves still middle-aged and who have optimistic evaluations of their present competence, who view the future with confidence and the prospect of death with serenity. Also favorable is an applicant's recollection of warm, strong relationships with his parents when he was a teenager and his expression of current satisfaction with his family and his friends. Less important are the number of activities in which he would like to participate and the fact that there is some organization which he would like to join.

Popularity with other residents, as a standard of adjustment, suggests quite a different approach. For selection to maximize popularity among peers, applicants who seem to feel they are better than other people should be eliminated, as should those likely to gossip. The nervous and easily upset should not be admitted. Effort should be made to screen out the untidy and disorderly, and to admit people who are scrupulously clean and neat and those who are esthetically sensitive and responsive to beauty. Preference should be given to married couples, to the younger applicants, and to those who had more education.

If administrators' judgments are to serve as the criterion of adjustment, the most promising applicant is the person who tends to make everyone's business his own. Outgoing sociability and readiness to take part in formal organizations and planned activities, as well as informal ones, also should characterize those admitted.

In any real situation, one or more of these definitions of resident adjustment would probably be used in determining selection procedures. However, it is interesting to note that when research interviewer ratings were applied as a criterion measure still a different set of applicant characteristics emerged as predictors.

The power of any one of the prediction systems developed in this study suggests that improvement of tenant selection for such facilities is feasible, even if the applicant group is relatively homogeneous and acceptee adjustment generally good. The first problem staffs will face is the definition of adjustment, since selection items and their weights will depend upon this decision. The second question will involve the equally practical matter of cost. Factual questions amenable to routine collection and simple clerical handling of responses should improve selection to a useful degree for any one of the statements regarding the nature of adjustment. For certain of them, other variables hold additional promise. Efforts should be made to develop measures of these relatively "expensive" items.

Social Processes in Victoria Plaza

During the first year of occupancy of the Plaza residents were polled every three months regarding their relationships with other people, and their reactions to them. The relative decline in importance of relatives and pre-Victoria Plaza friends was obvious. Development of interpersonal relationships within the resident group suggested that assignment within the building, in regard to floor or to location within the floor, had little to do with selection of friends, participation in activities in the ground floor Community Center, general popularity, or assumption of a leadership role.

All of these seemed to be determined largely by characteristics of the individuals. No consistencies were observed in regard to development of friendships. However, both general popularity within the resident group and perception as a leader within it should be fairly predictable on the basis of certain background information and personality characteristics of applicants. Those people generally chosen as leaders were not necessarily those sought as companions; the most popular residents might or might not be perceived as leaders. Formal office holding seemed to exert little effect upon the incumbents' nominations, either as leaders or as companions.

Some Additional Comments

Architects and builders of facilities for older people would see in the reactions of Victoria Plaza residents a justification for efforts to build in beauty. Safety, cleanliness, comfort, ease of upkeep were appreciated—and so were the patterns of light and shadow cast by the balconies and fire escapes, the strong colors in the recreation room, and the seclusion of the walled courtyard.

Planners should have no apprehension about the ability of old people to accept novel construction ideas and household appliances, if this group is any indicator. Planners might profit, particularly in regard to innovations in the interest of safety, by conferring with prospective residents or, if laboratory studies are made, by using such people as subjects. Special design features which make an environment safer for children may have no effect, or even an adverse one, for people with such different physical structures and sensory and motor capabilities. Simple changes in a plan in the interest of economy might also come from consultation with people such as those studied. Conversely, the additional cost to take their suggestions for such features as service elevators which do not debouch into the recreation area might be justified.

The common "living room" concept seems an excellent one. Optimally, this space should be planned to accommodate several groups involved in different activities, and its decoration should be informal. Comfortable seating or lounging should be provided, in view of activity areas but so situated that a person does not feel compelled to join an activity in order to justify his presence downstairs.

Designers might give some thought to the matter of privacy in apartments. Hungry as these people were for social interaction, they felt strongly about maintaining control over their relationships with others. They enjoyed having people in their apartments by invitation, but they disliked visibility to passersby. Views from many of the apartment windows were beautiful, and the residents prized them. Cross-ventilation in the building was generally good and was appreciated. People's sense of privacy, however, seemed to be violated in many cases by the window arrangement.

This matter of privacy also needs special consideration by the staffs of such facilities. Perhaps the need was exaggerated because these people had had so little in the way of material possessions—and many of them also in the matter of privacy itself. They were eager to share their good fortune in the sense that they wished everyone could be as satisfactorily housed as they were, but they had strong needs to control the doors and the windows of their own apartments. This problem was no doubt complicated by the old people's reluctance to displease staff members to whom they felt grateful and whom they liked personally, and also by the residents' own conflict between desire for privacy and enjoyment of attention.

The desire for self-determination seemed strong and pervasive, and it is probably worthy of special attention in regard to the housing and the activities of older people. Autonomy appeared early in this study as a strong motive for housing application, and it continued to affect the desires and behavior of residents. In general they preferred less formal, more spontaneous pastimes and would rather do, themselves, whatever planning or preparation was necessary. Availability of suitable space and equipment was appreciated and applauded, and residents exhibited little reluctance to seek help, but any intimation that someone else was trying to "get them organized" met with resistance. Obviously this situation speaks for subtle approaches by staff members and community service organizations. Also it is probably well to remember that old people like these usually know what they want to do and how to go about accomplishing it. Among this group there was an impressive fund of experience in organizing clubs, planning bridge parties, and managing teas.

Further, there was a reservoir of skills and knowledge which could benefit any community and a desire to be useful. Old people's opportunities to be of assistance to others are limited by finances, transportation, and by the reluctance of persons and organizations to make use of their services, either on a paid or a volunteer basis. In this way strong needs of older people are blocked, and perhaps other generations miss a certain enrichment.

The people studied were grateful and delighted that their society provided them a beautiful, comfortable place in which to live, one in which they could be with congenial persons according to their own desires and from which they could maintain good relationships with families and old friends. However, they did not let anyone forget that they were paying their own way, not accepting charity. The need to continue responsible participation often went beyond this, to the wish that the broader society would make some use of their time and experience.

APPENDIX A[1]

Data-Collection Forms

Interviews
Adjective Check List
Peck Sentence Completion Instrument
Seven-Day Diary
Interviewer Remarks and Reactions
Disengagement Index
Sociometric Questionnaire
Rating Scale for Adjustment to Victoria Plaza
Rating Scale for Resident Happiness
Ratings Used as Predictors of Adjustment to Victoria Plaza

[1] Unedited reproductions of forms used in the study.

Interview[2]

Date.......................... Code No..........................
Time: Started...................... Ended...................... Total..........................

General Information

1. Name 2. Address
3. Marital Status
4. Sex
5. Age at last birthday
6. Ethnic origin
7. Citizenship
8. In what country were you born?
9. In what country was your father born?
10. In what country was your mother born?
11. Can the subject speak English? How fluently?
12. What is your mother tongue?
13. What other languages do you speak? read? write?
14. How old were you when you left school?
15. What was the last grade in school you completed?
16. How long have you lived at your present address?
17. How long have you lived in or near San Antonio?
18. Where do you live now? (Own home, boarding house, etc.)
19. Where do you get your meals? (Indicate sociable-solitary conditions)
20. How does your present housing compare with what you had when you were 55?
21. What about your neighborhood?
22. What was the cost for your housing last month?
23. What were your eating costs last month?
24. During the past few months, who lived in your household?
25. Do you feel that, for what you are getting, the monthly cost is: very high, somewhat high, about right, low, very low?
26. How do you like your present housing?
27. Why are you interested in changing your housing?
28. Do you have any of the following services provided: housecleaning,

[2] The questions served as a guide to the interviewers, who were trained to elicit the material desired through open-end questions and discussion. Questions asked in the first interview but not in the second are marked with single asterisks in the left magin; questions asked in the second interview but not in the first, with double asterisks. Responses were categorized after data had been collected. These categorizations are available upon request, but their inclusion here would make the appendix too bulky.

cooking, shopping, maintenance, laundry, nursing, garbage taken out, other?

29. Which of the following do you own, have, or have access to: telephone, elevator, central heat, space heater, laundry machine, gas or electric stove, kerosene or wood stove, refrigerator, ice box, radio, T.V., hot and cold water, indoor toilet, other?
30. How are your arrangements for eating? sleeping? housecleaning? shopping? laundry? repairs and maintenance? garbage disposal? other?
31. In general, how do you feel about your present neighborhood as a place to live?
32. How do you feel about S.A. as a place to live?
33. What kind of furnishings do you own?
34. What do you plan to do with them if you move to the housing project?
35. How did you hear about the housing center? How did you come to apply?

Health

1. In general how would you rate your health at the present time?
2. Would you say your health is better or worse than the health of other people your own age?
3. How does your weight now compare with a year ago?
4. Do you own, use, need: eyeglasses, hearing aid, cane, crutches, leg braces, special shoes, dentures, truss, anything else?
5. Are you bothered by: vision, hearing, crippling, stiffness, heart trouble, heart burn, stomach trouble, cough, constipation, diarrhea, dizziness, headaches, shortness of breath, diabetes (sugar sickness), piles, sinus trouble, feet or legs swelling, backache, gas pains, belching, varicose veins, sleeplessness, bad dreams, tiring too easily, food not tasting good, feeling blue, nervousness, noise, health worry, forgetfulness, other?
6. During the past month about how many days were you: in bed because of a health condition, in and out of bed, kept indoors, not kept indoors but restricted in activity because of health? Explain.
7. How many days did you spend in bed last year? Explain.

*8. Have you had any serious accidents in the last five years? Explain.

9. During the past month did you see an M.D.?
10. During the past year did you see a dentist?
11. Would you have liked to? Which?
12. Did you see anyone else in the health line?

*13. What did he say?

14. Where was it you saw your doctor?
15. Did you pay for this visit? If so, how?

Family

1. What is your marital status?
2. How many times have you been married?
3. How old were you (each time)?
4. How do you rate the happiness of your marriage (each separately)?
5. If you had your life to live over again, would you marry the same person(s)?
6. How many living children do you have?
7. How often do you see your children?
8. What other close relatives do you have?
9. How often do you see these relatives?
10. How often do you communicate with them by phone? Letter?
11. How close (geographically) do your relatives and/or children live?
12. Do you help your children and close relatives in any way? How?
13. Do they help you in any way? How?
14. Do you feel that your family is a real help to you now?

Friends

1. How many people do you think of as close friends (whom you could ask to do you a real favor)?
*2. Name your three best friends.
3. How often do your friends visit you?
4. How often do you visit your friends in their homes?
5. Who comes to visit most often?
6. Do you see your friends more or less often than when you were 55? Why?
7. How often do you talk with friends on the phone?
8. How often do you write letters? To whom?
9. How often do you receive letters? From whom?

Leisure Activities

1. How much free time do you have?
2. During the past six months, what did you often do in your spare time?
3. Are there things you plan to do in the next year or so? What?
4. How much time each day do you spend reading?
5. What do you read regularly?
6. How often do you attend the movies?
7. How much time do you spend listening to the radio or watching T.V.?
8. Is there any particular place outside your household where you frequently spend the time of day for enjoyment or relaxation or to see friends?
9. What is this place?
10. What do you do most of the time you are there?

11. During the past six months did you take part in any social group, group church activities, or organization in the community?
12. What kind of group?
13. What was your role in the group(s)?
14. What groups or organizations would you belong to if you had the opportunity? Why?
15. What kind of activities would you like to take part in, if you had the opportunity? Why?
16. Do you give more or less time now than when you were 55 to these activities?

Employment History and Economic Security

*1. Have you ever earned money?
*2. Record chronologically, starting with respondent's last job, his full-time employment history. Include earnings.
*3. What was your husband's work most of his life *or* did your wife ever work? At what?
4. Comparing what you have done with the work of your brothers, sisters, and first cousins, would you say you have done about as well, not as well, or better?
5. Are you working now? Full time? Part time?
6. If so, at what?
7. How does work you do compare with what you did at age 55?
8. Are you in a better or worse financial position than at 55?
9. How would you describe your present financial position?
10. What is your chief means of support?
11. How much do you have in savings?
12. Do you feel that your present source of income gives you permanent security? Explain.
13. What kinds of things have you had to do since age 55 because of lowered income?
*14. During the past month, did you receive anything, not counting money, from organizations or from persons, for which you did not have to pay? What? From whom?
15. Do you own a car? Make. Year.

Religion

1. What is your religion?
2. Are you a church member?
3. How often do you attend religious services?
4. Do you attend services more or less often now than you did at age 55?
5. If you attend church less often now, why is it?
6. Do you believe in an after life?

7. Do you listen to church services over the radio or T.V.? How often?
8. How often do you read the Prayer Book, Bible, or other religious books?
9. Does anyone from your church call on you?
10. Do you go to social gatherings in your church? How often?

Early Life

*1. What was your father's occupation?
*2. Which child in the family were you?
*3. How many children in your family lived to the age of 5 or older?
*4. If your parents are living, how old are they?
*5. If not living, how old were they at their death?
*6. How was your health when you were about 12 years old?
*7. When you were in your teens, how did you feel toward your father?
*8. When you were in your teens, how did you feel about your mother?
*9. When you were in your teens, about how many friends of the same sex did you have?
*10. Opposite sex?
*11. What was the financial position of your family when you were about 12?
*12. How often did you attend some religious service when you were about 12?

Attitudes

1. What was the happiest period of your life? Why?
2. What was the least happy period of your life? Why?
3. As you look back over your life, what things were the hardest for you to bear?
4. As you look back over your life, in general would you call it: very happy, moderately happy, average, unhappy, very unhappy?
5. If you could have three wishes, what would they be?
6. How do you feel about what you have accomplished in life?
7. In which age group do you feel that you now belong? Why?
8. Did you vote in the last national election?
9. Do you have your poll tax or exemption certificate?

Use of Time

*1. What did you do yesterday? (Using time sheet for one day, be sure respondent sees how it is filled in, as discussion proceeds.)
*2. Would you take this other sheet and fill it out every day for a week? Then please mail it to me.

Closing

*1. What do you think are your major problems now?

2. What kinds of services or programs could you use?
*3. Have you ever participated in an interview like this before?
*4. What do you think about this kind of building?
*5. If you live there, do you have any preference, or aversion, for any part of the building? Why?
*6. How do you feel about this interview?
*7. Would you be willing to answer such questions again sometime in the future?

****Victoria Plaza and the Senior Center (Second Interview)***

1. What do you think of Victoria Plaza?
2. In what way(s) has it not lived up to your expectation?
3. How is it better than you thought it would be?
4. What effect has living in Victoria Plaza had on your life?
5. What are the best things about living in the Plaza?
6. What are the worst things about living in the Plaza?
7. If you could, what would you change about the Plaza?
8. Do you use the Senior Center? How?
9. How often do you use the Center?
10. What do you like about the Center?
11. What do you dislike about the Center?
12. If you could, what would you change about the Center?
13. What do you like about this kind of building?
14. Do you have an aversion to any part of the building?
15. Why do you have these aversions?
16. What do you think about a project such as this restricted to an age group?
17. Do you think you'd like it better if:
    a) people were not all in the same age group?
    b) you had your own yard?
    c) it was not such a show place?
18. Do you think you would like it better if some things were different? What?
19. What do you particularly like about the people living in Victoria Plaza?
20. How do you feel about your future now?
21. Do you ever think about the end of life? What?

Adjective Check List

I am going to say some words. For each one, answer either "Yes" if it fits you or "No" if it does not. (If person absolutely cannot decide, tell him "Don't know" is acceptable.) Let's try to do it quickly.

1. absentminded
2. active
3. affectionate
4. alert
5 bitter
6. bossy
7. brave
8. busy
9. calm
10. capable
11. cautious
12. cheerful
13. clear-thinking
14. clever
15. complaining
16. confident
17. confused
18. contented
19. cooperative
20. cowardly
21. dependable
22. disorderly
23. dissatisfied
24. dull
25. easy-going
26. enthusiastic
27. fault-finding
28. fearful
29. fussy
30. generous
31. gloomy
32. good-natured
33. healthy
34. helpful
35. high-strung
36. independent
37. irritable
38. jolly
39. kind
40. lazy
41. moody
42. nagging
43. nervous
44. optimistic
45. patient
46. pleasant
47. quarrelsome
48. realistic
49. sarcastic
50. self-centered
51. self-confident
52. self-pitying
53. sensitive
54. shy
55. sociable
56. stubborn
57. superstitious
58. tactful
59. talkative
60. tense
61. timid
62. tolerant
63. touchy
64. unselfish
65. weak
66. whiny
67. wise
68. worrying

Peck Sentence Completion Form
Form 2-D (Alternate)

Finish the following sentences by writing *one word, only*. Put down the first word that occurs to you, and go on. If you can't think right away of a word to finish a sentence, skip that item, go on to the next one, but *come back later* to finish any you have not completed. Remember, use only *one word* to finish each sentence. Please *use pencil.*

1. The average person is ______.
2. ______ makes me feel happy.
3. People think of me as ______.
4. When I let go, I ______.
5. ______ makes me feel sad.
6. My friends are ______.
7. The easiest way to get money is to ______.
8. My mother was ______.
9. What gets me into trouble is ______.
10. Being with other people is ______.
11. ______ makes me feel angry.
12. My best quality is my ______.
13. Bosses are ______.
14. Someday I will ______.
15. My father was ______.
16. My body is ______.
17. What I want to do most is to ______.
18. ______ makes me feel tense.
19. Most men are ______.
20. I'd like to be a child again so I could ______.
21. ______ makes me feel guilty.
22. Most people don't know I am ______.
23. It's exciting to ______.
24. My worst quality is my ______.
25. When I have some free time, I ______.
26. As a child I was ______.
27. When I'm put under pressure, I ______.
28. ______ makes me feel relaxed.
29. My mind is ______.
30. I hope I never ______.
31. Until now I have been ______.
32. I am ______.
33. ______ makes me feel proud.

Seven-Day Diary

	Monday	Tuesday	Wednesday	Thursday	Friday	Saturday	Sunday
1 AM							
2 AM							
3 AM							
4 AM							
5 AM							
6 AM							
7 AM							
8 AM							
9 AM							
10 AM							
:TC.							

Interviewer Remarks and Reactions

1. Was this respondent in general cooperative or antagonistic during the interview?
2. How alert was this respondent?
3. Did respondent have any difficulty in focusing on the interview?
4. Did respondent have any marked physical disability?
5. Did respondent show any evidence of confusion in dates, places, names, other?
6. At what part of the interview, if any, did respondent show signs of discomfort or anxiety?
7. How interested was respondent in the interview?
8. Did you get any insights or information about respondent that would aid in interpreting questionnaire? Please describe.
9. What is your prediction of respondent's success as a tenant, if accepted?
10. Personally, how well do you like respondent?

Disengagement Index[3]

1. More willing to let family run own lives
   ....0) no answer
   ....1) no
   ....2) yes
   ....3) don't know

2. Less interested in material things
   ....0) no answer
   ....1) no
   ....2) yes
   ....3) don't know

[3] The Disengagement Index required interviewer's estimates regarding change in the subject. For example, the interviewer would check "Yes" to Item 2, "Is less interested in material things," for a person who gave the impression during the interview that previously he had been more concerned with the way his house looked, the kinds of furniture it had, etc., but that now this meant less to him. Those who had mentioned during the interview continuing to want pretty clothes, to have their hair fixed every week, to have furniture, to "keep up with the Joneses," etc. would be checked "No." Also these are estimates of interest or willingness, not of performance, since in many instances the person seemed extremely interested in people but the circumstances of his life made it impossible for him to enjoy social participation. He would be checked "No" in Item 5. The score is the per cent of "Yes" answers.

3. Less interested in mental stimulation
   ....0) no answer
   ....1) no
   ....2) yes
   ....3) don't know

4. Less interested in taking part in activities
   ....0) no answer
   ....1) no
   ....2) yes
   ....3) don't know

5. Less interested in people
   ....0) no answer
   ....1) no
   ....2) yes
   ....3) don't know

Sociometric Questionnaire

Companionship Score (nominations by other residents on):

1. Name your three best friends.
2. Whom do you visit in his (her) apartment often? (3)[4]
3. With whom do you have a meal or snack? (3)
4. With whom do you spend the most time in the ground-floor Center? (3)

Leadership Score (nominations by other residents on):

5. If you were on an important committee whom would you want on the committee with you? (3)
6. Whom would you want as chairman of the committee? (1)
7. Who are the people most likely to take the lead when something needs to be done? (3)
8. Whom would you nominate to represent the Center in community-wide recreation planning? (3)

[4] The figures in parentheses indicate the numbers of nominations requested on the item.

Rating Scale for Adjustment to Victoria Plaza[5]

7	6	5	4	3	2	1
Is making good adjustment to living in Victoria Plaza.			Average	Is making poor adjustment to living in Victoria Plaza.		

[5] Each resident had two scores: (1) the average of his ratings by the two administrators (or the one administrative rating when only one was made), and (2) the average of his ratings by the two data collectors.

Rating Scale for Resident Happiness[6]

7	6	5	4	3	2	1
Generally happy.			Average	Generally unhappy; tends to be gloomy, sour.		

[6] Each resident's score was the average of his ratings by those of the eleven administrative, service, and research personal who rated him.

Ratings Used as Predictors of Adjustments to Victoria Plaza[7]

(Female Form)

7 6 5	4	3 2 1
From a purely personal point of view, I like this person.	Average	From a purely personal standpoint, I dislike this person.

1 2 3	4	5 6 7
"Superior" and "above" people in building, rarely associates with them.	Average	Congenial with neighbors and people in the building.

7 6 5	4	3 2 1
Nosy and a gossiper.	Average	Minds own business and refuses to gossip.

7 6 5	4	3 2 1
Sensitive, easily gets overwrought. Shows occasional signs of "nervousness" (Fidgeting, tremor, digestive disturbances, poor memory). Worries.	Average	Rarely seems to get upset. Goes on with what she is doing regardless of distractions or interrupt-tions. Rarely shows any "nervousness."

7 6 5	4	3 2 1
Tidy, overprecise, especially over details. Drives other people to be the same. Strict, fussy, pedantic. Insists on everything being orderly. (In these respects rather "uncomfortable to live with.")	Average	Rather careless of detail. Lazy.

7 6 5	4	3 2 1
Artistically sensitive to surroundings, art. Fastidious, not too easily pleased.	Average	Not showing artistic tastes. Not interested in artistic subjects. Insensitive to esthetic effects.

[7] Each resident's score for these items was the average of his ratings by those of the eleven administrative, service, and research personnel who rated him. Ratings on the last two items were averaged together to comprise one predictor score.

APPENDIX B

Housing Authority Admission Standards

Unedited

Eligibility Standards at the time of data collection:

The San Antonio Housing Authority interpreted the Federal, State Housing Administration and local Authority documents to set up the following eligibility requirements for elderly persons*:

Admission Requirements:

A. Qualifications as an "elderly person or family" defined as
   1. A family with male head 65 years of age and over or *female head 62 years of age and over.**
   2. Single men 65 years of age and over, and *single women 62 years of age and over,** living alone.
   3. Men 65 years of age or *women 62 years of age** who may live with a related or unrelated person who is of similar age and of the same sex.
   4. Exceptions are made in the case of people totally disabled according to the Social Security Disability Benefits requirements. In this case a person can be admitted at age 50.

B. Income Limit

   The net income of families of 1 or 2 persons may not exceed $2,500 a year. This limit is set by the Housing Authority with the approval of the Public Housing Administration and is therefore subject to change after research has demonstrated that such a maximum is not feasible.

C. Assets

   The net family assets shall not exceed $2,000, unless such assets together with the net income of the family are insufficient for it to obtain and maintain adequate accommodations on the private market. When families have only assets out of which to take their support, a welfare budget for a typical family is obtained and used as the basis for determining the amount of rent the family should pay. This limitation is set up by the Housing Authority with the approval of the Public Housing Administration.

D. Residency

   An applicant must have resided within a 5-mile radius of San Antonio for at least six months immediately prior to admission, except that this requirement may be waived in case of extreme hardship.

E. Previous Housing

   For normal families, it is required that families be living in substandard housing or be families of veterans or servicemen in order to qualify for public housing. Congress recognized that in the case of the elderly, there might be other unsatisfactory housing arrangements (such as standard housing in the home of other family members) and therefore waived the necessity of substandard housing as an admission requirement (San Antonio Housing Authority, 1959, Sec. I, p. 1).

* Italicized provisions first included in the Housing Act of 1959. In June of 1961 men also became eligible at age 62 and income limit was raised to $2,700 for one person, $2,900 for 2 persons and $3,100 for 4 persons.

Methods for Selecting Elderly Tenants for Public Housing

A. ELIGIBILITY ACCORDING TO LAW
Requirements for residency, income, assets are met, and preferences for Veterans' families used.

B. DATE OF APPLICATION
All else being equal, date application is placed is considered.

C. NEED FOR DECENT HOUSING
Reported condition of housing condition, with special attention to bathroom facilities, poor repair, fire hazards, stairs, etc., is given very great consideration.

D. ABILITY FOR ADJUSTMENT TO CLOSE COMMUNITY LIFE

1. Mental Alertness.
Interviewer watches closely for reactions to questions, comprehension as shown in answers, understanding, and general alertness—which is noted on application.

2. Health Determination.
Obvious general health condition noted, especially as to applicant's ability to keep house and look after himself. Special health questions are asked where indicated.

3. Appearance.
General appearance is noted, with special reference to good grooming, cleanliness, etc., which would indicate housekeeping ability and acceptance in the community.

4. General Attitude.

(a) Acceptance of reduced income.
Healthy acceptance of financial status is easy to detect in the questions and answers about income.

(b) Acceptance of reduced activity.
Adjustment to limited physical activity of older age, or resentment of them, is indication of happy attitude or otherwise.

(c) Possible contribution to community activity.
Interest in group activities, hobbies, interest, past interest, and activities which might indicate both leadership and participation is noted.

(d) Sense of humor.
Outlook upon community life is indicated by sense of humor—or lack of it—as disclosed in application interview.

(e) Selection to round out normal community.
Often a male applicant is selected to place in a neighborhood top heavy with lone women, to round out a normal community rather than an old ladies' home situation.
Couples are often selected to place in a neighborhood overabundant in lone occupants, to achieve a normal situation. (San Antonio Housing Authority, 1959, Sec. III, p. 2.)

In addition to information routinely collected during application for admission or continued occupancy in any San Antonio Housing Authority facility, the following items were added for elderly persons: (1) name of private physician or clinic used; (2) name of person other than doctor to notify in case of emergency; (3) signature of a sponsor who thereby agreed to be responsible for the elderly person "if he/she should ever become unable to care for self, and further agreed to be responsible for moving him/her out of his/her apartment if such action should become necessary"; (4) size of apartment for which the individual might qualify; (5) amount of furniture presently owned; (6) plans for acquisition or disposition of furniture; (7) chronic illness or physical disability; (8) recreational interests; (9) church affiliation. Regarding the latter, Housing Authority personnel were instructed to explain that this was a matter of interest only, having no bearing on eligibility or selection. (San Antonio Housing Authority Supplement.)

APPENDIX C

Experimental Design and Statistical Treatment of Data for Assessment of Housing-Change Impact

To assess the impact of residence in Victoria Plaza over the period of a year to fifteen months covariance analysis was used. This allowed taking into account initial between-group differences. (Though, in this instance, they were few and slight, this fact could not be anticipated. In any event, those existing were taken care of.)

Further, the design provided for simultaneous testing of change for four subgroups: male residents, female residents, male nonresidents and female nonresidents. It was possible that residential-change effect for men might be different from that for women.

The regression model (Bottenberg and Ward, 1963) was selected because it involves a minimum of assumptions regarding the nature of the variables, and because it seemed particularly well suited to the experimental problem. For any given variable the question was whether there was a tendency for the level of an individual's score to shift during the period between interviews and, if so, in what direction.

Generally, the model asks the question: What is the relationship between initial and final scores: did they tend to show increment or decrement or no change? In addition it asks: Can one conclusion be drawn for the entire group of subjects as a whole, or was there a tendency to change during the year which was related to whether the subject lived in Victoria Plaza, or to his being a man rather than a woman? Further, did the change seem to depend upon the value of the person's initial score on the variable?

Data-processing output was in terms of the regression line(s) which related the initial to the final score. If the regression lines for the four subgroups were identical, change from 1960 to 1961 was not affected by moving to the Plaza, nor was it different for men and women. (The .05 significance level was accepted throughout.) If one regression line represented both male residents and female residents, while a second regression line represented male and female nonresidents, there was a residence effect which had similar impact on people regardless of their sex. There was the possibility of one regression line for three of the subgroups and a second line for the remaining group. Four separate regression lines indicated change over time which was affected both by sex and by residence.

Effects of residence and sex were determined by the number of regression lines. Extent and direction of change, in each case, and dependence of change on size of initial score, were represented by the slope and intercept of the regression line.

For each regression line a test was made for the hypothesis that the parameter slope = 1.0. Any slope other than 1.0 indicated deterioration or improvement which was different at various points on the initial score scale. A slope greater than 1.0 showed that individuals with high scores generally improved more, or lost less, than those with low original scores. A slope less than 1.0 represented the situation in which individuals initially scoring high tended to drop in score, or to improve less, than those beginning with low scores. When the hypothesis of slope = 1.0 was accepted, this was used in interpreting the item. Otherwise, the sample slope was used.

In the same way, a test was made for the hypothesis that each parameter intercept = 0. When this hypothesis could be accepted and the slope = 1.0, not only was there no general shift in level of scores, but also individuals tended to maintain the same score levels from 1960 to 1961.

A slope of 1.0 and a positive intercept indicated general improvement throughout the score range, from initial to follow-up contact. A regression line with a slope of 1.0 and a negative intercept represented a consistent deterioration, or lowering of score, throughout the score range over that period of time.

As the slope departed from 1.0, the statement which could be made about overall shift in score was less clear-cut. For example, a regression line with slope greater than 1.0 and a positive intercept represented a situation in which general improvement had taken place, but in which individuals with high initial scores improved more than did individuals at the low end of the score scale at the beginning. On the other hand, one with slope greater than 1.0 but a negative intercept indicated that individuals with high initial scores tended to improve, while those with low original scores generally showed score decrement over the period between data collections.

For situations in which the slope of the regression line departed in either direction from 1.0, determination was made of the initial score which tended to show little change. Generally, in this situation, the more extreme an individual's original score from this one, in either direction, the greater the change to be expected in his 1961 score.

This use of the slope and intercept of the regression line(s) relating 1960 to 1961 information seemed preferable to an analysis using only means of initial and follow-up data. Compensating changes in different individuals are not reflected in the latter, so that outcomes may be masked. For example, improvement during the interval by a person at one end of an original score distribution and reduction in score by an individual at the other end might produce a mean change of zero, though the conclusion of no tendency for scores to change would be erroneous.

Here the major purpose was to compare residential status groups in order to determine the effect of Victoria Plaza on various indicators. Each residence status group was further divided into men and women, to test differential effect of residence condition by sex. For any indicator the question was whether individuals' scores tended to shift during the period of observation, the direction of shift that occurred, and the consistency of score stability or change from subgroup to subgroup. The regression model seemed ideally suited to answer these questions.

APPENDIX D

Results of Data Processing

Characteristics of Applicants (Tables 1 through 8)

Changes Associated with Residence in Victoria Plaza (Tables 9 through 17)

Prediction of Adjustment in Victoria Plaza (Tables 18 through 26)

Regression Weights of the Twenty-Seven Predictors for Optimal Prediction of Each of the Four Criteria of Adjustment (Table 27)

Characteristics of Applicants[1]

TABLE 1

Sex Differences on Religious Items

	Chi-Square	*df*
Frequency of Church Attendance	17.11 ↓	5
Frequency of Bible Reading	51.71 ↓	4
Calls from Church People	18.74 ↓	2

[1] In Tables 1 through 8:
M = 75
F = 277
All differences significant at the 5% level.
↑ Higher scores for men.
↓ Lower scores for men.

TABLE 2

Sex Differences in Health Problems

	Chi-Square	*df*
Number of Accidents in Last 5 Years	14.21 ↑	4
Constipation	10.43 ↓	1
Cough	7.15 ↑	1
Dizziness	11.16 ↓	1
Forgetfulness	6.36 ↓	1
Sleeplessness	6.03 ↑	1
Swelling	15.77 ↓	1

TABLE 3

Sex Differences in Employment History

	Chi-Square	*df*
Job Level (last level)	68.68 ↑	6
Employed by Others vs Self	47.63 ↑	2
Satisfaction with Present Ability To Work	32.42 ↓	2
Current Work or Obligation To Look Forward To	13.64 ↓	1
Earned Money	13.42 ↑	1

TABLE 4

Sex Differences in Amount and Use of Leisure Time

	Chi-Square	*df*
Too Much Free Time	18.24 ↑	2
All Day Free	15.84 ↑	3
Days Too Short	11.35 ↓	2
Sewing	70.00 ↓	1
House Work	50.25 ↓	1
Shop Work	28.35 ↑	1
Correspondence	27.29 ↓	1
Telephone Conversations	21.65 ↓	1
Sports	19.45 ↑	1
Sit and Think	16.04 ↓	1
Naps	9.44 ↑	1
T.V.	8.30 ↑	1
Church	6.73 ↓	1
Voting	15.87 ↑	1
Poll Tax	14.86 ↑	1
Frequency of Letters Written	50.20 ↓	4
Frequency of Phone Conversations	27.78 ↓	8
Frequency of Letters Received	22.74 ↓	4

TABLE 5

Sex Differences in Self-Attitudes

	Chi-Square	*df*
Cause of Greatest Unhappiness	45.31	8
Adjectives as Applied to Self		
Active	13.77 ↓	1
Affectionate	17.65 ↓	1
Bitter	21.32 ↓	1
Brave	9.48 ↑	1
Busy	18.02 ↓	1
Clear-thinking	14.85 ↑	1
Easy-going	8.81 ↑	1
Nervous	8.53 ↓	1
Sarcastic	11.03 ↓	1
Self-centered	15.80 ↓	1
Self-pitying	10.87 ↓	1
Sensitive	8.61 ↓	1
Sociable	11.66 ↑	1
Tactful	18.65 ↑	1
Tense	8.63 ↓	1
Unselfish	10.31 ↑	1

TABLE 6

Sex Differences in Desire for Services and Organizational Contacts

	Chi-Square	*df*
Want Membership in More Organizations	23.34 ↑	1
Number of Services Desired	15.26 ↓	3

TABLE 7

Sex Differences in Interviewer Ratings

	Chi-Square	*df*
Ability To Change Plans	11.56 ↓	1
Negative Talk of Past	5.19 ↓	1

TABLE 8

Activities Desired Should Conditions Permit
(Percentage Distribution)

Activity	*% of Applicants*	*Activity*	*% of Applicants*
Card Games	35	Hunting and Fishing	5
Dominoes	24	Jigsaw Puzzles	5
Book Reviews	21	Sewing	5
Monologues	20	Bowling	4
Discussion Groups	17	Football	4
Lecture Groups	17	Horseshoes	4
Skits	16	Painting	4
Crafts	13	Piano	3
Charity Works	12	Playing Pool	3
Gardening	10	Washer Tossing	33
Modeling	10	Quilting	2
Shuffleboard	9	Shop Work	2
Group Singing	8	Swimming	2
Dancing	7	Tennis	2
Visiting	7	Writing	2
Baseball	5	Reading	1

Changes Associated with Residence in Victoria Plaza[2]

TABLE 9

Cooperation

Index	*F*	*Chi-Square*	*Res x Sex*
Interviewer's Evaluation	6.28**		

TABLE 10

Satisfaction with Housing and Living Arrangements

Index	*F*	*Chi-Square*	*Res x Sex*
Major problem: Housing		79.23**	
Satisfaction with Living Arrangements	19.76**		
Evaluation of Housing	31.28**		
Evaluation of Neighborhood	12.78**		

TABLE 11

Services Wanted

Index	*F*	*Chi-Square*	*Res x Sex*
Number		123.12**	
Recreational		114.45**	
Instructional		31.17**	
Housekeeping		94.31**	
Transportation		13.46**	
Medical		10.80**	
Cafeteria		51.62**	
Beauty Shop			64.15**

[2] In Tables 9 through 17: * indicates significance at the .05 level; ** indicates significance at the .01 level.

TABLE 12

Living Costs

Index	*F*	*Chi-Square*	*Res x Sex*
Cost of Housing	91.11**		
Evaluation of Present Housing	31.28**		
Housing Value for Cost	15.26**		
Eating Costs	6.62**		
Eat Alone—with Others		9.39**	
Financial Situation	5.49*		
Financial Security		91.00**	
Attitude: Money	35.28**		
Major Problem: Money		31.29**	

TABLE 13

Activities and Relationships with Others

Index	*F*	*Chi-Square*	*Res x Sex*
Memberships		11.05**	
Time at meetings	5.93**		
Leadership		11.98**	
Memberships wanted		81.19**	
Activities compared to those of age 55	30.67**		
Number of Leisure Activities	9.41**		
Per cent Active Activities	6.01**		
Per cent Social Activities	12.83**		
Time at Hobbies	8.31**		
Time Sleeping	7.86**		
"Lost " Time	23.02**		
Number of Close Friends	13.88**		
Frequency of Visits to Friends	24.33**		
Frequency of Visits from Friends	11.42**		
Friends: Neighbors vs. Others		55.60**	
Visitors: Neighbors vs. Others		47.55**	
Phone Calls to Relatives	11.81**		
Attitude: Family	10.37**		
Attitude: Friends	42.76**		
Major Problem: Companionship		10.42**	

TABLE 14
Religion

Index	*F*	*Chi-Square*	*Res x Sex*
Radio, TV, Church Services	13.18**		
Church Socials	6.79**		
Attitude: Religion	7.36**		
Calls from Church		31.71**	

TABLE 15
Morale

Index	*F*	*Chi-Square*	*Res x Sex*
Age Identification		6.50*	
Feel about Accomplishments in Life	5.79*		
Attitude: Work	13.87**		
Attitude: Usefulness	8.06**		
Attitude: Happiness	24.79**		
Attitude: Total	45.78**		
Major Problem: Personal Adjustment		5.18*	
Happiest Period	15.51**		
Per cent of Favorable Adjectives	8.68**		
Number of Major Problems	5.52*		

TABLE 16
Health

Index	*F*	*Chi-Square*	*Res x Sex*
Rating of Health	6.41*		
Attitude: Health	5.93*		
Major Problem: Health		5.90*	
Neurotic Problems	5.98*		
Time on Health Care	5.53*		

TABLE 17

Disengagement

Index	*F*	*Chi-Square*	*Res x Sex*
Disengagement Index Score	6.74*		

Prediction of Adjustment in Victoria Plaza

TABLE 18

Predicting the Happiness of Residents after a Year in Victoria Plaza[3]

Prediction System	*Correlation Coefficient*
Using All Four Types of Predictor	.56
Using Only Three Types of Predictor:	
Application Blank, Interview Item, and Interviewer Judgment	.55
Application Blank, Interview Item, and Trait Rating	.52
Application Blank, Interviewer Judgment, and Trait Rating	.39**
Interview Item, Interviewer Judgment, and Trait Rating	.54
Using Only Two Types of Predictor:	
Application Blank and Interview Item	.50**
Application Blank and Interviewer Judgment	.31**
Application Blank and Trait Rating	.36**
Interview Item and Trait Rating	.49**
Interview Item and Interviewer Judgment	.52*
Interviewer Judgment and Trait Rating	.33**
Using Only One Type of Predictor:	
Application Blank	.26**
Interview Item	.47**
Interviewer Judgment	.22**
Trait Rating	.24**

* Significantly different from .56 at the .05 level.
** Significantly different from .56 at the .01 level.
[3] Tests of significance of difference are in Appendix D, Table 19.

TABLE 19

Tests of Significance of Difference between Predictors of Happiness after a Year's Residence in Victoria Plaza

	dfl	*df²*	*F*
All predictors vs:			
Application, Interview Item, and Interviewer Judgment	5	176	1.88
Application, Interview Item, and Trait Rating	13	176	2.13
Application, Interviewer Judgment, and Trait Rating	15	176	12.00**
Interview Item, Interviewer Judgment, and Trait Rating	23	176	0.68
Application and Interview Item	10	176	4.21**
Application and Interviewer Judgment	18	176	24.20**
Application and Trait Rating	18	176	12.50**
Interview Item and Trait Rating	10	176	5.42**
Interview Item and Interviewer Judgment	10	176	3.00*
Interviewer Judgment and Trait Rating	18	176	18.83**
Application	23	176	26.50**
Interview Item	15	176	5.33**
Interview Judgment	23	176	38.33**
Trait Rating	23	176	25.75**

* Difference significant at the .05 level of confidence.
** Difference significant at the .01 level of confidence.

TABLE 20

Predicting the Popularity of Residents after a Year in Victoria Plaza[4]

Prediction System	*Correlation Coefficient*
Using All Four Types of Predictor	.58
Using Only Three Types of Predictor:	
Application Blank, Interview Item, and Interviewer Judgment	.45**
Application Blank, Interview Item, and Trait Rating	.55
Application Blank, Interviewer Judgment, and Behavior Judgment	.55
Interviewer Item, Interviewer Judgment, and Behavior Trait	.55
Using Only Two Types of Predictor	
Application Blank and Interview Item	.40**
Application Blank and Interviewer Judgment	.36**
Application Blank and Trait Rating	.54
Interview Item and Trait Rating	.52*
Interview Item and Interviewer Judgment	.40**
Interviewer Judgment and Trait Rating	.52**
Using Only One Type of Predictor:	
Application Blank	.30**
Interview Item	.32**
Interviewer Judgment	.29**
Trait Rating	.50*

* Significantly different from .58 at the .05 level.
** Significantly different from .58 at the .01 level.

[4] Tests of significance of difference are in Appendix D, Table 21.

TABLE 21

Tests of Significance of Difference between Predictors of Popularity after a Year's Residence in Victoria Plaza

	dfl	*df²*	*F*
All predictors vs:			
Application, Interview Item, and Interviewer Judgment	5	176	24.30**
Application, Interview Item, and Trait Rating	13	176	1.00
Application, Interviewer Judgment, and Trait Rating	14	176	1.00
Interview Item, Interviewer Judgment, and Trait Rating	23	176	0.76
Application and Interview Item	10	176	18.77**
Application and Interviewer Judgment	18	176	13.62**
Application and Trait Rating	18	176	1.75
Interview Item and Trait Rating	10	176	3.50*
Interview Item and Interviewer Judgment	10	176	18.55**
Interviewer Judgment and Trait Rating	18	176	2.13*
Application	23	176	21.20**
Interview Item	15	176	25.33**
Interviewer Judgment	23	176	21.40**
Trait Rating	23	176	2.50**

* Difference significant at the .05 level of confidence.
** Difference significant at the .01 level of confidence.

TABLE 22

Predicting the Administrations' Rating of Residents after a Year in Victoria Plaza[5]

Prediction System	*Correlation Coefficient*
Using All Four Types of Predictor	.78
Using Only Three Types of Predictor:	
Application Blank, Interview Item, and Interviewer Judgment	.51**
Application Blank, Interview Item, and Trait Rating	.78
Application Blank, Interviewer Judgment, and Trait Rating	.76
Interview Item, Interviewer Judgment, and Trait Rating	.77
Using Only Two Types of Predictor:	
Application Blank and Interview Item	.49**
Application Blank and Interviewer Judgment	.34**
Application Blank and Trait Rating	.75
Interview Item and Interviewer Judgment	.48**
Interviewer Judgment and Trait Rating	.75
Interview Item and Trait Rating	.77
Using Only One Type of Predictor:	
Application Blank	.22**
Interview Item	.44**
Interviewer Judgment	.30**
Trait Rating	.75

* Significantly different from .78 at the .05 level.
** Significantly different from .78 at the .01 level.

[5] Tests of significance of difference are in Appendix D, Table 23.

TABLE 23

Tests of Significance of Difference between Predictors of Administrations' Ratings of Residents after a Year's Residence in Victoria Plaza

	dfl	*df²*	F
All predictors vs:			
Application, Interview Item, and Interviewer Judgment	5	176	46.86**
Application, Interview Item, and Trait Rating	13	176	0.23
Application, Interviewer Judgment, and Trait Rating	15	176	0.84
Interview Item, Interviewer Judgment, and Trait Rating	23	176	0.20
Application and Interview Item	10	176	26.85**
Application and Interviewer Judgment	18	176	40.24**
Appication and Trait Rating	18	176	0.90
Interview Item and Trait Rating	10	176	0.84
Interview Item and Interviewer Judgment	10	176	29.92**
Interviewer Rating and Trait Rating	18	176	0.93
Application	23	176	82.00**
Interview Item	15	176	25.63**
Interviewer Judgment	23	176	45.80**
Trait Rating	23	176	0.58

* Difference significant at the .05 level of confidence.
** Difference significant at the .01 level of confidence.

TABLE 24

Predicting the Interviewers' Rating of Residents after a Year in Victoria Plaza[6]

Prediction System	*Correlation Coefficient*
Using All Four Types of Predictor	.82
Using Only Three Types of Predictor:	
Application Blank, Interview Item, and Interviewer Judgment	.52**
Application Blank, Interview Item, and Trait Rating	.81
Application Blank, Interviewer Judgment, and Trait Rating	.81
Interview Item, Interviewer Judgment, and Trait Rating	.81
Using Only Two Types of Predictor:	
Application Blank and Interview Item	.43**
Application Blank and Interviewer Judgment	.45**
Application Blank and Trait Rating	.80
Interview Item and Trait Rating	.80
Interview Item and Interviewer Judgment	.49**
Interviewer Judgment and Trait Rating	.80
Using Only One Type of Predictor:	
Application Blank	.25**
Interview Item	.37**
Interviewer Judgment	.41**
Trait Rating	80

* Significantly different from .82 at the .05 level.
** Significantly different from .82 at the .01 level.

[6] Tests of significance of difference are in Appendix D, Table 25.

TABLE 25

Tests of Significance of Difference between Predictors of Interviewers' Ratings of Residents after a Year's Residence in Victoria Plaza

	dfl	*df²*	*F*
All Predictors vs:			
Application, Interview Item, and Interviewer Judgment	5	176	52.73**
Application, Interview Item, and Trait Rating	13	176	0.24
Application, Interviewer Judgment and Trait Rating	15	176	0.24
Interview Item, Interviewer Judgment, and Trait Rating	23	176	0.16
Application and Interview Item	10	176	43.54**
Application and Interviewer Judgment	18	176	5.36**
Application and Trait Rating	18	176	0.41
Interview Item and Trait Rating	10	176	0.63
Interview Item and Interviewer Judgment	10	176	32.92**
Interviewer Rating and Trait Rating	18	176	0.41
Application	23	176	87.66**
Interview Item	15	176	44.00**
Interviewer Judgment	23	176	24.22**
Trait Rating	23	176	0.44

* Difference significant at the .05 level of confidence.
** Difference significant at the .01 level of confidence.

TABLE 26

Zero-Order Correlations between Predictors and Criteria of Adjustment

Predictors	*Criteria of Adjustment* *Happiness*	*Popularity*	*Interv. Rating*	*Admin. Rating*
Age	.22	—.22	—.10	—.16
Education	.06	.09	.03	.07
Marital Status	—.14	.17	.07	—.01
Teen Friends	.02	.03	.02	.04
Church Attendance	—.15	.10	.14	.15
Confusion Rating	.05	—.27	—.28	—.22
Rating as Tenant	—.04	—.10	—.32	—.19
Physical Disability	.17	—.07	.03	—.03
Income	—.14	.20	.15	.10
Active, Social Pastimes	—.14	.22	.21	.33
Neurotic-Type Health Problems	.12	.01	—.14	—.01
Senility Index	.08	—.15	—.39	—.21
Disengagement Index	.07	—.14	—.23	—.45
Teen Relations with Parents	—.20	.22	.23	.34
Job Level (Working Years)	.00	—.02	.19	.13
Attitude to Self	.30	.09	.16	.15
Attitude Toward Others	.26	.07	.16	.12
Memberships Desired	.05	—.01	—.13	.01
Feeling about Future	—.29	.06	.11	.07
Likability	—.10	.21	.68	.16
Nosiness, Gossip	—.07	—.23	—.13	.53
Congeniality	—.24	.36	.63	.50
Nervousness	—.18	—.24	—.52	—.30
Tidiness, Sensitivity	.10	.26	.28	.19
Number Activities Wanted	—.12	.17	.10	.23
Age Identification	—.23	.13	.12	.15
Number of Friends (Squared)	—.10	.07	.09	.17

TABLE 27

Regression Weights of the Twenty-Seven Predictors for Optimal Prediction of Each of the Four Criteria of Adjustment

Predictor	*Criterion*			
	Happiness	*Popularity*	*Interv.*	*Admin.*
Age	+.1154	−.8129	−.2198	−.0612
Education	+.0190	+.2864	+.2062	+.2721
Marital Status	−.3462	+.4957	+1.0845	−2.3388
Income	−.0082	+.1047	+.0566	+.0894
Job Level	+.0051	−.1870	+.4160	+.7229
No. of Friends (squared)	−.0026	+1.8980	+.1715	+.4469
Teen Friends	+.0706	+.1748	+.0356	+.4925
Church Attendance	−.0928	+1.0302	+.4004	+1.0692
Active, Social Pastimes	−.0052	+.0195	+.0077	+.0799
Neurotic Problems	+.0775	+.0813	0	−.0741
Attitude to Parents	−.0085	+.0362	+.0286	+.0471
Attitude to Self	+.1405	+.6195	+.6034	+.0904
Attitude to Others	+.0084	+.0475	+.0182	+.0225
Desired Membership	+.1201	−.1972	−.7415	0
Activities Wanted	−.0334	+.0697	+.1069	+.1400
Age Identification (middle-aged)	−.1993	+.5209	+.1527	+.5797
Feel about Future	−.4751	+.2461	+.1296	+1.3241
Confusion	+.0176	−.2953	−.0123	−.1573
Disability	+.1515	−.1884	+1.5490	−.5174
Senility Index	+.0012	−.0403	−.0326	−.0540
Disengagement Index	+.0015	0	−.0123	−.0339
Desirability as Tenant	−.3292	−1.2644	−.6808	−.6044
Personal Liking	−.0007	+.0209	+.3711	+.0462
Congeniality	−.0162	+.3481	+.3687	+.5297
Nosiness	−.0018	−.2661	−.0047	+.6495
Nervousness	−.0067	−.1433	−.1454	−.1473
Tidiness, Sensitivity	+.0035	+.2357	+.0919	+.1653

To obtain a resident's overall predictor score for any criterion, his raw score on each predictor variable was multiplied by the appropriate weight in this table, and to the sum of these was added the constant value associated with the criterion: for happiness, 5.60; for popularity, 7.01; for interviewer rating of adjustment, 3.43; and for administrator rating, 3.20.

The constants and weights in this table applied only when the full set of predictors was used. The regression analyses based upon subsets of predictors resulted in different values.

These constants and weights are specific to these data and, furthermore, are dependent upon the particular system of item scoring and combination. Details of the scoring system, and regression constants and weights for subsets of predictor measures in relation to each of the criteria, are available from the author. Even with these, application to new situations and people must be tentative; cross-validation is prerequisite to practical application.

BIBLIOGRAPHY

Blau, Zena Smith. " Changes in Status and Age Identification," *American Sectological Review,* Vol. 21 (1956), pp. 198–203.

Bottenberg, Robert A., and Joe H. Ward, Jr. *Applied Multiple Linear Regression.* 6570th Personnel Research Laboratory, Aerospace Medical Division, Air Force Systems Command, Lackland Air Force Base, Texas. An unclassified technical documentary report, March, 1963.

Bradshaw, Homer. "Differentiating Characteristics of Superior Old People," in Ohio State University Dissertation Abstracts, 1956, Vol. II.

Britton, Joseph, William Mather, and Alice Lansing. "Expectations for Older Persons in a Rural Community: Living Arrangements and Family Relationships," *The Journal of Gerontology,* Vol. 16 (1961), p. 156.

Burgess, Ernest, Ruth Cavan, Robert Havighurst, and Herbert Goldhammer. *Personal Adjustment in Old Age.* Chicago: Science Research Associates, 1949.

Burgess, Ernest, Ruth Cavan, and Robert Havighurst. *Your Activities and Attitudes.* Chicago: Science Research Associates, 1948.

Carp, Frances M. "High School Boys Are Realistic about Occupations," in *Occupations,* Vol. 27 (1949), pp. 97–99.

Carp, Frances, and Abraham Carp. *Demographic and Psychological Characteristics of Applicants for Public Housing for the Aged in San Antonio, Texas.* 1961. A mimeographed working paper.

Cavan, Ruth Shonle, Ernest W. Burgess, Robert J. Havighurst, and Herbert Goldhammer. *Personal Adjustment in Old Age.* Chicago: Science Research Associates, 1949.

Cumming, Elaine, and William E. Henry. *Growing Old: The Process of Disengagement.* New York: Basic Books, Inc., 1961.

Droller, H. "Falls and Accidents in a Random Sample of Elderly People Living at Home," *Old Age in the Modern World.* Edinburgh: E. & S. Livingstone, 1955, pp. 374–384.

Flyer, Eli. "Prediction by Career Field of First Term Airman Performance from Selection and Basic Training Variables." Lackland Air Force Base, Texas: Air Force Personnel Research Laboratory, March, 1964 (Research Report AFPRL–TDR–64–5).

Flyer, Eli, and Frances M. Carp. "The Picture Test: Rationale and One Validation of the Method," *The Journal of Applied Psychology,* Vol. 46 (1962), pp. 226–227.

Gough, Harrison. *The Adjective Check List. Berkeley*: University of California Printing Department, 1952.

Hall, C. S., and G. Lindzey. *Theories of Personality.* New York: John Wiley & Sons, 1958.

Hathaway, S. R., and J. C. McKinley. *Minnesota Multiphasic Personality Inventory.* Beverly Hills, California: Sheridan Supply Co., 1949.

Kelly, Lowell. "Consistency of the Adult Personality," *The American Psychologist,* Vol. 10, (1955), p. 659.

Lorge, Irving, "Gerontology," *The Annual Review of Psychology,* Vol. 7 (1956), pp. 349–364.

McClusky, Howard, and Gale Jensen. "The Psychology of Adults," *The Review of Educational Research,* Vol. 29 (June, 1959), pp. 246–255.

McGuire, Carson. "Index of Status Characteristics," *Social Status, Peer Status, and Social Mobility.* Chicago: University of Chicago Press, 1949.

McNemar, Quinn. *Psychological Statistics.* John Wiley: New York and London, 1962, 3rd edition.

Murray, H. A. *Thematic Apperception Test.* Cambridge, Massachusetts: Harvard University Press, 1943.

Netter, Lola G. *The Use of Housing Authority Criteria in Tenant Selection for Victoria Plaza, an Apartment Building for the Elderly.* An unpublished Master's thesis, Trinity University, 1962.

San Antonio Housing Authority. *A Discussion of Admission Criteria, Apartments for the Elderly.* San Antonio, Texas: San Antonio Housing Authority. A mimeograph.

——— *Supplement to Application and CO's for Elderly Persons.* San Antonio, Texas: San Antonio Housing Authority, 1959. A mimeograph.

Sells, J. B., ed. *Tri-Service Conference on Research Relevant to Behavior Problems of Small Military Groups under Isolation and Stress.* Fort Wainwright, Alaska: Arctic Aeromedical Laboratory, March, 1961. A mimeograph.

Shanas, Ethel. "Family Responsibility and the Health of Older People," *The Journal of Gerontology,* Vol. 14 (1959), p. 208.

Sheldon, H. D. *The Older Population of the United States.* New York: John Wiley & Sons, 1958.

Shelton, Florence and Robert Kastenbaum. "Wishes in Later Life," *The Journal of Gerontology,* Vol. 16 (1961), p. 404.

Shore, Herbert, ed. *The Newsletter of the Texas Society on Aging.* Dallas, Texas: July, 1961.

Sward, K. "Age and Mental Ability in Superior Men," *The American Journal of Psychology,* Vol. 58 (1945), pp. 443–479.

Tuckerman, Jacob, and Irving Lorge. "Classification of the Self as Young, Middle-Aged or Old," *Geriatrics,* Vol. 9 (1954), p. 534.

Tupes, E. C. "Relationship between Behavior Trait Ratings by Peers and Later Officer Performance of USAF Officer Candidate School Graduates." Lackland Air Force Base, Texas: Air Force Personnel and Training Research Center, October, 1957 (*Research Report* AFPTRC-TN-57-125).

Tupes, Ernest C., and Raymond C. Christal. "Stability of Personality Trait Rating Factors Obtained under Diverse Conditions." Lackland Air Force Base, Texas: Personnel Laboratory, May, 1958 (*Research Report* WADC-TN-58-61, ASTIA Document No. AD 151 041).

United States Bureau of the Census, 1958.

von Mering, Otto, and Frederick Weniger. "Social-Cultural Background of the Aging Individual," in James E. Birren, ed., *Handbook of Aging and the Individual.* Chicago: University of Chicago Press, 1959.

Wacker, Marilynn, ed. *Victoria Plaza Apartments.* San Antonio: Clegg Publishing Company, 1960.

Wechsler, David. *The Wechsler-Bellevue Intelligence Scale.* New York: Psychological Corporation, 1946.

Whelpton, P. K., and Ronald Friedmon, "A Study of the Growth of American Families," *The American Journal of Sociology,* Vol. 61 (1956), p. 595.

White House Conference on Aging. *Aging in the States.* Washington, D.C.: United States Government Printing Office, 1961.

Wilner, Daniel M., Rosabelle Price Walkley, Thomas C. Pinkerton, and Matthew Tayback. *The Housing Environment and Family Life.* Baltimore: The Johns Hopkins Press, 1962.

INDEX

DOYLE